REMEMBER WHO THE FUCK YOU ARE

Who Were You, Before the World Told You What to Be?

KATIE DICKIESON

LANDON
HAIL
PRESS

Copyright© 2023 Katie Dickieson
All Rights Reserved

Cover design by Rich Johnson, Spectacle Photo

Paperback ISBN: 978-1-959955-19-1
Hardback ISBN: 978-1-959955-12-2
Published by Landon Hail Press

DISCLAIMER: This book is memoir. It reflects the author's present recollections of experiences over time. Some names and characteristics have been changed, some events have been compressed, and some dialogue has been recreated. Although the author and publisher have made every effort to ensure the accuracy and completeness of information contained in this book, we assume no responsibility for errors, inaccuracies, omissions, or any inconsistency herein. Any slights on people, places, or organizations are unintentional. The material in this book is provided for educational purposes only.

This book is dedicated to the eccentric, erratic, odd, outlandish, peculiar, singular, unique souls that are crazy enough to change the world. It is people like you who have the greatest chance. We need you. More than that, you need you. So, love yourself and all that you are because it is you that makes this world worth fighting for.

TABLE OF CONTENTS

Foreword _____ 5
Prologue _____ 7
Introduction _____ 11
Chapter 1: And So it Begins… _____ 21
    Origin Story _____ 24
    Don't Let Me Get Me _____ 27
    Preachers and Pot _____ 40
    Resilience: I Always Find a Way _____ 43
Chapter 2: Those Who Fight for their Limitations Get to Keep Them _____ 50
    Birthmarks and Breakaways _____ 56
    My Friend, Janis _____ 65
    Too Much _____ 75
    Letting Go of Our Limitations _____ 77
    Method in the Madness _____ 82
Chapter 3: Solitary Creates Clarity _____ 89
    Seeing the Bigger Picture _____ 90
    Blue-Sky Mindset _____ 92
Chapter 4: Settling the Debt of Hustle and Grind _____ 95
    Protesting For Joy _____ 105

Chapter 5: You are Not What You Do _____ 111
    My Superpower is Breaking Down Structures __ 112
Chapter 6: Always Be Advocating _____ 115
    Advocate for Yourself _____ 122
    Me, Too. _____ 124
    You Have the Face of Someone Who Would Go Missing On the News _____ 126
    Past Trauma _____ 132
    Becoming a Champion of Health _____ 154
    All the Small Things _____ 160
    Privilege _____ 164
Chapter 7: Revealing Magnifies Healing _____ 170
Chapter 8: The People Who Make Us _____ 178
Chapter 9: Seeking Your Own Attention _____ 184
    Who Am I? _____ 187
    Triple Point _____ 195
Chapter 10: We're All Somebody's Bad Guy _____ 197
    Homewrecker _____ 199
    Lab Rats _____ 207
Chapter 11: Get to Know Yourself Enough to Love Yourself _____ 219
Chapter 12: When the Way you Love is Different _____ 227
Chapter 13: Happiness is the [Hard] Choice _____ 247
Chapter 14: Fuck Personal Development _____ 270
Chapter 15: This World is Not Fair, but There is Peace in the Chaos _____ 276
    Evolving With Integrity _____ 285
    The Road Less Traveled _____ 288

Chapter 16: Change is a Drug Unlike Any Other ___ 290
Chapter 17: The Synergistic Flame _____ 296
Chapter 18: Disruptors Get a Bad Rap _____ 304
Chapter 19: Remember Who the Fuck You Are ____ 307
Chapter 20: The Great Dance of Nostalgia _____ 312
    Move Dates _____ 316
References _____ 317
    Additional Resources by Mental Health Condition
    _____ 317
    LGBTQ Resource List _____ 321
    Anti-Racism Books to Read _____ 322
Thanks _____ 323
About the Author _____ 324

KATIE DICKIESON

What People are Saying about *Remember Who the Fuck You Are*

"Katie's stories beautifully weave messages of healing and resilience through her own journey, where she faced trials and setbacks while rediscovering herself. Her words have the power to evoke both tears and laughter, ultimately leaving you with a profound message of hope. As a trauma specialist, I've encountered many narratives of survival and growth, and Katie's storytelling spoke to her heart. Her ability to share her experiences with authenticity and vulnerability is not only relatable but also deeply touching. This is a must-read for those looking to embark on their path towards hope and healing."

—Lauren Auer, Trauma Therapist

"An explosion of emotions that will leave you processing Katie's processing as you process your own process. Her vulnerability and willingness to dive into the tidal wave of her psyche will have you swimming into the abyss of the human condition. Katie's desire to relate to herself and others will serve as your life preserver and save you from drowning in the sea of human despair."

—Toni Nagy, Comedienne

Foreword

Dear Reader,

You are about to read the story of the little girl who saved my life in the seventh grade. We were just two kids fantasizing about escaping our reality; so loved and yet misunderstood. Our paths somehow collided, and to be honest, it's a miracle we're both still here.
Oh, but Katie. This little girl was extraordinary.
This author was different than the other kids in our wealthy, suburban environment. She was playful, curious, empathic, and sad; so very sad, navigating the world with such big feelings and such small boxes. Imagine Matilda meets Junie B. Jones—so much wonder and torment. Where the rubber meets the road.
And she was mine, my friend, and I imagine, by the end of this book you'll think of her as your friend, too. Imagine us, a little Black girl in a White, suburban world and an eclectic White girl in a hyper-religious world.
We passed thousands of handwritten notes, interrogating our beliefs and searching for a deeper meaning of life. We were eleven years old yet countless years before our time.
Katie was the first person I ever told about my self-harm, and I was the person with whom she first spoke of her childhood torment. We saved each other.

I hope, after reading the words that follow, Katie and her story will help save you as well. So, to all of the little girls who feel queer in a colorless world, let this story inspire you to shine.

Camille "Cammie" Williams
Self-Love Behavioral Scientist
Becoming Unfuckwithable

Prologue

TRIGGER WARNING: I cover a lot of trauma ground in the following pages. I have given myself permission to go through all the emotions that arise during the act of writing this book. So please, be prepared, and take care of yourself.

My goal with this book is to give the most accurate details I can of the events that happened in my life, so others are able to learn and grow through experiencing and processing them with me. I am not a doctor, therapist, or specialist in the area of psychology. If you have experienced any of the traumas I write about in these pages, I advise you to seek professional help. I also list references, to assist with that. Please be kind to yourself and to others. This shit is hard, and you never know where someone is, either mentally or emotionally.

* * *

I want to write this right now while I'm okay. I want to write this in a clear state of mind so that those of you who will read this can understand that this didn't come from a place of erratic emotion or one day in sadness. I've written this letter more times than I can count, the only difference today is that I am writing in a moment of happiness because it is the only way I can convey how alone I am without being told I'm overdramatized, crazy, or unaware of reality. The reality is; this is it. In the happiest days I am reminded that I'm not. That the highest level of happiness I can attain is forgetting how sad I am and that it just becomes a reminder of how I actually feel. I spent the longer part of my life feeling and showing everything that courses through my bones and because of it was made to look like a "crazy liar" which in this day & age I guess I get...but not really. I never understood this because I would never be one of those people. I know a few of you believe this but for some reason the majority see the real as the insane because it's easier to go with the grain. I've never been completely innocent but innocent enough to not deserve the way I was treated. Yet, this is not the reason still. You see, I always loved who I was, and no matter how much a person could possibly hate me it wouldn't break me as long as I knew I was true to myself. What broke me from the very beginning of my life was never understanding. You see I grew up believing and spent my entire life believing in the good in everyone. When they were wrong to me I was hurt because it hurt me to think of how they were hurting. That I could have such a beautiful relationship with someone become so ugly for no reason. I am not wishing or placing blame on anyone by writing this. I am hoping that by writing this, you, whoever you are, will live the rest of your days seeing the good in the people around you especially those who have done you wrong. It would be so easy for me to tell you "fuck them, and fuck it all..." but the truth is that mentality will only make you worse and more unhappy. Unless you are one of those people that live solely for money, material possessions and status, then ya know what...keep fucking moving because you won't realize until it's too late.

What is the point in living? What is the point in us having this gift of life if we don't use it to create something better for our future generations?! What is the point if we don't make an impact on the lives of those we love most? It's impossible for me to believe that in the core we don't all possess a want, a need, a necessity for what is beautiful and passionate for all living creatures. We are all a part of this life together yet hide in our homes of solitude as though someone else couldn't possibly understand who we are.... I get it, for the majority of people reading this knowing I took my own life are screaming "HYPOCRITE" right now... and ya know what it's fucking true. I am a hypocrite, an idiot, and human... I was only human.

But, I won't take my life tonight, the night of June 13, 2019. And I will keep this promise for tonight, but when you do find this after I am gone please call the first person that comes to mind.

Don't question it.

Just do it.

Whether or not you ever know, you could be saving a life. And that one life could hold the most beautiful song you've ever heard, the cure for ANYTHING, the best snuggle buddy, brunch date, chess opponent, movie companion, bowling nemesis, tubing combat partner, chem lab TA, professor, president, yoga instructor, sommelier, chef, pizza maker, or any other trait that makes this world a beautiful, diverse, and magical place. That one life is a human that you're thinking about because they are necessary to the development of this world and you don't want to do life without them. So, promise me you will call them.

Immediately.

You may be crying. Even better. Let the world know and those you love that it's okay to feel, and maybe if we all allow ourselves to do it a little bit more other people wouldn't be so afraid to as well. I have a lot to live for, I know. I'm really smart, I'm extremely capable of all the things I could want to do in this life, I have the most incredible family, amazing friends, and the best dog in the entire world. I know it's selfish. I used to think, if I killed myself, I would be doing the world a favor, but that's not it at all. I did it for me. Because it doesn't matter if I ever become an actress who makes enough money to save thousands of children, a doctor who cures genetic disorders through space altered genes or a scientist who figures out what we can do with greenhouse gas emissions. I can't save the world, because I can't even save myself.

If I get into NASA will you guys ask them to take some of my ashes to space?

Introduction

FOR YEARS, I HAVE PLAYED around with what the title of this book should be.

I started writing it when I was in middle school, and I kept rewriting the first page over and over again every year, until I hit twenty-six years old. It never had a title. It never really had a point. All the layers to my life seemed so scrambled. Yet I felt the need to meet the perfection in me, because the only way to write a book is to start with page one and then, linearly and manically, write until the finish line, which is the last page.

That's not even close to how this fucking works. And life is just as non-linear. This book has been titled *Katie in the Gnome*, *The Best Book I've Ever Written*, *You Can't Put Me In a Box*, *Homeless to Mars*, *I Might as well be Who I am*, *The Others*, *Breaking the Mold*, *Different*, *Innovating Katie*, *Bonafide With Pride*, *Gay Enough*, *Too Much*, *Feeling Seen*, *The Unseen*, and *You're Welcome*, plus many, many more names I can't even remember. Each of these titles is connected to a specific part of my life.

When I first became serious about writing this book, I felt as though I needed to make it palatable to the general reader. Ironically, I felt my book needed to fit into a box, in order to be seen as acceptable. Which doesn't make any sense, because I am not someone who is easily accepted. I don't easily accept things in my life, and I certainly don't want this book to just be accepted.

Being accepted is like being tolerated, and I don't accept just being tolerated. I want to be celebrated, and I think we all deserve to be celebrated.

I have noticed a pattern when discussing, in everyday conversations, the big ideas I put forth in this book. I have an inherent need to feel validated and throughout much of my past, especially my childhood, my environment made it feel nearly impossible for me or my opinions, thoughts and ideas to be considered valid without having an adequate co-signer. Someone whom other people respected or deemed worthy of listening to, to even acknowledge any worth in what I had to say. So, in conversation, I tend to add citations to my statements.

"Well, when talking to my therapist the other day we talked about this..."

"In conversation with so-and-so, we discussed this..."

"My leadership professor, who's been doing this for forty years, explained this about me..."

"In this book about 'fill in the blank,' to describe why someone would act like me..."

"I am a 6/2 Manifestor, with an Aries Sun, Libra Moon, and Capricorn Rising, so..."

I am not criticizing the use of titles, definitions, or research to back up what you're trying to say. I am a scientist, after all. I get off on puzzles, connections, and understanding how and why things, people, and situations work. I can't help but wonder, though, if we didn't put so much emphasis on only believing how the rest of the world views us and describes us, and instead truly listened to others and their experiences, we might be able to find deeper understanding, grace, love, and validity in who that person is.

The second someone sticks a label on me, I feel claustrophobic. The desire to prove them wrong, to do the exact opposite, the need show them "who's really the boss," swells within me. To be seen as the full human spectrum of who I really am. That I can be fierce, stand my ground, and stick up for what I believe in. That I can be the advocate, while not losing myself to the rage that so often tries to consume me.

So, I practice softness and empathy. I am learning how to lean into my feminine, so that my constant evolution makes it impossible for anyone to put their labels on me, to put me in a box. I think the same goes for everyone.

I am not a saint. I watch *Real Housewives,* for God's sake. I totally get off on drama, it's my guilty pleasure, but I also get off on watching those women heal their trauma and mend their relationships.

Whether you believe reality TV to be real or not, I think there is something to be said about watching people navigate difficult conversations and be able to come out better on the other end. Does this happen all the time on Bravo? Absolutely not. But we're also not here to discuss Bravo.

I think the bottom line here is to recognize that, while I believe some things are black and white, a lot of things are also on a spectrum, and figuring out and navigating which is which is not the easiest process. What I have witnessed, though, is that the people who acknowledge this truth and continue to dig deeper into the issues, without automatically naming everything as black and white, are usually the people who engage in the hard conversations that make this world a better place for all of us.

This book is exactly for those people and those hard conversations. Conversations surrounding sexuality, femininity, masculinity, and how to honor both sides of who we are. Conversations about racism, what it means to be humane, about spirituality/religion and why it is something so personal to each and every one of us. Conversations about love and what its definition is for each of us. About what infidelity means to you, boundaries, trauma, death, friendship, dreams and aspirations. Recognizing our oneness, and accepting that it's okay to not enjoy everyone, but to be willing to see their humanness, either way.

I love being able to feel as deeply as I do. Feeling is a constant reminder that I am human, that I am alive. I don't believe in telling other people what is right for them, but based on the many, many times I have been put on antidepressants (there's a specific reason they do not work for me; I am not against them), I have learned that to feel nothing at all isn't a life I want to live.

Pain has created the magical life I live just as must as pleasure. I am now learning to accept the equilibrium of these two opposites. To experience pleasure and pain in life's quiet and still moments and to not only allow myself to accept but to embrace these moments. I am grateful for this rollercoaster that I now get to choose.

So, this book could have had any of those titles. Or each of those titles could apply to individual books that come after this one. Sometimes, I forget I am not just writing this book for other people but also for myself, and that I am not supposed to be perfectly healed by the end of this.

Sometimes, I forget one of the biggest reasons for writing this book is to remind other people just how normal, and not just acceptable but beautifully magical, it is to be everything, everywhere all at once.

I have known that I have something to say my entire life. My gut has led me to this moment. Trusting my gut blindly has brought me to the most impactful moments in my life. This is the first time I have ever really questioned that gut feeling, though. *Who am I to think what I have to say is important enough for the rest of the world to hear? Why would anyone read this book? I am a nobody to the world.*

Through this process of opening up to others about my experiences and my journey I am continuously reminded of exactly why it is I am doing this. It is because I am a "nobody."

We're all nobodies who are actually somebody. We're all human. We all are experiencing what it means to be human together, yet we never talk about it. We never talk about the opportunities we're missing, when we don't recognize the humanness in everyone around us and what kind of change that could create in this world. Why not? We all have the power to create change. We are all nobodies who are somebody, and those who are considered somebodies seem to be acting a whole lot like they're nobodies.

Without recognizing the power that we hold individually, we do a disservice not only to ourselves, but to the entire world. Which is why it is important that you *Remember Who the Fuck You Are!* Which is why it is important to remind the people we know *Who the Fuck They Are,* and that, as a collective, we all *Remember Who the Fuck We Are.* Because we are all somebodies who usually feel more like nobodies.

We must become more capable of first telling ourselves who we truly are, in order to enable and embolden our abilities to remind others of this fact. The more we are reminded of our own power, the more we are capable of being exactly who the fuck we were meant to be on this planet and in this life. When we are more aligned with who we are meant to be in this world, the higher we vibrate, and the higher our energy vibrates, the higher the collective energy vibrates. The higher the collective energy vibrates, the better this world becomes.

I know we are all tired. For those of us who have been doing the work on ourselves and who are at the point of protecting our own energy, I totally get it. Gathering the tools and knowledge to help pick and choose the worthy battles is crucial. We do need to protect our energy, but unfortunately right now, we are in a war on consciousness. And for this exact reason, we need to be protecting our energy so that, when the battles rise that are worth our energy, we have it to blow the enemy out of the water.

I am fucking tired, man. I am fucking exhausted. As I write this I am holding back tears, because I wish I was a person who knew how to give up. I wish I was a person who knew how to quit. I wish I was a person who knew how to turn a blind eye, use my privilege for personal gain, and ignore the pain of our collective.

But I can't. I am not that person. We, as a collective, are in survival mode right now. I wish we could all "thoughts and prayers, and love and happiness" the world's problems away, but we can't.

As critically acclaimed author, world-renowned speaker, educator, pastor, and my favorite motivational speaker of all time, Eric Thomas, PhD, says, "Sometimes in life you have to hit back."

Sometimes we have to fight for who we are, and sometimes we have to fight to keep even the bare minimum. It is necessary. It is exhausting. Advocating for yourself feels like a constant fight between your higher self and the demons who have been telling you that you aren't worthy. I get it. But the more you advocate for yourself, and the more you advocate for others, the easier it becomes. Thus, empowering you to recognize the bystander effect has become the norm of everyone who's just trying to get by.

I am fucking done with just trying to get by. And I am fucking done watching the whole world just try to get by. It's time for us to *Remember Who the Fuck We Are*. It's time for you to *Remember Who the Fuck You Are*. It's time to recognize who you are without labels. It's time to re-meet your soul.

Because this whole credit-checks, power/poverty battle for survival, drugged-up, numbed-out, and disassociated way of living is not it, man. We are better than this. If the ego is what's driving you, then maybe recognizing that the window is closing on your chance to make your mark might light a fire under your ass.

I know none of us came into this world with the intentions of making a living, getting good health insurance, creating a family, and then dying. Honestly, if that is what you believe your intention is in life, I don't believe you, but I'll pretend you're speaking truth. You need to get out of the way of the rest of us though because we've got more important work to do.

Remembering Who the Fuck You Are is not a one-and-done process. It takes multiple meetings of the self at different spaces in time during your life. It is a lifelong process. It is not easy, and much of it entails accepting that it is a difficult and dirty process. And in the famous words of Michael Rosen from the children's book *We're Going on a Bear Hunt,* "We've got to go through it."

Remembering Who the Fuck You Are entails a lot of self-reflection, self-awareness, grieving, anger, forgiveness, acceptance, and learning to let go, so you can be the person you were always meant to be, before the world taught you who you "should be."

I don't want to belittle people's experiences. Through this book, you will read the stories of my journey. I understand some of these stories will seem like nothing in comparison to things you might have been through. On the opposite end of the spectrum, they may seem like stories too insane to believe. Wherever your experiences land on this spectrum has no impact on your ability to survive and get through to the other side. Everyone's spectrum is different so don't allow insidious bullshit to suffocate you.

Your experience is valid. You are valid. Being a person of color, queer, disabled, neurodivergent, female, in poverty, or anything else I have missed that places you in any minority category, does create a disadvantage in this world. This world is not fair or kind to those in the minority, right now.

My hope is that, one day in the future, there will be someone reading this book as though it is a part of history and no longer the norm. My wish is that the people living in this world at this very moment, November 2023, are the last people who ever have to go through personal development. Since personal development was created because we were never taught how to love ourselves properly as children, in my ideal future, loving ourselves will become second nature to all. And no one will ever have to *Remember Who the Fuck They Are* again, because they were never forced to forget who they were in the first place.

I have to believe the reality of this is true. Or at least possible. I have to, because I believe this is why I am here. I have had this belief for a long time, that *if I am capable, then I should.* The problem is, for a while, I used that mentality toward things such as school, debating bosses who did not care to change how they treated employees, doing extra work for businesses I never planned to stay at, and fighting my parents about who I was at every step of my childhood. I used my survival as a badge of honor.

I realize what I am capable of is much greater than these things. I realize my reach is far wider than I have allowed myself to accept in the past.

I've had this inherent need to save the world since I was a child. It's not about saving the world, though. It is about saving humanity. I saw from a very young age what worked and didn't work: in school, family, society, and relationships. I am not perfect but I am efficient and empathetic.

The problem is, no one person can save humanity. We need to work as a team. And the first step in this process is getting everyone on board with the idea that it is possible.

I need you to believe. I need you to see every single negative, depressing, and infuriating moment in life, take a step away for however long you need, and feel it. Feel it as hard as you need to feel it and then let it the fuck go.

Ignore the news; turn off the fucking news. Cancel any service provider you have that allows the news to exist in your household. Fuck it all. Fuck the noise. Fuck the noise from every single angle it comes in from. You only have time for believing in the possibilities now. No more time for limitations.

Become a blind optimist. Not in the sense of "I am a divine creature made of light and sunshine, sprinkling fairy dust over everything," bullshit. "Let me live in false reality to make myself feel better." *No*! We are the optimists that choose to be blind. Blind to all the bullshit the world tries to feed us.

We know the darkness that exists. We've lived in the darkness, and we might even still be in the darkness. We know just how strong the darkness is, but we choose not to accept the darkness.

Cue Rage Against the Machine's "Killing in the Name."

"Never accept the world as it appears to be. Dare to see it for what it could be." (Dr. Harold Winston, *Overwatch)*

Chapter 1

And So it Begins...

"To live would be an awfully big adventure."
—Peter Pan, *Hook*

I DIDN'T KILL MYSELF.
I can't kill myself. This human being that I am cannot kill herself because she has a purpose to fulfill...

Who am I? Who is the human being who is writing this?

She's straight from the hip, cut to the chase, I/she/her is Katie, and I was born this way, baby.

I've been writing since I was a kid, writing journals, writing poetry, writing songs. As a girl, I was inspired by Jo in *Little Women*. We would play olden days, although now I cringe at how privileged that sounds coming from a White woman. I always imagined myself moving to New York City, writing a book, and falling in love. I wanted to write manuscripts. I wanted to be an actress. I wanted to be Winona Ryder. (Spoiler: I am *not* Winona Ryder, not even close. Though I did get caught shoplifting rings from an art fair one time, so birds of a feather or something like that.)

I am writing this for all the people who have a Katie in their life. I am writing this for the Katie out there whom I have never met, most likely will never meet, and who quite possibly would annoy the living hell out of me if we did, but I would still like her to stay alive all the same.

I am writing this for people who are looking for signs to get started or to make a change, for people who believe there is something more out there for all of us.

I am writing this for all the dreamers who still believe in love, although their hearts have been broken five hundred times, and for the people who still believe in the good of humanity, while they walk around battered and bruised. I am writing this for all the people that know it's not easy and need that extra push or memo to remind them just to make it to tomorrow.

I am writing this book because I used to look at many of my idols who committed suicide, and I took comfort in knowing they understood how I felt. That in the end, it would make sense if I went out the same way.

I don't see it that way anymore though. I want to be the person who became all the things they could have been, had they chosen to stay alive. This is not a bash on these lost idols and who they are/were. I still understand what it feels like to have had enough, to feel done, to want to leave everything behind, to be ready to say goodbye to the world. But I have more to give, and I'm not done yet.

I cry every time I reread my suicide letter, because I still mean it, and I still feel it. I also feel the pain of the girl who wrote it as though that girl isn't me. That girl isn't just me, either. I know there are hundreds, thousands, probably even millions of people who have felt the exact same way. So, when I read that, I feel the pain of anyone else who ever felt as alone as I have at so many times in my life. We stand together in our desire to understand why the world works the way it does. Why so often we as humans choose to avoid the hard questions that mean so much to all of us, and instead to focus our attention on greed, excess, and things that ultimately never make us happy. It is madness.

That letter was the last suicide note I wrote. I hope never to write another. I am doing everything within my power to stop myself from ever feeling the need to write another. One of those things includes writing this book.

In writing this book, I am giving myself a greater chance of living, because, to be honest, I know myself. I know, if I tell people I am contemplating death, I will feel too guilty to ever do it. I would never want someone to think, even for a second, that it was their fault for not doing anything. It has taken me a very long time to get to this point, though.

One particular event, which we will come to later, happened during my teenage years and stopped me from speaking about these suicidal and melancholic emotions for over a decade. Why? Because I was afraid of what "they" do to people who talk about stuff like this.

Well, I'm fucking sick of it. I'm fucking sick of the stigma connected to mental health, which is so engrained in us, I can't even trust my own emotions sometimes. I am fucking sick of people being afraid to talk about something that could literally save their life as well as countless other people's lives. I'm fucking sick of losing some of the best-hearted people in this world, because we, as a human race, don't know how to treat one another properly. And maybe, just maybe, if I talk about my story as bluntly as I possibly can, people will start listening to others, too.

In the moments when I feel the darkness, I sometimes find myself begging and pleading for signs that everything will be okay. That, if I knew what the future held, it would be easier to hold off until tomorrow. But if someone had told me ten years ago about the events that would unfold in my life, I wouldn't have believed them, and more importantly, it would have dulled the moments to come. It would have ruined my anticipation of the steps along the journey that led me to where I am now. You know how all those super-corny and dramatic motivational speakers are always talking about the journey and not the destination? Well, they're right. And I am just as corny and dramatic.

As is my life.

Origin Story

I discovered Eric Thomas Ph.D., world-renowned motivational speaker, in 2016, when I set out to run my first and only half marathon. I used the app 8tracks back then to find motivational playlists to run to. When I stumbled upon, "When you want to succeed as bad as you want to breathe," it changed my life forever.

I was inspired even more when I found out both Eric Thomas and I grew up in Southfield, Michigan, battled homelessness, and took twelve years to get a four-year degree. I must point out, though, Eric Thomas is a Black man and I am a White woman, which makes our experiences vastly different.

At this point, I hadn't gone back to university yet. It didn't take long for that to change. When Eric Thomas tells us the story of the lion and the gazelle and how it's about the process and not the prize, he's right. Real lions love the hunt. Learning to love the hunt is a process in itself.

Sometimes, the words *magical* and *unexpected* feel like forced lies used to create a false sense of hope, making me want to punch myself in the face for how annoyingly positive I sound. Except it's not a lie, because, on my best of days, that is exactly who and how I am, but on my worst days, I somehow don't even deserve life anymore. This is the battle, and it didn't start overnight.

Everyone has a beginning to their story, and the narrative of that story can change at any given moment. My narrative has changed too many times to count, but that's me. That's the way I like it and I'll keep changing it up as long as I live.

I was born March 24, 1989, on Good Friday. And what a Good Friday that must have been, although I wasn't quite all together there yet. However, being born into a Catholic household, they must have really thought I was truly a gift from God, and I agree... was I ever!

I lived in the same house my entire childhood and adolescent life. While pregnant with me, my mom was so sick of house hunting, she declared that the next house they found would be "the one." To this day, my parents still live in that house in Southfield, Michigan, a suburb of Detroit. And although it is wonderfully nostalgic to go home for a visit, I wish they would just move on.

I don't really remember life before my sister was born, as I was only two. My father was a professional photographer, though, so my entire childhood was documented on video. The first blip in my ever-so-perfect life was the day Erin was born. I have been told constantly that I didn't like her from the second they sat her next to me. So, what did I do? Well, I punched her in the stomach and spit on her face, of course. From then on, I stole and hid all of her binkies and bottles and proceeded to tie all of her baby clothes around my body and limbs. My oft-repeated line was, "Hold da baby," while lifting my arms toward my mother and grasping at the air.

I was the baby, and this stranger came in and messed it all up for me. How did I deal with this pain...? I stole tubs of Country Crock margarine and bricks of cheddar cheese from the refrigerator. I would hide them under the dining room table or behind the living room curtains, which would allow me to devour them both in peace. Recently, my brother informed me that somehow my young niece had inherited this delicious yet larcenous trait from me. I had no idea anyone even knew about this and thought I'd gotten away with that all these years.

I've been mad at my parents for so long at this point that it has become my normal state whenever they are around. I realize that's not fair, and I'm working on it, but when you're the only person in a relationship who ever does any self-work, it makes connection and growth almost impossible. So, we learn how to implement boundaries. The concept can be stated many ways, but the mental health platform, *The Minds Journal,* relates it clearly and concisely:

"The more you heal, the more comfortable you are with being the villain in the story of people who don't want to do the work to heal themselves."

My family has spent the last thirty years laughing at these stories. Even I have spent the last thirty years laughing. Laughing became my coping mechanism. Because, if I didn't laugh, if I didn't go along with how everyone else felt, more often than not I was accused of being dramatic, seeking attention, and faking emotions. In my family, explanation of my feelings or emotions was ridiculed and forbidden.

It is hard for me to laugh when my family talks about "hold da baby" at this point, because all I want to do is go back in time, pick that little girl up, and love her as hard as I possibly can. I needed that. I needed someone to love me, not laugh at me.

I know this created a great deal of animosity within me that I have carried for much of my life. I know this also created a sense of independence at such a young age, as I could not rely on my parents to give me what I needed. Sometimes, I wonder how I might have turned out, if given the proper loving and nurturing environment I needed.

It's hard not to dwell on the past. Though, it is easier to dwell on a past you cannot control, because you never have to take responsibility for where you are now. You can make the choice to blame it on someone else and stay in your "woe is me" space forever.

That's not said to illegitimatize your experience. But at some point, you have to take control of your own life and say, "I'm not going to be a product of my environment. I don't want this to control me any longer."

I don't think it takes a different kind of person to be able to do this. I think we are all capable of being honest enough with ourselves and looking at where we need to let go, in order to create real change. The problem is, it's terrifying. It is so much easier to latch on to our limitations and to the narratives we've been telling ourselves for years if not decades. Accepting these beliefs and stories for how it has to be, using them as excuses for why we don't have all the things we want and why we aren't and never will be the person we want to be.

I think it's all bullshit. It's all bullshit for anyone who is capable of reading this book. Anyone who has the capability to obtain this book and actually read it has the ability to decide, "I am not going to be that person anymore." You just have to decide and put in the work.

Don't Let Me Get Me

The first time I ever fell in love, I was four years old. The whole world of Bingham Farms Preschool supposedly knew about my love story. For my birthday, my mom made pumpkin muffins for the entire class, a strange choice for a March birthday. This was a time before ever present allergies and awareness of gluten intolerance, so I assume I just loved pumpkin cupcakes, which makes sense, being the basic bitch that I am. When it came time to tell my mom what I wanted for my class, she must have reminded me how much I loved them, which immediately excited me about doing something different!

I did not know at the time that Sawyer, my love, absolutely despised pumpkin cupcakes, which obviously resulted in me believing that he hated me forever. I mean, kids are kids. If they think something is gross and that thing can be correlated to a person, it therefore makes that person gross, too. Back to Sawyer, who clearly hated me, and now I was labeled as gross, which broke my little four-year-old heart.

Pretty soon after the pumpkin muffin incident, Sawyer moved away, and no one told me. I went to class one day and couldn't find him anywhere. I was told he wouldn't be coming back. Ann Smyth (my best friend's mother) had to physically drag me out of the building as I screamed and cried.

I am assuming my four-year-old brain told itself Sawyer hated me because of the pumpkin muffins and never wanted to see me again. No one told me differently.

This could be a pretty good explanation of my never-ending need to please my male interests, as I grew up. Always living with the fear that they would not like me or would abandon me, if I did anything "wrong" or something they didn't like. Add in the familial trauma and *Bam!* You have the perfect storm for an elder millennial, stricken with anxiety, trying to reverse the effects of generational trauma in a world that seems on the edge of nonexistence on a daily basis.

I always wanted to be cute and girly. But from a young age, I recognized I wasn't the cutest girl by any standard definition. My family didn't have the money to keep up with the Joneses, so I was automatically classified into categories such as, "decent-looking," "lower-income," and "weird."

The *weird* label was actually and inherently me, and I think it was the easiest aspect to identify with, because it was the only real attribute that was part of the human being I was and still am, at heart. So, I not only rolled with it, but once again, I embraced it. And part of embracing the weird side of my nature was to acknowledge the positive and negative reinforcement toward my new behavior.

I didn't realize I was doing this at the time, still being a young child, but it is definitely what was happening. Most likely these internal and external interactions inaugurated my dramatic black-and-white view about things. Being intensely different meant getting the attention I craved at home, from the outside world, at school, and from friends.

"Katie, this song always reminds me of you!"
As though that's a compliment.
The song was "Don't Let Me Get Me" by Pink.
Is this what everyone thinks about me?

"I'm a hazard to myself."

It reminds me of me, too.

Several incidents stick out in my mind as moments when I recognized how my economic status as a child consistently impacted me. The first came during Christmas, when I was in middle school.

I have always loved dressing up, even as a young child. Another running joke in my family was that my godmother, while holding me during baptism, whispered in my ear, "You were born to shop." Which is ironic, because I hate shopping, most likely because it is directly tied to money, which I was always taught to hate due to our family never having enough of it. Nevertheless, this struggle never deterred my love of dressing up.

So naturally, between my desire for attention and my love of dressing up, I was voted as Most School Spirited in middle school. When you are named as something like this during the formative years, you create a need to live up to the title that has been bestowed upon you.

Well, Christmas was coming, and on the last day before the school break, I *had* to dress up, in order to get everyone excited. Ya know, like ya do.

I knew exactly what I wanted to wear. A pair of red pants, this velvet, green turtleneck T-shirt of my sister's, and to complete the ensemble, tied a big bow around my body, so I could be a walking present for everyone before they left for the holidays.

There was only one problem, the green-velvet shirt was dirty. This was during a time when my sister wasn't yet old enough, about eleven, or self-aware enough to think of putting on deodorant every day. Needless to say… the shirt reeked. But I couldn't let this get in my way of showing up for the people. So, I doused it in perfume and rubbed deodorant all around the inside and the armpits, which ruined the texture and created pit stains. Yet still I persisted.

I didn't have anything else to wear that fit me or would be Christmasy. I can still imagine walking down the hallway, not wanting to lift my arms to say hi to people as they passed and being able to smell myself all day long, just waiting for the moment I could leave to avoid anyone else having to smell me.

Why wouldn't my parents buy us deodorant or razors? Why did I have to sneak in to use my dad's deodorant? Why did I have to sneak shaving my legs for the first time and end up slicing my leg from knee to hip? Because my mom refused to teach me how, saying I wasn't old enough, while at school and on trips with friends, I was made fun of incessantly for how long my leg hair was at my age. Why did I have to share clothes with my sister? She wasn't the "sharing is caring" kind of sister, anyway. So, in addition to being smelly, I had to worry all day about going home and getting yelled at for wearing my sister's shirt, since she was bound to see me in it at school.

During this time in our lives, I would take the bus to school most days, while my sister would get driven to school and dropped off by our dad. She made him drop her off down the street, so kids wouldn't see the car she got out of or who she was related to, especially if I happened to be in the car that morning, as well. She was friends with all the rich, popular kids and therefore needed to have all the stylish clothes they owned and wore, which of course she would get.

I was trained to make things easier and to want less, so I pretended not to want or like nice things, and this made it easier to be happy with what I did have. If the girls in seventh grade knew how heartbroken I was over the only pair of dance pants my parents afforded me, which shrank after the first time I wore them because my mom didn't know not to dry them, then they would also know I couldn't afford more than one pair.

As I continued to wear my favorite yet flooded dance pants, they became a constant reminder of our financial limits and created a sense of scarcity. I spent entire days pulling them down over my feet in the middle of class, hoping, if I just held them stretched long enough, they might go back to the length they were supposed to be. You'd think I would just stop wearing something that made me feel so uncomfortable, but I couldn't. Once a week, groups of girls planned matching outfits where dance pants were the main event.

During that same year, I was prescribed glasses for the first time. My first thought: *I will change my entire look!* I would start wearing Polos and khakis and wear my rectangular-framed silver Tommy Hilfiger glasses constantly. A person who wears glasses doesn't need dance pants! I decided I would be smart and beautiful like the women in the pictures at the ophthalmologist's office. Then, I would look put together, and people wouldn't think I was poor.

The problem was, my khakis were also flooded, and the Polos I wore were off-brand and far too small for me. I was wearing hand-me-downs from my younger sister. I repeat, my *younger* sister!

In less than a month, I lost the glasses, and my parents couldn't afford to get me another pair. I didn't get another pair of glasses until I was thirty-three, once I had my own insurance and own money, so I could afford another pair. I kept my glasses case in my pencil case for the rest of the school year, empty.

Not only was I battling my issues at school, but a lot was going on in my private life, as well.

I tend to connect a lot of things to the people in my life who have died. In 2002, my Aunt Nancy had been living in the Cleveland Clinic hospital for over a year. By this point, she had suffered two major heart attacks and several strokes. For a woman in her early forties, this wasn't normal, but they couldn't seem to figure out what was wrong with her heart, so she was placed on the heart transplant list.

The week before she found out she would be getting a new heart, I was supposed to go visit her with my dad. I hadn't yet visited her at the Cleveland Clinic, but everyone kept talking about how she was going to get a heart and we wouldn't have to worry. My aunt was going to be fine.

I chose not visit her that weekend, which happened to be around my birthday, and I didn't want to miss spending time with my friends. But also, we'd been assured a new heart had been "found," and she would receive the transplant the following week. Being an adult now and knowing how the world actually works, there is no way I would not have gone, had I known what would come next. When you're a kid, who hasn't been given the explanation of what a heart transplant really involves, it can just come across as a simple, easy fix.

"She's getting a new heart, and she's going to be all better? That's wonderful!"

As a child, if no one explains to you the reality of a surgery like this, you have no reason to have any concern or worry, because all you know is what everyone has told you, time and time again: "Don't worry, everything is going to be fixed and wonderful again.

Nancy went into surgery for a heart transplant on March 19, 2002, and bled out right there on the table. She never made it out of surgery. The day before her surgery, she'd called my mom in tears, and my mom tried to comfort her, believing she was afraid of what might happen on that table. However, my Aunt Nancy told her she wasn't crying because she was afraid of dying, she was crying because the surgeons were going to cut out her breast implants, and she was afraid my Uncle Todd wouldn't love her without them. I think about that a lot.

Then, I think about a conversation I overheard, years prior to my Aunt Nancy's death, at my Nana and Papa's house, after my other uncle, Joe, had started dating our now Aunt Patty. My mom proceeded to tell everyone about how my sister wasn't able to decide which uncle's house she liked going to more: my Uncle Joe's, to see

Patty, or my Uncle Todd's, to go on his boat. I might have been the only one to notice my Aunt Nancy murmuring under her breath about that being a nice thing to say to everyone, while she sat right there.

I was twelve years old when my Aunt Nancy died, over twenty years ago, and it still saddens me to think about how alone she must have felt, for her to be more worried about breast implants than her life on the day before heart transplant surgery. I just wish I could have been there for her, even as a child.

I look back now on my naivete as a child and really wish people (especially my parents) had been more honest with me. I didn't understand death. I didn't understand the abruptness of it. Or why I never got to say goodbyes. I think I knew, without entirely knowing, that adults weren't being honest with me. So, from a very young age, I felt extreme betrayal in the hardest moments of my life.

I lost my best friend's mother in September 2001, my aunt in March 2002, and my grandpa in November 2003. Every year of middle school, someone close to me died. Additionally, 9/11 rocked all of our worlds during the same time. I came to believe that this is how life works. Every year, someone else important to me dies without warning, and that is how the rest of my life will be. I am getting a picture of how so many of the things I did during this time of my life might have been reactionary or cries for help.

I realize, as important as all of those people are to my story and to who I am as a human, those people are not me. I am who I am today because of the decisions I have made for myself. For better or worse.

During this time, another pivotal moment of my life occurred. It was 2002, I was in eighth grade, and Avril Lavigne had just topped the TRL countdown. I was raging with prepubescent hormones and a longing to belong (which seems even funnier now, putting it into perspective). I wasn't in the popular group, but I wasn't not popular.

It was fourth period Language Arts, taught by Mrs. Warren, who wasn't exactly the sharpest tool in the shed. Boys spent most of the period mooning kids in the trailer classroom outside without her ever noticing, so it was easy to get off task.

Darlene Steedman sat in front of me and loaned me her scissors. Because, ya know, kids just always have a pair of shears handy anytime you need them. Well, accept for me. I was definitely the kid constantly borrowing things from other students.

I actually asked Mrs. Warren if I could cut my hair in her class, which just proves the whole suck-up theory everyone has about me with my teachers. But I don't know if it's really considered sucking up or more of just being honest. She obviously said no, so I asked if I could go to the bathroom.

I walked into the bathroom on the second floor in the most southeast corner of Berkshire Middle School that afternoon, and I cut off my entire pony tail.

There was a sense of bullshit that covered my entire adolescent life and I don't know what it was about, precisely, but I was tired of trying to understand it. I decided, without understanding the concept very well, being a thirteen-year-old, that I would rather see action than hear useless words. And if my friends felt like bullshit to me, well, they could prove to me they weren't by the way they treated me, after I no longer had hair.

What thirteen-year-old does that?! I sometimes don't even think I know who that person was!

I should mention two life-changing movies for me, as a kid. One of my favorite movies to this day is *Empire Records,* and the other is *Wild Hearts Can't Be Broken.*

So, during fourth-period language arts, in an attempt to experience the orgasm that I'd felt the first time I watched Robin Tunney shave her head in *Empire Records,* I created my own moment of freedom. That moment changed my life trajectory forever. I look to *that* girl, who went into the bathroom, for strength in my times of weakness.

The first time I ever saw *Empire Records* was one New Year's Eve in elementary school. All the big kids were watching the movie in a bedroom upstairs at our family friend's house. The only little kids at the party were my sister and me, so the big kids hid us in a closet, so we could watch the movie through the cracks in the doors.

Whenever the parents came looking for us, the big kids lied; our parents got drunk enough never to realize the little kids were watching a PG-13 movie. One that would inspire their daughter to cut off all her hair in the middle of class at school.

I have always been someone who runs against the grain. For one year, I switched schools before rejoining my elementary classmates at our new middle school. The new experience had taught me one thing: I knew I didn't want the same friends I'd had before. Nothing against them; I just needed to branch out.

I walked into the first year of middle school and started pointing my finger at everyone I wanted to be friends with, as though I was picking a team for dodgeball during lunch. But you know, not for the Cobras Team, but for the Average Joes Team. That is how I met one of my best friends to this day.

Gina was sitting alone on the bleachers at lunch. I don't remember every detail, but Gina can still recall my outfit (I guess details stick harder when you're alone and someone else notices you). When she describes it, I can remember exactly how that red sweater felt around my neck, how it was too hot and too itchy. Also, how those khaki pants were too tight and always showed my butt crack, if I tried to move in any way at all.

(Isn't it funny how hyper-aware you are of all those things as a middle schooler? Nowadays, I'll wear a pair of genie pants with a ten-inch hole in the crotch and butt with no underwear and think, "Well, I guess I hope no one notices.")

Gina is the only person from that time in my life who has remained one of my best friends.

I was thirteen when I got my first real job. I had been babysitting family friends since middle school, but my first "real" job was working on the weekends at a movie theatre called The Palladium in downtown Birmingham.

Because I was only thirteen years old, the laws were strict about when I was and was not allowed to work. Shifts were a specific length of time, as well, so I couldn't work after school on weekdays. On weekends, I worked long shifts, eight hours with one required thirty-minute break. At thirteen, I was only allowed to rip tickets or work the concessions, both being the most brutal positions in a movie theatre. There were waves of people for five to ten minutes and then nothing to do but stand there or clean for an hour or so.

Time passed so slowly, I felt like I was in prison but worse, because I was surrounded by all my favorite things and not allowed to have any of them. Pizza, pop, movies, popcorn... It was torture. If we wanted anything to drink, we had to use a disposable cup and fill it with an inch of liquid, walk out of concessions, down our shot of pop, and get back to work.

My brother also worked there at the time, but he was older, so he was allowed to do the cooler jobs like cleaning the movie theatres (doesn't sound cool, but you could hide in the theatre and watch the movies). Plus, he had access to all the leftover food at the end of the night, so he would take the black trash bags filled with leftover popcorn and bring them home.

I can't remember how long I worked at that movie theatre or how I even quit. That is how much I hated working there. I do remember, my first day, not knowing I had to pay for my own meal, and not having any money, so I didn't eat; how bad my feet hurt when I had to stand in the same spot for eight hours ripping tickets; those shots of Cherry Coke, and finally getting to see the new *Peter Pan* (2003) for free. That was it. Today, I fucking love Cherry Coke, on the rare occasion I do drink it I allow myself to enjoy it entirely, wherever I want. Never let anyone ruin the things you love and enjoy, even if it's just a shot of pop.

My next job was working at an A&W, one with a big parking lot that looks like people should deliver your food to your car on roller skates, but they don't.

I was very excited to get that job, because I *loved* A&W. Big pop and fast-food guy over here. I very quickly learned just how terrible it is to work in fast food. Especially fast-food franchises owned by families.

On my very first day working at A&W, I learned that I was the only person in the business who was not a family member. They taught me how to make milkshakes and the difference between real root beer and the fake carbonated stuff we're accustomed to. I made root beer floats and learned how to organize the food into their given bags for delivery. It was pretty simple, but it was also my first job where I was put on the spot, with everyone watching to see if I was even capable of doing the tedious tasks that they gave me.

At one point, I reached to grab a just-wrapped burger and throw it into the bag for delivery when my elbow hit a paper cup next to me, and it fell to the ground. *One. Cup.*

"*Mommmm! The new girl knocked over alllll the cups!*" yelled the son in charge of the flat-top as he gave me a smirk. He was half my size, at least two years younger than me, and a little shit. What a fucking douche canoe.

The mom came over, confronted me about the cups, yelled at me about how much each cup costs and how they would have to throw all of them away for touching the ground. She then told me I was finished for the day.

This happened on Labor Day weekend, and I was supposed to train for three days in a row. Saturday, Sunday, and Monday. The next day, my friends and I all gathered at Beverly Park. I was pissed that I had to go back to that awful place; I was supposed to work at 1 p.m. It was around 11 a.m., and none of my friends at the time had jobs, so they were all in the middle of planning the rest of the day outside. It was beautiful.

Fuck A&W and that family! I never wanted to go back there again. I didn't think twice. I didn't even plan what I was going to say. Before I knew it, the phone was ringing and douche-canoe's mom answered the line.

"A&W on 12 Mile in Berkley. How can I help you?"

"Hi, yes. This is Katie Dickieson. I had my first day training with you guys yesterday. I won't be able to make it into work today."

"Okay. Are you okay? Is there a reason you won't be able to make it in?"

"No, I just can't."

"Okay, will we be seeing you tomorrow?"

"No. Thank you for the opportunity, but I'm never coming back there again. Bye."

I hung up the phone, jumped in line to hit the joint my friends were passing, and had an incredible day in the sun. Every time I look back at that move I made, I think of how big of a little badass I was for doing that.

It makes me wonder, at what point in my life did my anxiety change from, *I'm not going to allow anyone to disturb my inner peace,* to *I must do everything I can to make these awful people happy.* Maybe, the freedom of being a kid and knowing I could get a part-time gig like that anywhere was helpful. I knew no one was going to be calling an A&W for references.

Preachers and Pot

I was raised Catholic. Baptism, catechism, first Communion, Confirmation, church every Sunday—you know, the whole shebang. As I moved into high school, our family found a new church that wasn't Catholic. It was nondenominational. It had lights and a band, and every Sunday, we got to watch a skit, as if we were at the theatre. I began to enjoy church more.

The week before starting high school, I got caught smoking pot for the first time. I was immediately grounded and only allowed to go to church things. So, I dove in head-first to the Monday night teens club called The Edge. My brother had already made friends there and was part of the popular group.

We lived a thirty to forty-five-minute drive away from the church. It was in a completely different school district. The only way I got to hang out with people from church was if my brother drove me.

He never liked me hanging out with him and his friends, so he left me behind a lot. I wasn't allowed to be friends or hang out with the people I wanted to from school, and I had no way of reaching the people I wanted to be friends with at church.

I believed in God but not in the way everyone else seemed to believe, which really didn't work in my family or in our church. There was always a "right" way and a "wrong" way to do things in those spaces. I didn't believe that either, though, and my own relationship with God told me that wasn't true. I trusted my relationship with God over other's opinions of my relationship with God.

I also liked girls and guys but knew without having to be told that wasn't going to be accepted. Ironically, I can't remember any specific moment when I was told or showed that the world around me was homophobic. I think I was just breathing in the general climate of unacceptance in our town, the culture, my family, and the church. It was just unexplainably clear that I wasn't safe to be who I was/am.

The Edge gave out Xboxes and pizza every week and the popular groups were just as cliquey as school. The only difference, I noticed at church, was that the overwhelming majority seemed to be rich and elitist in the name of God. That never sat well with me. I went there for connection.

I became a leader in that group, so I could help spread that connection and help others who felt alone feel like they had somewhere safe to go. I was fourteen! Debating the leaders of the church about what was right and what was wrong and what actually mattered. I spent every morning before school handing out flyers for my church group at the front doors. I debated my Vice Principal for the right to post notices in hallways, and I won on the basis that the boys' county hockey team was able to hang their posters, although they were not associated with the school, either.

I fought everyone. And because of that, I was made the "example" by every authority figure who was terrified by their inability to control me. By the church, the school, my teachers and especially in my own home. My parents wouldn't put it that way, but my youth pastor and my band teacher certainly did. Their reasoning: I was capable of handling it.

Almost twenty years later, I would get into a similar argument with a co-worker, when he said the same exact thing: "Well, I know you can handle it better than other people."

"That doesn't mean I have to."

I left the Edge after the youth pastor, who had made me his example for over a year, left the church. He was gone, but all the people who stood by and let him treat me that way were still around. It was those bystanders with whom I had more of an issue. The people, the bystanders, who let bad things continue to happen.

One day, while dropping my sister off at youth group, I was approached by another youth pastor whom I liked. He asked me how someone with faith as strong as mine could leave the church. I wrote him a thirteen-page email with everything I knew that was wrong with the church. No surprise, money being the major factor.

Years later, while in hair school, I got a Facebook message from the same pastor. He was reaching out to let me know my Small Group leader had passed after a brain aneurysm. He remembered I had been close with her. While catching up, I learned that, very soon after I wrote him that email, he left the church and went back to work as an engineer, while becoming the pastor at a different church. He worked at this new church for free. Sometimes, I wonder if my letter might actually have helped inspire that change. I was seventeen when I sent him that email.

Resilience: I Always Find a Way

I am not exactly sure when I first learned what it meant to be resilient but I can tell you I have been practicing resilience for longer than I can remember and not happily. I actually got to a point in my life where I became very resentful of that word. It was presented to me as though it was a badge of honor but one that I had no time or use for. It felt like every day I had a new person saying the same thing to me:

"Well, you're resilient. You always find a way," with a smirk and a pat on the back.

Seriously? Fuck you!

I felt like my mishaps were everyone's entertainment, as though I was the court jester.

"What's the drama today, Katie? There's always *something* going on with you."

I learned to use humor about my resilience as a defense mechanism and why not, my life had been nothing but one survival mindset to the next. That's how I was taught to deal with anything serious in life.

So, I created the *Lavish Homeless Lifestyle.* I made a list of everyone I had ever fucked (including all the men who had raped or sexually abused me), along with their astrological signs. I mocked my childhood abuse to make sure I never became the Debbie Downer in any situation, due to my status in this world and what cards I had been dealt.

I never wanted to be resilient. I never asked to be a badass. I became one out of pure survival instinct.

I was labeled difficult but also very smart, at a very young age, so I was ignored like so many other children given these labels. Because, when you are a difficult child, you are seen as doing anything and everything you can to get attention, as though there is something wrong with just wanting to be loved.

When I was a child, my parents would lock my sister and me in our room. If we needed to go to the bathroom? Well, they tossed in a large popcorn bowl to be used as a toilet. When I later confronted my parents about this, I was told it had been a joke just like everything else. (See the pattern?) Abuse as a joke. I was told time and again to "lighten up" and to not take things too seriously.

As I lay in the dark, trapped in my locked room, screaming bloody murder, pounding my feet against the walls, and begging to be let out, my sister learned it was not beneficial to be like me. From this early age she knew, as long as she didn't act like me, she would be rewarded.

I knew I was hurting. I knew I was scared. I knew I needed comfort. I knew I deserved all those things, and when my needs as a child were not met, I learned how to be resilient.

I emptied my small closet. Into it, I pushed my nightstand full of books and a child-size director's chair. I sat down and slid the doors shut. I created a safe space for myself to go. A place I could escape to. I created my own home.

I have lived this way my entire life. I will say there may be a slight advantage to developing resiliency for those who experience traumas such as these at a young age. Anyone who experiences having to grow up much earlier than they should will understand this best. This is called adultification.

> *"When notions of innocence and vulnerability are not afforded to certain children."* (Davis and Marsh, 2020)

When this happens outside of the home, it is always grounded in bias and discrimination. Certain aspects of that child's personal characteristics, socio-economic situation, or lived experiences are met with discriminatory responses. This means that, rather than being seen as children experiencing abuse, they are viewed as either responsible in some way, or as more resilient and able to withstand maltreatment.

It is important to point out that black children are much more likely to be subject to adultification bias. Black boys and girls are often perceived through the lens of racialised stereotypes. The roots of these stereotypes can be linked back to the dehumanising racial attitudes of colonialism (Goff et al, 2014*).*

I, however, do not believe in the tough-love mentality. I can look back on my past and appreciate the lessons I learned as a result of what I've gone through, but I would have rather had the choice of feeling loved than not.

When you grow up without feeling loved, you tend to look for love anywhere you can get it, without ever really accepting or feeling like you deserve it. You constantly feel like you're a permanent resident on the island of misfit toys.

People like us tend to pride ourselves on our ability to, in the words of the punk band, Chumbawamba, "Get knocked down, but I get up again," without ever really letting ourselves heal from those times we've been knocked down. We do not allow ourselves to accept that it was never okay for those things to have happened to us. Instead, we wear our pain and trauma as another badge of honor. As though we're going through life trying to one-up each other, based on how much pain we've endured and how far we've come.

Countless times, I have cried out about my hatred of resilience and begged to no longer be forced into it.

At age thirty-one, I was diagnosed with Premenstrual Dysphoric Disorder (PMDD) and while speaking with my therapist, I lost it. After years of going to doctors, trying to find out what was wrong with me, I finally figured it out, only to learn there was no cure. Being a scientist, I was ecstatic about finding out the reason behind the problem, because that meant I could control/fix/solve the puzzle—*anything*! But PMDD isn't that easy, and it doesn't just affect you; it affects every aspect of your life, including those you love most.

It has been three years since my diagnosis of PMDD, although I have lived with the effects of it my entire post-pubescent life. But, if it weren't for my resilience, I am not sure I would be alive today. I have spent the past three years tracking my cycle and researching holistic ways to mitigate symptoms; I am living with a manageable form of PMDD now that I never thought possible.

. The definition of resilience, the ability to withstand or recover quickly from difficulties, doesn't capture just how arduous and painful it is to be resilient. The definition makes resilience sound like a rubber band or a Slinky springing right back into place as though nothing was affected in the process.

To me, resilience is more like constantly getting snapped by a rubber band while being forced to walk a tightrope across the Grand Canyon with no safety net. Or have your skin caught between all the Slinky wires as someone squeezes it back together, over and over again, while you're on a trapeze. And though you may accomplish both, you still hurt afterward, because your body has been subjected to consistent pain throughout the process. Instead of being able to celebrate your accomplishment, you end up licking your wounds. You tell yourself, "That wasn't as good as it could have been, because imagine if I didn't have X, Y, and Z working against me."

Like, you still fucking *walked a tight rope across the Grand Canyon and trapezed with no safety net!* Isn't it insane what we put ourselves through, mentally and emotionally, in order to prove our worth to people? People we don't even like, people who have wronged us and we wouldn't even want in our life?

I did this to myself in such an extreme way that my body eventually physically reacted. In 2020, I experienced what my neurologist, at the time, called a pseudo-seizure. I lost all vision and control of my body. I didn't know where or who I was for over two hours.

How did I get to this point? Well, it took some time. In 2017, I decided to go back to school for a nursing certificate. I was twenty-eight years old. I took eighteen credits a semester while working three jobs for two years. The most important people in my life were my grandparents, Nana and Papa. I wanted to make them proud of me more than anyone in my life.

I wanted to create a life like my Papa had given to my entire extended family, so that, when I was older, I could afford to take all of us on vacations and keep the family close, like he had done for us.

I was late to the game (so I believed) so it was hard for me to think I was allowed to "shoot for the stars."

"Just do enough to make a decent amount of money, Katie." That's what I had been taught by my parents throughout my life. When things changed along my educational path, I lied to everyone in my family about what I was really doing.

All I wanted more than anything in the world was for my Nana and Papa to see me graduate. My best friend and I planned the event together. Once graduation day arrived, she would go to their house and live stream it for them, as they were in their nineties and couldn't travel.

I was set to graduate with my bachelor's degree in December, 2019. In September, 2019, I became homeless. In October, my Papa passed away. A few weeks later, and only a week before my graduation date, my Nana passed. I had a cap specially made that said *For Nana and Papa.* I walked the stage on Friday the 13th, in December, 2019. I received my bachelor's in Biological Sciences Pre-Med, finishing in two years while working three jobs and living the *Lavish Homeless Lifestyle.*

I didn't know how to feel my emotions. When I became homeless and Papa died, I told myself I was allowed to do anything I needed to do, in order to survive and make it to that graduation date. I picked up smoking again and was taking Adderall every day.

After I graduated, I didn't even know how to be proud of myself. I had no idea what the future held, and I didn't know what to do. To keep myself busy, I got a fourth job and re-enrolled in more courses I didn't even need.

Two months later, in the last week of February, 2020, I walked into my bartending job at Copperpoint Brewery in Boynton Beach, Florida, and I collapsed on the ground in front of my good friend and manager. I spent two hours on the floor, shaking and unable to see. I had no idea who I was, where I was, or how to effectively breathe.

My resilience without reward had caught up to me, and my physical body wasn't going to let me go any further until I slowed the fuck down.

My doctors had me take the next week off from school and from *all* work. Coincidentally, the following week, my friend Frances had already planned and paid for me to visit her in California. My brother and his family also lived there at the time, so I would be able to see my niece and nephews. I didn't know it at the time, but the universe had my back and was about to change my life forever. The catalyst, the tipping point, was the lowest point of my life, as I sat on the ground on that day at Copperpoint.

Chapter 2

Those Who Fight for their Limitations Get to Keep Them

"We got no food, we got no jobs, our pets' heads are falling off!"

—Llyod, *Dumb and Dumber*

I WAS IN SECOND GRADE the first time my mom took me to a therapist. I remember being confused about why I was there and about the questions the doctor asked my mom.

"Does your family have a history of mental illness?"

"Yes, my grandmother committed suicide," my mother sheepishly replied.

That's the day I learned what the word *suicide* meant. And I learned it in a room where I would be forced to look and examine myself far more than anyone else in my family.

Does this mean me and my great-grandmother are the same? Am I going to commit suicide? Why won't anyone talk to me about this?

In order to be persistent, one must also have resilience. The reverse, however, is not true. You could be resilient and just be surviving, no forward momentum, just getting by from one moment to the next. To *persist*, though, to be a persistent person, means you've already married and divorced resilience a couple of times. At this point, you have unhappily accepted that you and resilience will have a relationship for the rest of your lives.

Kind of like the relationship I have with my mother. I love her, but it has taken me a long time to understand that and appreciate her in my life.

Looking back at my story about being locked in my room as a child, you could say that might have been my first experience with persistence. The part where I screamed and pounded my feet on the wall, even getting to the point of desperation, when I opened my windows and yelled out to my neighbors, to at least have someone to talk to. I also thought, maybe if my neighbors became aware of how my parents were treating me, they would stop it. Maybe my neighbors would save me.

I am not really sure how intricate my thoughts were about that at such a young age, but nevertheless, I persisted. I was going to be heard. I was going to be seen. Even if my parents weren't going to be the ones on the receiving end, I was going to make sure someone was.

Luckily for me, people outside my family loved me from a very young age. Or maybe I forced my way into their lives, and by default, they learned to love me. Either way, it is the families that I created throughout my life who have really saved me. These are the people who helped to pave my way to survival and, then, to thrival.

I spent much of my younger life trying to prove people wrong. I can still be guilty of this today, but luckily, I have learned how to tune in to myself and understand whether I am fighting for something I actually believe in, or if it's just my ego showing off. It's hard to tell the difference when you're younger, filled with rage and passion. Feelings I was filled with to the brim.

I figured out creative ways to persist through life. I look back at the young girl I was and think what a badass she really was.

I have always had a zero-tolerance policy for bullshit. The lack of communication in my family led me to type up pages and page of letters to my parents. I would then print them out, staple them together, and put the letters on their pillows at night. Again, I was begging to be heard. I'm pretty sure every single one of those letters I wrote ended up in the trash.

I felt a similar way with my friends at school. I always had a problem feeling accepted and included into groups. I even switched schools to follow people I thought were my friends in fifth grade, only to experience one of the hardest, most embarrassing, and loneliest years of my life. Come sixth grade, I switched back, and everyone thought I'd found my "real parents." Probably because, in fourth grade, I had told everyone I was adopted whenever people noticed I looked nothing like my siblings or parents. (I assumed this was my green light to totally separate myself from them mentally.)

Looking back on those middle school years, I see a very "normal," White, suburban girl with her group of friends. I see a young girl getting her first period, playing MASH, talking shit, and experiencing her first kiss on a Friday night, at Y-Night in seventh grade. I sure seemed like I had it good, man.

I *was fucking dying inside.*

At eleven years old, I wanted to die. I drank Pine-Sol for no particular reason other than it felt like a way out. I survived, but after that I was called "Pine-Sol girl" over AOL Instant Messenger (AIM) by a mean girl I am still not fond of today.

I was sick of my "friends" telling me what to wear, how to act, who I could be friends with, and which boys to date. The structure of what was acceptable to a teenage girl made me want to vomit. I felt like I was in a psychological prison I couldn't break free from.

Cutting my hair off during the most formidable years of my life definitely taught me about persistence. I wanted to know whether people liked me for who I was as a person, not for what I looked like or what they could get from me.

It worked.

It completely polarized my life in all areas. What I did not think about, though, before taking this action, was becoming "that girl." I had already spent my entire life begging to be seen and to be loved by my parents, while being told that everything I did was just for attention. Now, to any observer, I had just exacerbated that.

"The attention-seeking drama queen."

"She does anything she can for attention."

It wasn't until years later, when my mom and I discussed the hair-cutting incident, that she told me one of my friend's parents actually contacted her, telling her she believed my action was a cry for help. I confirmed this belief, and I told her it certainly *was.* Even in that moment, as two adults talking, my mom couldn't accept what I was telling her as truth.

It *was* a cry for help, Mom. When I walked into the house after school that day and found my dad folding laundry, all he did was ask how school was. I had to tell him I'd cut off all my hair. And even though he could physically see me standing in front of him, his response still was, "No, you didn't."

So, I persisted.

My parents saw me as the problem child for many reasons, but one reason specifically was how often I quit and started new things. They saw me as a quitter, as opposed to someone who stuck up for themselves. Instead of having my back in these moments, I would often hear from them, "What did you do to deserve this?" And they became more inclined not to allow me to start new things, because I would just end up quitting them anyways.

Regardless of my reasons for quitting everything I ever started as a kid, I don't think there is anything wrong with it. In reality, I believe kids need more of this freedom in order to figure out what it is they actually enjoy doing! What's with this whole attitude of forcing kids to play the same sport or instrument from the time they're born and never letting them try anything new? It's stupid, man.

Here's the thing. I am sharing all these short stories from my life so you can see how I persisted through my life. Although it may not look the same in your stories, what will be similar is inherently knowing right from wrong for yourself.

I knew from a young age what I was okay with and what I wasn't, and I followed that. Unfortunately, a lot of people don't let themselves be guided this way, and they end up having to unlearn a lot of shit as adults, in order to even understand that they have an inner compass they haven't been following this whole time. When you learn to listen to that inner compass and to accept that whatever you choose for happiness is right, no matter what, no one can fuck with you. This is living as your authentic self.

Persisting, to me, means pushing every boundary in your life that rejects or resists your fullest, most authentic self. Every time someone or something tries to push you in a direction that doesn't align with who you are as a person, you have to say, "Fuck that shit" and go the other way. Any way is better than the way of someone who wants you to conform. You must be willing to blindly have faith, though, in the universe and in your authenticity and your own ability to get through what the world throws at you.

My mentality my entire life has always been: Ya know what...? Fuck it! Whether it's the mentality of being homeless is better than living by the rules and regulations of my Catholic parents, or that being unemployed is better than being enslaved to a fucked-up system or countless other examples throughout my life. I'm telling you, fortune favors the bold, dude. You've just got to be willing to take the leap.

I like to play this game with myself now, when I start to have anxiety about anything in my life. It's kind of a twist on the game Randall and Beth play on *This is Us*: "Worst-Case Scenario." Being someone who has suffered from suicidal ideation my entire life, it usually comes down to will the worst-case scenario make me want to kill myself.

At this point, the biggest threat to my existence is my own mind, but if I can persist through my own worst-case scenario... I think, *Fuck it. Let's find out what happens when I take this leap. Worst-case scenario; I will survive.*

The more you give yourself the opportunity to trust your badass-ness, the stronger that intuition becomes. Your survival-to-thrival instincts become sharper and more fine-tuned. I suggest you start small, but by all means necessary just start jumping, man!

If you are a person who has never jumped in your life, understand that I am an extremist and my mentality aligns more with the way I attack a theme park. Specifically, Cedar Point, because it's the only theme park that matters.

Always start with the ride that scares you most. When you ride the Millennium Force first thing in the morning, everything else seems like a cinch. Life is the same.

I think we are able to use physical actions to jump-start these mental barriers in our life. Afraid to go live on IG? Go sky diving. Don't know how to quit your job you hate? Go bungee jumping. Do something physical to jump-start the mental. Seriously, go jump out of an airplane and tell me you're not a different person after that experience. I might have lived multiple lifetimes on this planet, but I know I want to experience everything I can in this one that I've got right now. So, I persist.

I've gotten to a point in my life where my drive is so in parallel with persistence and resilience that, as my life has become easier, it's actually become more difficult to persist, because I don't have to fight as hard. Now, I must learn a new form of persistence. What used to look like four jobs, a full load of courses, and an alcohol/cigarettes/Adderall habit to survive has transformed into meditation, manifestation, and the constant process of unlearning. I can now see life doesn't need to look like the former for me to be someone who is worthy of happiness.

Persistence doesn't have to be painful. The more you know who you are and are comfortable with who that person is, the less painful persistence will be. You will no longer settle for anything less than what you desire.

Persistence doesn't have to be painful. Remember that.

Birthmarks and Breakaways

I was seventeen years old and summer had just started. I should have been hanging out with my friends, but instead, I was on my way to therapy with my parents on a Friday night.

They'd promised me I could go see my boyfriend after that, though, so I obliged. I should have known something was up with both mom and dad taking me to my therapy session. Another appointment just for me, not for anyone else in the family. The message was clear: I was the problem, I was dysfunctional.

As I have mentioned, I 'd been forced to go to therapy since second grade, while no one else in the family ever went and certainly had never been forced to go. In some way, shape, or form I knew I could blame the Catholic Church for this, in part. My mom didn't get her ideas from nowhere.

Even if I wasn't on my way to therapy, I really didn't have friends to hang out with anymore. My friend Gina went behind my back and fucked my boyfriend, while my other close friend, Jessica, had just given me an ultimatum: my boyfriend or her but not both.

I love how everyone gets to pick and choose who and how others forgive. Fuck that shit! In addition to the previously mentioned mess, another friend, Janis, had just died of fentanyl-laced heroin. So, ya know, I must've been doing heroin, too...

As my parents and I pulled into the parking lot, I remember looking at the English Gardens plant store next door and noticing we were at the corner of a major crossroads. An intersection six-lanes wide, with a huge outlet mall on one corner. I believe there was a Joe's Crab Shack attached to the mall. If you're from the Midwest, you know exactly what I am describing.

My therapist, Dr. W's office was in a gray, three-story building, but located in the basement. My parents sat on the couch in her waiting room as I walked away and entered into the pit of hell with the devil herself. My parents would not be joining. Remember: *I* was the problem.

I sat down, and at first, Dr. W seemed fine. We were talking about school and friends and my jobs, of which I had three by junior year and would later have five, if that tells you anything about how badly I wanted out of my family's house.

The conversation took a turn when she started using the names of people I had yet to mention, and it hit me. *This is Jessica's psychologist. This isn't legal. We just learned this in psychology class.*

She wasn't allowed to accept me as a patient, so, I stopped engaging. She had lost all of my trust, and I could feel the room getting smaller. This was an attack, and I was not prepared. Here's how it went next:

Dr. W said, "Katie, I want you to go somewhere with me. It's called Havenwyck."

I knew what Havenwyck was. I'd just met a girl who was sent there last summer.

I replied, "Okay. What will we do there?"

"I want you to meet some girls who are not going down the greatest path in life right now. So, you can talk to them. And it might possibly help you."

"Okay, I am fine with that."

"Okay," Dr. W said. "Then, let's go."

I protested. "It is eight o'clock on a Friday night. Those girls are put to bed before nine. There is no way you are taking me to talk to them right now."

Dr. W demanded, "What's the matter? You're not strong enough to handle the situation?"

"It's not that I am not strong enough," I said. "It's that you are a liar. I know what Havenwyck is. I know that you are Jessica Johnson's psychologist, and it's completely illegal for you to accept me as a patient, knowing you have a biased point of view on the situation. So, no, I will not go with you anywhere."

I got up to storm past her through the door. Just as I reached her, though, she grabbed my wrist and swung me around, staring me dead in the eyes.

"Janis Joyce was alive one day, and three hours later, she was dead."

This was my friend who had just died from fentanyl-laced heroin not even a month prior and whom I had been working with for the past year at Little Caesars, a girl I had known since kindergarten. Dr. W knew exactly what to say to push me over the edge, and I fucking exploded.

I bolted, running past my parents in the waiting room and screaming, "*How fucking dare you?*" I ran as fast as I could, crossing the six lanes of oncoming traffic and into the strip mall. I didn't have my phone, which I had lost the prior night at a party.

There was a hair salon. I asked the receptionist to use the phone and call my boyfriend. He was at work on the other side of town, but he said he'd get there as soon as he could.

I walked to a window and watched the parking lot while I waited for him. Then I saw it: three cop cars entering both entrances of the shopping mall parking lot. The pit inside my stomach was impossible to ignore. They were there for me. I knew it.

I ran back to the salon to call my boyfriend as quickly as possible, tears pouring down my face. I was frantic. I didn't even bother to notice an entire salon, fully booked on a Friday night, bearing witness to the most terrifying moment of my life.

I decided I was going to run out of the mall, hop the fence behind the building, and race through the neighborhoods to get to my boyfriend's house. That was my new plan. I hung up and ran toward the back exit.

As I was about to walk out the door, two cop cars pulled up in front of it. On my left was Coney Island, so I dipped inside and headed for the bathroom. If you're from Michigan, you know how jam-packed any Coney Island restaurant is on a Friday night.

I sat in the bathroom, staring at myself in the mirror. I was wearing blue-and-beige checkered bell bottom pants (my favorite), a lacey, white long-sleeved top, and was carrying an oversized bright-orange Bob Marley beach bag Gina bought me on my birthday, as an apology for fucking my boyfriend. I calmed myself down, took a deep breath, and walked out of the bathroom.

There they were: two cops, arms crossed, standing in front of me.

Officer One asked, "Katie Dickieson?"

"Yes, that's me."

Officer Two said, "You're going to have to come with us."

"Why? I am seventeen years old, I don't have a curfew, and I haven't done anything against the law."

Without warning, the two officers took hold of me and handcuffed me. Then, Officer One threw me over his shoulder like a sack of potatoes.

Officer Two continued, "Your psychologist said you would be difficult. You're not of right mind to be in society at this time." This line still haunts me to this day.

He carried me out, through the crowded Coney Island and out the mall entrance, and threw me in the back of the cop car. I tried to sit up, but the plastic seat was huge, and I kept slipping. When I finally got upright, I looked out the window just as my boyfriend's best friend pulled up next to the cop car and stared at me. He was so close.

The cops drove me back to Dr. W's office, where an ambulance was waiting. They pulled me out and uncuffed me, only to shove me into a straight-jacket (one of my worst fears) and strap me to a gurney. They pushed me into the ambulance like I was a pizza going into an oven and about to go up in flames.

Six cop cars escorted my ambulance to the hospital, while my parents followed in their car. I was taken to a room and left with a police officer.

"I am so sorry this is happening to you," the officer said. "My sister was sent to Havenwyck, and it was the worst thing my parents could have ever done."

Holy shit. Is this police officer my saving grace?!

"So, let me go then."

"I would if I could," he replied. "But I am not in charge here, and if my lieutenant found out, I would be fired."

"Can I use your phone to text my boyfriend?"

The officer handed me his cell and let me text Brian.

They got me. I saw Zed, but it wasn't in time. I'll contact you when I can. I love you. This is a cop's phone, don't text back.

"Thank you, Officer."

Then, the officer said, "Your psychologist is here."

"What psychologist?"

"Dr. W."

"She's *not* my psychologist. I just met her an hour ago."

"Then how was she capable of doing this?"

I declared, "I don't know. You tell me."

"So, you don't want to see her?"

"Absolutely not."

The officer asserted, "Okay then, I will tell them to have her leave."

All of a sudden, I could hear commotion down the hallway, and for a split second, Dr. W's face appeared. I couldn't make out what she was saying, but she was hysterical.

"Get her the fuck away from me now!"

The cops detained her, and the officer in my room pushed her out. She was escorted off the property while I was left to suffer the consequences of her and my parents' actions. Somehow, this was what protecting your child looked like.

I was drug-tested, and when my mom came into the room, she demanded to know, "When did you start using cocaine?"

I had tested positive for cocaine? I knew this couldn't be true, because while I smoked weed all the time, I'd never done cocaine at that point in my life. I demanded a retest, but they ignored me.

Great, so now I am also a cokehead.

At this point, I didn't know what time it was, probably past midnight. They put me back in the ambulance. This time, my parents wouldn't be following us. They informed me of this as though it was somehow going to upset me to hear that the people who had put me in that situation would not be coming along for the ride.

The drive was long, and I was exhausted and had no idea what was in store for me. When we arrived at the facility, because it was the middle of the night, no doctors were present. So, I was greeted by intake personnel.

They had me strip down naked and made me stand in the middle of a cement cell so they could stare at me, taking note of every inch of my body.

When they made it to my ass, they asked,

Intake: What is this?

"My birthmark."

Intake: That isn't a birthmark. Birthmarks aren't that color.

"It's my birthmark. Call my parents if you want proof."

Intake: We know you did this to yourself. It's only going to be harder for you if you lie to us.

"You think I tried to kill myself by cutting my ass?"

They handed me an orange jumpsuit, suggesting I'd graduated to prison, and then led me to the bathroom and ordered me to shower. They gave me one type of soap to wash my entire body and hair and nothing else. The entire complex was uncomfortably sterile. Everything smelled like sanitizer.

My hair was a wet Brillo pad, and even if I'd had a comb, there was no way to pull it through my hair after what that soap did to it. There was no lotion, my skin felt tight and dry every time I moved, like I was getting a rug burn over my entire body. After I put on the orange jumpsuit, they led me to my bedroom. It had two twin beds and a double-plated window that didn't open (obviously). Time to sleep.

I woke up to a blood pressure cuff around my arm and two strangers poking and prodding at me. Once they left, I got up and headed to the common area. My room was the first one on the left side of a long hallway of rooms. To the right of my room was an open space with a desk, like in your principal's office as a kid. To the left, the common area was basically like a waiting room in a doctor's office. The bathroom was past the common area.

My parents hadn't given them any clothes for me, so my daily attire was the orange jumpsuit, which, in that place, meant you were on suicide watch or had tried to kill someone. So, I had that going for me.

The staff assigned to watch us were no more than glorified babysitters, with no medical experience whatsoever. They all knew what the orange jumpsuit supposedly represented and treated me accordingly. The only Black girl in the facility intentionally acted out the moment she woke up, knowing she would be taken to the "no camera" room, injected with a booty dart, and left sedated for the entire day. At first, I didn't understand why she would intentionally behave that way, but quickly I came to understand that all too well.

A fourteen-year-old girl named Ashley had been in Havenwyck for over two years. She stayed locked in her room with tube socks duct-taped to her hands for the first week I was there. I found out it was because her dad had raped her and her entire family, giving them all herpes. She didn't understand what that was, so she just scratched and scratched her entire body until she was covered head to toe in blisters. So, they couldn't let her out.

After two days, they finally introduced me to my doctor. Dr. S was an incredible man. He was overworked and trying to do the best he could for as many children as possible. I could tell he really did have our best interests in mind, but the facility was understaffed, without the means to do what was actually needed for anyone who came to that facility. The place was riddled with abuse and negligence, like forcing unnecessary antipsychotic drugs on patients.

Dr. S began, "So, you're here because you're an alcoholic and very promiscuous."

"What? No. I have only drank a handful of times. And the only person I've had sex with is my boyfriend of three years." (I didn't think this was the moment to also admit I had been raped before Brian).

"Well, this is what your file says from your psychologist."

"What psychologist? Dr. W? She's not my psychologist. I just met her thirty minutes before she sent me here. She is also my best friend's psychologist."

Dr. S asked, "How was she able to send you here then?"

"You tell me, Doc."

Dr. S put in for another drug test on my request, after hearing my story. I tested positive for weed and nothing else. Although I felt validated, it didn't change the position I was in.

I was informed of my parents' plan to send me to boarding school in Arizona. For the first time in my life, my parents were forced to have family therapy with me. I explained to my parents that if they thought I really had a problem, if they thought I was a drug addict, a drunk, a slut and they sent me away, how did they ever expect me to become strong enough to overcome the issues I'd face throughout my life?

Dr. S explained to them that they could send me away, but when the day came when I turned eighteen, I could remove myself from boarding school and never talk to them again. So, if they were afraid of losing their daughter, sending me away was their worst option.

They listened to him, and after a few weeks, I was released from Havenwyck to spend the rest of my summer before senior year with my mother sleeping in my bed while I attended outpatient therapy every day. This while everyone else I knew was visiting potential universities and planning their futures.

While in Havenwyck, I was force-fed Lexapro, Trazodone, and Zoloft. If you refused any medications while in Havenwyck, they took you to the no-camera room, strapped you down, gave you a booty dart, and forced it down your throat anyway, so I obliged. My parents continued to force the medications even after I was back home.

My Friend, Janis

It was first period on May 25, 2006, right before I was sent to Havenwyck. I was sitting in my math class next to Steve Benowitz. Our principal came over the loudspeaker to announce some upsetting news.

Steve turned to say, "I know what this is about," as though he was proud.

I was about to ask him about it when I heard overhead, "Janis Joyce passed away last night."

I froze. The whole room froze. I still felt frozen as I turned away from the loudspeaker, as if I could make the moment never have happened.

I'd known Janis since preschool. We were in Girl Scouts together and always had friends in common. She was always really shy to most, but she was one of those people who, once you got close to her, made you feel like the most special person in the room. She gave you her undivided attention and no one else.

While growing up, Janis and another girl, Mary Noble, were inseparable. The saying, "connected at the hip," doesn't even begin to describe their friendship. It was as if they were one person with one impenetrable brain.

On one of the only Girl Scout trips that I remember going on, most of the other girls ignored me and left me out of their clique, so I tried to tag along with Mary and Janis. Surprising to me, they actually let me. For that one day, they let me into their special world. It's weird to write about this now, realizing how neither of these two girls could ever have known how much that meant to me. Enough for me to still remember, over twenty years later.

Once in middle school, I drifted further and further from the girls I'd called friends during elementary school. I always stayed acquaintances with everyone, but I definitely lived in my own world. Katie, the friendly loner. Janis continued to stay friends with the original girl group from elementary school, and of course, she and Mary continued their friendship.

When we all started high school, things rapidly began to change. Not just for me, but for everyone. One of the jobs I had in high school was working at the local Little Caesars. A group of about seven or eight of us from school worked together: David, Anthony, Enrique, Samson, Allen, Jessica, myself and Janis.

During this time, Janis had several dramatic interactions, perhaps shameful or embarrassing, with some of the males in this group. Incidents she may not have been able to process and move past at that adolescent time of life. Kids at school made fun of her, and I made fun of her. Janis was made fun of for being the first to do things that all of us were too afraid to do but wanted to. She was slut-shamed, because she was brave and didn't care what other people thought of her.

I don't really know what the catalyst was for her. I do believe she genuinely just loved to get high. But I can't help but wonder how much of an effect the gossiping had on Janis. How much the judgments of her supposed best friends affected her, causing her to create more and more distance between herself and those who loved her most.

What secrets was she keeping? Not the secret of her drug addiction. *We all knew* she was addicted. We were seventeen years old, and every single one of us knew she was addicted to heroin yet couldn't do a thing about it. Her girlfriends abandoned her, because of her drug use, not wanting to be associated with her. So, she was left with Us, the "potheads" of our high school. Maybe others would have labeled our group as "druggies" or 'addicts' too... But at the time, we thought, if the shoe fits...

The truth was, although we smoked copious amounts of weed, none of us were doing heroin. Janis had started dating Allen, and I think he really believed he could save her. I think we all believed he could save her. None of us thought about the possibility of life actually being taken from her. That just doesn't happen. Not in Birmingham, Michigan.

I was really curious about heroin, though. I badly wanted to understand its allure and its stranglehold but never had the guts to actually try it. We all watched *Requiem for a Dream* and saw how that ended.

But Janis never shot up, she only snorted heroin, so there was nothing to worry about. Snorting was safe: we didn't have to worry about her using dirty needles or overdosing, because that can't happen if all you're doing is snorting a drug, right? Right?

It made me sad that Janis and Mary weren't close anymore. I couldn't imagine what that must have felt like for the both of them, letting go of that friendship. I thought Janis must feel so alone, and I didn't want her to feel that way. I began trying to hang out with her more, but again, the problem was everyone knew Janis was a heroin addict, including my parents, and there was no way I was going to be allowed to spend more time with her. This dilemma led me to start cutting out of work with her. We always worked similar shifts. Whenever it was dead, we would both fake sick and then drive around neighborhoods in her GMC Jimmy, smoking weed out of an apple.

I remember asking her what heroin felt like. I watched as her face lit up when she talked about it, like it was the love of her life, because it was. We talked about going to the house where she always got it, and I played along with her and the idea of doing it together, despite knowing I never would.

I didn't want her to be alone. I didn't want something bad to happen to her. I thought, if I could just be her friend, if I could get her to spend more time with us, maybe we could get her away from that shit. Then, she would call us when she was on heroin, and it was like she already didn't exist. The boys would put her on speakerphone and laugh at how fucked up she sounded. I would just sit there like an asshole and say nothing.

There was one guy at our high school who brought the heroin in. He was older and addicted but still a teenager, himself. He was one of the richest kids in the entire school and spent all of Daddy's money on heroin for himself and all his girlfriends in the younger grades.

Although he and Janis hung together, they never dated, because it was strictly about the high for her. People had caught on to what was happening between Janis and Zane, as had clearly many other kids at school, so the high school police set up a sting the day before spring break started.

Janis and Zane had been driving to score drugs in Detroit every day at lunch, while, unbeknownst to them, an officer had been following. On this day, he was going to get them, and he did. Officer Miner followed, observed the exchange, waited until they returned to his jurisdiction, and pulled them over.

He found heroin in the car. It was Zane's car, but both he and Janis were arrested. Other officers raided the drug den that day, but the targeted dealers just happened not to be home and present at the time.

Both Zane and Janis came from well-off families, so both were sent to rehab facilities until trial. Zane's dad also happened to be one of the top attorneys in the state of Michigan. Rumor had it the plan was to place the blame on Janis. Let her take the fall for the heroin that was found in the car, and get Zane off. Which I am certain would have happened if the plan had actually played out in court.

As the school year came to a close, Janis left rehab and was still awaiting trial. She had been clean during her time in rehab and after getting out. The last time I saw Janis was at school, in the middle of the day.

Coincidentally, we both had left class. She and I walked toward each other on separate sides of an empty hallway. No one else was there, and neither of us even acknowledged the other.

I remember the look on her face as she just stared forward, pretending I didn't even exist. We weren't fighting. I know she wasn't mad at me; she was just in her own world, and I never became part of that world.

Sometimes I wonder, "What if I told someone?" But everyone already knew. Then I wonder, "Well, what if I went to the house with her?" As if that could have made things better or changed something. But I know that's not true.

I could have stuck up for the girl when people made fun of her, myself included. I could have not done that. But would any of those things really have saved her? Did any of those things have anything to do with this? Probably not, but maybe the snowball effect of everything did. I don't know. I will never know. Maybe she was happy; maybe this is what she wanted but I don't think so. I think she got herself into a corner and then was pushed to stay in that corner and only saw one of two options.

She went back to the house two more times. The first time, she was followed. The second time, no one knew. The same weekend Janis died, over 300 people in Detroit lost their lives to fentanyl-laced heroin. Janis never shot up. Janis was sixteen years old in a heroin house in Detroit when she went unconscious from snorting laced heroin.

The people in the house didn't know what to do, so they took off all of her clothes and threw her into an ice-cold bath, in hopes of shocking her out of it. When that didn't work, they called a woman known as "Mama," a regular at the house who was known for holding ice to men's balls to bring them back from similar accidental ODs.

It was too late, though, or so they thought. So, they paid Mama fifty dollars to drive Janis's GMC to the middle of Detroit and leave her there to die. Over two hours after Janis initially snorted the heroin, Mama pulled up to the hospital in downtown Detroit and dropped Janis at the emergency room. It was far too late, as too much time had passed for anyone to be able to resuscitate Janis. She died.

That morning, after the PA announcement about her death, people kind of lost it. I remember being really mad at the girls from elementary school who had abandoned her and now were crying, looking for support from people. I remember thinking, "Where the fuck were you when she needed you most?"

We were all looked at like criminals, or so it felt. When we went to her funeral with our friends and everyone who worked at Little Caesars together, it felt like the entire room was staring at us, thinking we were the kids she'd done drugs with, that we were at fault and to blame. Really, though, we were just the ones who'd tried to stay and help but who had failed.

I remember walking into Janis's funeral, expecting to see a body, like at Ann's, my Aunt Nancy's, and my grandpa's funerals. When I saw the urn, I lost my breath. It was hard for me to comprehend that the last time I would ever see her was that moment in the hallway, when we'd both pretended not to know each other. I had hoped to see her at peace in a casket, but she was just gone.

A year later, the *Detroit Free Press* did a front-page exposé on the heroin problem facing the Midwest. More specifically, it documented the 300-plus people who had died during that fatal week. The article included Janis' entire story, along with interviews with Mama. They busted the source of the fentanyl-laced heroin in Mexico. A video appeared online that chronicled the entire raid and bust. From this one source location, thousands of people across the Midwest died from fentanyl-laced heroin.

Another year later, while I was in hairdressing school, I met a girl who was on methadone, a former heroin addict trying to get clean. I still couldn't shake what had happened to Janis, and I needed to talk to this girl. I hoped I might understand more about the way Janis was thinking during her struggles, her addiction, and her loneliness.

I didn't get much from her, but what I did learn was that there are two possibilities when a person overdoses on heroin. They either die instantly or they lose consciousness. If they lose consciousness, it's a good thing, because they have about an hour or so to get to the hospital, where they can usually be revived and survive. Meaning, if the people at that house had just immediately taken Janis to a hospital, when she lost consciousness, the chances of her surviving were pretty high. The thought made me sick, and it still makes me sick.

The song "Anthems of a Seventeen-Year-Old Girl" will forever be me and Jessica's song for Janis. We used to listen to it and cry, imagining Janis left to die alone in her car.

> *Used to be one of the wretched ones and I liked you for that...*
> *...Now you're all gone, and you're not coming back*

At this point, after leaving Havenwyck, I was a ghost of a human. I looked at myself in the mirror and saw I was nothing but skin and bones. I stood there, on summer vacation at a cottage in northern Michigan, as my bikini hung on boney points and sagged off of me, and I realized the last thing I wanted was to be in the sun. Instead, I got into bed, pulled the covers over myself, and I slept all day. I slept every day.

My mom attended one family therapy session at my outpatient facility, but after five minutes, she stormed out of the room and never came back. In this facility, I met Dr. P. He observed me doing tasks he assigned over multiple sessions and diagnosed me with ADHD. I told him the drugs they were forcing on me made me a zombie, unable to feel my emotions, which in turn made me feel more depressed. He talked my parents into finally letting me come off the unnecessary medications.

I went into my senior year of high school rail-thin, with no friends, no future plans, on 40 mgs of time-release Adderall. A venti white-chocolate mocha Frappuccino with four extra shots of espresso in one hand, and chain smoking two packs of Marlboro medium 100s a day with the other. Somehow this was the epitome of health. This was how I was saved.

I took on five jobs, so I never had to be home. I began suffering panic attacks upon walking into school. I couldn't be somewhere I felt I couldn't get out of. The second I sat down in class, I felt like I was in prison all over again.

Luckily, all of my teachers always loved me, including my counselor. They all knew what I had been through that summer. We didn't talk about it, but when I made eye contact with my first-period teacher, ten minutes after arriving to class, she just nodded, which was my cue to go. I went to the counselor's office, and without having to explain myself, he excused me from my classes for the day. This happened on seventy-five percent of the days during my senior year.

So, I worked as much as I possibly could and threw myself into survival mode. I became a machine. Productivity leaves no room to feel pain, and so long as you don't stop, it can't catch up to you. I missed so many days of school that by the time my dean found out, there were only two weeks left. He gave me a detention, but I was a no-show, so he gave me a Saturday detention. I never went to school again.

On graduation day, my mom woke me up and announced that I had two weeks to find a new place to live. I'd met a girl the night before at a bar, where I went to watch my coworkers from Guitar Center play a show. I texted her what was happening, and she offered to let me live on her couch. I moved out that day. I didn't attend my high school graduation and found out they actually did let me graduate when my diploma showed up in the mail.

This was the first time I experienced homelessness. I had a roof over my head, but this was not home. I wouldn't really say living with my parents ever felt like home either, though.

Over the next ten years, I failed out of my first year of college due to working eighty hours a week, moved eighteen times, went in and out of homelessness twice, worked at Jet's Pizza, at a music lesson studio, Guitar Center, became a licensed hairstylist in two states, was a private investigation search specialist, a pharmaceutical sales rep, a nanny, a cleaning lady, a personal assistant, a certified holistic health nutritionist, a bartender, a server, and failed to start my own wellness company twice, before going back to university at twenty-eight years old.

I also had numerous toxic relationships with men, which included five who raped me, an ex who beat me before slitting his wrists with a chef's knife, almost bleeding out on the floor in front of me, consistent infidelity, and an unwanted abortion that failed and led to my needing a second abortion for the same fetus.

At some point, it gets to be too much. For me, too much felt like the theme of my life. If I wasn't being too much, then there was too much happening to me, and at some point—at many points for me—you feel there is just no way out.

Too Much

It was August 2016. My on-again, off-again boyfriend had just broken up with me, again, after cheating on me, again.

When I stood in front of the mirror, I could see the veins on the side of my head grow larger as they pulsed and became darker and darker blue. My face was turning darker red by the second, and I could feel my lips tingling from the pressure of blood building up. I was holding the belt around my neck and knew I wouldn't be able to kill myself that way, but I continued to watch myself in hopes it could.

I kept hoping this would be enough effort to do the job, because I was too scared to put in the real effort it would take to off myself.

I cannot count how many times I had been cheated on by this point. All I knew was I hadn't had a single boyfriend who hadn't done it, and I couldn't help but believe it was me who was the problem.

It wasn't that I had done anything wrong. It was that being who I am innately was the problem. Even if I am a good person, even if I like who I am, it was still not enough for the rest of the world. So, I thought, how about I just make this easier for everyone by leaving?

I'd tried to kill myself as many times as I had been cheated on. I wasn't even upset about the cheating. I was hurt by the lies. I was devastated by the person whom people are when they're with me and who they become without me. Why do they lie? Why can't they communicate?

It was too much, and I was too embarrassed to tell anyone what I was going through. The last thing I needed was my friends telling me, "I told you so," or, even worse, to negate my feelings because once again I'd allowed myself to be in this position.

I knew there were guns in this house, but where? This was the first time I ever had access to a gun while I was in this mental state. It was too easy.

I went to the main bedroom, to the master closet, to check the safe, but I didn't know the code. I turned to see a long plastic case, but the gun inside was too long to do the job. Then, I noticed a camo-print bag lying next to the case. Inside was a small revolver.

I'd never held a gun before. It was so small but so heavy and cold. I could see there were no bullets in the chamber. *But how the fuck do I open it and load it?*

I fumbled with the gun, tears rolling down my face, and couldn't seem to figure it out. I threw the gun to the ground and pulled up YouTube, typing: *how to load and shoot a revolver...* The video was eight minutes long and not the same gun.

I gave up and called my best friend. I couldn't get any words out and sobbed for what felt like an hour until she finally calmed me down enough to catch my breath...

Letting Go of Our Limitations

I was not a victim. I would have been doing this place a service by leaving the world. At least, that was what I believed in those moments, and that is a belief I have fought my entire life, until recently. It is still a battle from time to time, but I never come close to where I was on that day.

For years, I used the ways people treated me and betrayed me as a means to hold on to the belief that there was something wrong with me. If I could believe I was the problem, that meant I would never have to step into the power and strength of the person I knew I actually was and could be. Because stepping into that power would mean I was in charge of my life, in charge of my actions, in charge of myself, and that is a really scary place to be.

The day you decide you won't let anyone else tell you who you are ever again is the day you stop fighting for your limitations. That is the day you start fighting for the space you deserve in this world. Which is a hard place to claim, after you've spent so much of your life being taught you don't deserve anything. Or that you should be happy with just getting by. Or if you were taught not to ask for too much or try too hard, because it's not worth it or too risky. The fight transitions to demanding your space on this Earth right alongside the new and constant battle of reaffirming that you deserve to fight for that space on Earth.

It's pretty impossible to go backward after you start recognizing the limitations you've put on yourself. Simultaneously, as the walls from the cage you've created for yourself crumble, the real you naturally begins to evolve and shine. The more we step into our authenticity and out of the rubble, the less we are protected from going with the grain.

The moment you step out of that box, the world is ready to fire. They've been ready. They've been trained to react when someone steps out of line, and they're always looking for their next victim. I have found it easier to deal with the pain of these kinds of attacks by recognizing the patterns that create them. Self-hate, insecurity, fear, and shame are terrifying enemies to battle. As humans, when we are too afraid to battle the anchors that we personally carry, we tend to use them as weapons against those willing to be honest about the battles we all face.

There is limitless space for people looking to take advantage of you, once you become your authentic self, especially by those who don't know how to be honest with themselves or others. When someone like this meets me, we usually become fast friends, because suddenly, this person has someone else they can trust to be their true self with; *me*.

For someone who's been living their life constantly hiding, being able to break free is like crack. It took me a long, long time to figure this out in my life, because I don't have the capacity to not be myself. I just am who I am in the moment, every moment, and that's how I always have been. So, to be a person who often brings this side out in others makes it hard to understand why they would ever *not* be their self.

I think I only see the authentic side of people once they are a part of my life, which, with me, only takes one conversation. So, usually, when someone doesn't like me or they are not themselves around me, it's because they haven't even talked to me yet. This sounds and comes off as pompous as hell and might sour someone reading this, but remember, you've never actually met me.

Which is the problem with social media right. Especially when you are deemed a "polarizing person." Just because I am "polarizing" based on my beliefs and the types of things I post online doesn't mean I am incapable of having a rational conversation with someone who thinks differently than me. And more often than not, I will be able to connect with you on a personal level no matter what, because, at the root of this entire thing is our existence as humans, sharing our human experience on this Earth. There is not a single emotion that you have felt that I haven't felt and vice versa.

We are all experiencing life. The problem is, when people aren't authentic, it becomes harder for them to see the humanness in others, because they are not being their true human self.

I am no expert in this. I am not a behavioral analyst, although that was my first dream career. These are simply my observations, made through the lens of my own human experience.

People who are not living authentically tend to have a harder time creating and living their dream life. These people live in cages created by what society tells them they are supposed to be and do, allowing this to control their existence. These rules become so ingrained in people, they create persistent and preprogrammed reactions and responses.

This cage puts limits on whom a person can become. Without a person always knowing it, these limits are typically used as safety parameters. Believe me, though, the unknown is truly terrifying to everyone. Some people have created an easier path for themselves into the unknown by repeatedly putting themselves out there, trusting in themselves, the universe, or whatever you want to call it, and through this process, they feel more protected. That despite how terrifying the unknown is if something bad happens, they have a way to come back from it. There are people who aggressively push toward the unknown because they know that anything is better than what they are experiencing, which is typical of survival mode.

For those who don't live authentically, this is much harder, because they have yet to allow the world to see their real self. So, how could they possibly push beyond the cage when they're too scared of being seen inside of it? They use their limits as a mechanism to stay safe.

This is where the excuses come, right?

"I can't lose weight because I can't work out because I have a bad knee."

"I am too old to go back to school. They won't take me seriously."

"I can't stop smoking weed because my anxiety is so bad. I have to smoke weed all day long to make sure I don't have anxiety."

"I can't move because I have lived here my entire life. How would I survive?"

We create these totally made-up scenarios, based on zero evidence, because we haven't tried them out yet.

I used to spend a lot of time talking to my friends, family, and partners about the limitations they put on themselves, trying to make them see what they are capable of. But after a while, I began to realize that most of these people didn't want to change. They want to believe in their limitations, because it means it's a waste of time for them to try at all, and they can feel better about never trying by "knowing" it would never work in the first place.

It sucks falling in love with the potential found in every single person you meet and realizing you can't love their potential more than they do, and you certainly can't remove their limitations. Even if we could remove people's limitations for them, the mind has a funny way of creating things that are not there.

I have come to realize the best thing I can possibly do is ignore all of my limitations. They don't exist. The more I live my life with that mindset, the more frequently and efficiently I continue to bulldoze right past them. People tend to stare and watch in amazement. Maybe, as these people watch me give up my limitations, they will be inspired to do the same.

My pain was a limitation I fought for. The more pain I felt, the more I could retreat and lean on others to help me feel better about myself. My pain was my excuse for procrastination in life, and I used it every chance I got.

I so badly wanted someone to save me, but I was unwilling or unable to see that the only person who could do it was me. I thought so much about the pain I was feeling, I never wanted anyone to experience the same pain I did. But I never thought about how, by giving myself permission to let go of the pain, I might just give other people the permission to do the same.

A lot of us like to give advice about other people's experiences, as though they'll listen, but we know that is not true, because we never listened. People more often than not learn through their own experiences. It's not our job to tell people what they should and shouldn't do with their lives.

I thought, by expressing my pain and by explaining my pain over and over again to people, they might be capable of avoiding the things I had been through, but that, too, is not possible. We cannot control the things that happen, but we can control how we react and what things we give meaning. Forgiving and letting go have been the only true ways I have learned to lessen the weight of that pain. By showing other people we are capable of forgiving and letting go, we can give them hope that it is possible for them, as well.

Allowing yourself to move on from your limitations does not negate that they existed in the first place. Forgiveness does not mean you have to ignore all the things that have ever happened to you. But if you did, would there be anything wrong with it? Does holding on to things that have happened to us really do us any good? What would your life be like if you had a neutral response to all the terrible things that have happened to you?

Method in the Madness

I was sitting on the leather couch in the corner of the bar at 3rd & 3rd in Delray Beach, Florida on November 30, 2019. My bartender, Dan, set the ninth drink in front of me. It was 9:41 p.m., and I had two hours and nineteen minutes left to submit my application essay to graduate school.

Every drink was lined up on the table, not a single one of them touched. I hadn't even ordered any of them. Twenty-four hours ago, I hadn't known I was allowed to apply to graduate school. But there I was, racing the clock at my local bar to make the deadline.

Nothing inspires a college student more to finish their work than watching all their friends have fun without them. My bar mates trickled in one by one, joining me on the couch, amused by the assortment of drinks I had collected.

Finally, Stacey, the manager, who over the years had become my best friend, mother, therapist, and number-one confidant, sat down with all of us at the couch.

"I got into law school at Stanford, Katie. I can edit your admission essay."

I was shocked to learn this and confused as to why she was the manager of my local bar and not a lawyer.

But I had no time to waste, so I didn't question her, just handed my laptop over. We could discuss the details of that knowledge bomb later.

"What school is this application for, Katie?"

"Harvard," I said with such confidence, the entire group burst into laughter. But Stacey knew I was not joking. She gave me a look I will never forget. *The audacity to go to a bar last-minute and type up my admission essays for graduate school, let alone Harvard!*

I didn't get into Harvard, but as you might know, I did get into Cornell. Every application I sent was free, because if you don't make enough money to pay for them, you can reach out to the universities for fee waivers. So, I reached out to every single Ivy League University for a fee waiver and applied to every single one. I did this because I could and because I wasn't going to let someone else tell me I wasn't good enough. If anyone was going to tell me I wasn't good enough, they could tell me themselves.

I applied to Cornell on a last-minute essay (below), while I was homeless, just weeks after my Papa passed away and one day before my Nana died, and I got in. It's pretty easy to imagine what might have happened had I fought for my limitations, but can you imagine if I'd never had those limitations to begin with?

> *Imagine sitting in the classroom where the first discussions of going to the moon became reality. Imagine being a part of the breakthrough of space travel and knowing you were a part of a history that would forever change the future.*
>
> *Throughout my entire childhood, I'd yearned for that moment. The only problem was, as I'd grown older and tried to decide what I would do with my life, everything I had imagined had*

already been created. Each new idea I thought of was simply something that had already been built or discovered. I craved that first space flight moment; the kind of moment that would change the world.

I was sitting in my Human Mission to Mars class, listening to Dr. Sian Kelly speak, and that's when it hit me. All of a sudden, I was transported to the 1950s, and suddenly, I was sitting on the precipice of space travel. Mars terraforming, atmospheric pressure, and beyond. The impact this would make on our world was bigger than the moon landing. I was there, experiencing the plans for human life beyond Earth.

When I was a child, my dad took me outside of our house in suburban Detroit, and we would look at the stars every night. They were untouchable, yet all-encompassing. The questions no one could answer yet were before us.

I always knew my deepest passions lay far beyond the Earth. It wasn't until I went back to school at the age of twenty-eight that I realized it was possible to find what I was looking for. I had come to an epic realization: I wanted to do something different with my life.

While I was examining my blood under a microscope one day, my life changed. I immediately changed my lifestyle and went back to school for holistic nutrition.

Given my upbringing, I never believed I could be who I wanted to be. All I ever wanted was to understand the secrets of the universe and everything it entails, including how the world and human beings work. I just never believed there was enough time or that I was truly capable of it.

Once I finished my program in holistic nutrition, I very quickly realized it wasn't enough and that I was capable of so much more. I decided to go back to university for nursing. I aced every class. I had a 4.0 grade average, taking six classes while working full-time, and I knew I was on the path I was always meant to be.

When it came time to apply for nursing school, I was asked by my counselor why I wasn't going for my doctorate. I had the grades, the drive, no husband, no family, and nothing holding me back but my own insidious mind. So, I went for it.

I was set on pediatric oncology. I wanted to help merge Eastern and Western medicine to give families the option of both and to help change medicine. I realized the only way for me to do that would be from ground zero: through research.

I took organic chemistry with Dr. Druyan at Florida Atlantic University, and he changed my world. The class I despised most became my biggest passion. Chemistry is at the very core of all science, and for the first time ever, I was passionate, falling in love with chemistry.

There have been crossroads at every point in life that have forced me to look inward and decide what it is I truly want; to ask myself, "What is the dream?" Once I went back to school, as cliché as it is, the sky was the limit. I knew I wasn't going to stop until I'd made it.

I think it is extremely important to have the capacity to evolve and adapt to your surroundings. To reassess your situation and make decisions based on where you come from, as well as what makes sense to your future. I have changed my mind too many times to count about what it is I want to do in my life, but it is because of those changes that I found what I was looking for. Now, I am more focused than ever.

My goals at this point are to do research in synthetic biology and biomedical engineering, and to work toward sustaining life on Earth and Mars. I understand these things are far-reaching, but this is my passion, and I understand the steps it will take in order to get to where I want to be. I am looking forward to each of those steps in attaining my goals. As science and technology change, I realize my goals and ideas will change. I am ready to adapt and evolve to meet the needs necessary in order to make progress.

Cornell is a dream unparalleled to reality. The idea of going to Cornell never crossed my mind until I was introduced to Dr. Ata Kelly, who put me in contact with Dr. Eve Neal at Harvard, which is how I met Dr. Scott McAuliffe. I want the best, because I want to be the best. Applying to Cornell has opened my eyes to a level of research of what today offers and made me realize how committed I am to the concepts of science and biology and their advancement. Not for money, not for show, and not for my ego, but so that I can have the best potential to make the biggest change I can. I am not swayed by money. I am swayed by ideas, passion, and unlimited potential for growth and change. I believe Dr. McAuliffe is the best fit for my thesis advisor, because it is his research that has inspired me to get to this point.

I know what I want, I know how to get to where I want to be, and I'm not willing to let anything stand in my way. I am ruthless with passion and have a fire in my soul that will never *burn out. There are many people out there with higher GPAs and test scores than I, but they lack my drive. Who I am as a person is what makes all the difference in you choosing me over them. The cutting edge is where I belong, so that my efforts can be focused on what needs to be, rather than what most people haven't even realized is the now.*

Letter of Recommendation for Katie Dickenson

I first met Katie Dickenson at Florida Atlantic University in November 2019. But she had apparently met me a lot earlier, via my writings. She approached me, and what impressed me was both her knowledge and enthusiasm for the field of human space settlement. *I am a biology major. What can I do to move things forward that could really matter? How about synthetic biology? It seems to me it would have a lot to offer.*

You are right, I said. And she is. With synthetic biology, all sorts of vitally necessary products could potentially be made – fuels, plastics, fabrics, food, drugs, etc., etc., - via self-replicating systems that could allow a small extraterrestrial settlement to meet its needs separated from the vast global division of labor that supports the production of such necessities now. Developed for Mars, such technologies could subsequently provide enormous benefits for life on Earth too.

She sees that. She wants to do it. She is on fire. She may have to scramble a bit to make the grade at a school like yours, but she will do what it takes. Motivation is everything. You can't miss with this young woman. I strongly recommend you accept her.

Yours truly,

In the immortal words of Nike, "Just do it," especially when you don't feel like doing it. And even if your mentor doesn't spell your name correctly on your recommendation letter. It has always been when I *really* did not want to do something, but showed up anyway, that I have experienced the greatest results. Even if you are unprepared, show up anyway.

We are all human, and more than likely you are not the only person unprepared. The only difference is that you showed up and they didn't.

You get more opportunities when you show up. Especially when you show up and you are not at 100%. People appreciate and respect authenticity. When you can show up without being "perfect," people like that shit.

I fought for my limitations for a long time. Sometimes, I still find myself fighting for my limitations. The difference now is that I am aware of when I am doing it. I pay attention when that feeling begins creeping back in, and I stop. I stop, and I remind myself of who the fuck I am and who I became, once I stopped fighting for my limitations and instead started fighting for all my possibilities.

Chapter 3
Solitary Creates Clarity

"6:30, dinner with me. I can't cancel that again."
—The Grinch, *How the Grinch Stole Christmas*

I WAS SEVENTEEN years old and had just gotten back from Havenwyck. My mom was sleeping in my bed with me every night, and I was not allowed to see anyone or leave the house.

Unfortunately, or fortunately for me, all the times I have experienced a solitary existence were never my choice. However, in those moments of solitude, I have learned the most about myself, while metamorphosizing time and time again, each time coming out smarter, more beautiful, and more in tune with my true self than previously imagined.

While being imprisoned by my parents in solitary confinement, I watched so many doomsday documentaries, I began to believe in the possibility of the world ending on December 21, 2012. So much so, I lost any sense or hope of planning for a future. I never thought I would live past age eighteen, anyway. I'd never thought about getting married and having kids. Not that I was against it; it had just never crossed my mind. I didn't think I would make it that far.

I was the kind of little girl who made her Barbies have full-blown, steamy, dramatic sex, while the neighbor spied at the window, waiting to surprise Barbie after Ken left, not fall in love.

My pretzels and pens were cigarettes, destined to be a smoker from the age of two, candy cigarettes from the ice-cream man surely did not help. I dreamed of cigarettes, orgies, and working as a boss-ass bitch who banged her coworkers to get what she wanted, like Lieutenant Einhorn in *Ace Ventura Pet Detective* or Ms. Hyde in *Dr. Jekyll and Ms. Hyde*. Which should come as no surprise to me now, realizing how both of Sean Young's roles in those movies feature her transitioning into a woman after being born biologically as a man. We didn't have enough education to help me understand my fantasies back then, but as you can tell, they were always there.

Anyway, I was seventeen years old and thought the world was going to end at any moment, and I already felt life as I'd known it as a teenager had already ended for me. I was alone during a time when I very much needed someone to be there for me. I definitely didn't know how to be there for myself, but I had no one to trust.

Seeing the Bigger Picture

It was November 4, 2020, and the ballots were still being counted to determine our next president. I'd ripped off all of my toenails, and while trying to stop the blood with one hand, I was gnawing at my cuticles on the other. I was sitting on my dark-green futon, so at least I didn't have to worry about visible stains.

I was in my apartment on University Avenue in Ithaca, New York. My only friend in town, Alicia, lived above me. She is a Black woman, and I didn't want to trouble her with my anxiety.

I'd moved to Ithaca summer of 2020, at the height of Covid, my fourth move since March of the same year. I was lucky, though, having yet to catch the virus. What an achievement. Honestly, I would have gladly taken some long-term Covid, so long as that Cheeto Mussolini would never be our president again.

Little did I know I had nothing to fear on that day compared to what was to come on January 6, 2021, just two months later.

I emailed my professor for a second time that semester to request an extension. Shamelessly and manically, I described my anxiety about the day's events. How could anyone possibly function "normally" with what was going on in this country on a daily basis? Let alone what the outcome of today's events could mean? *What the fuck was wrong with us?*

The Cheeto lost. That was all anyone could really ask for at that moment. To ask for anything more would just have created even more division.

I'd been off antidepressants for fourteen years, but I was having serious thoughts about giving them another shot. Being force-fed pills after I was Baker Acted at seventeen hadn't really given me the best appreciation for prescription medicines, but at that point, I needed something.

I hadn't been home since August, a few months prior. My only connection to the outside world was one dude I'd met on Bumble, where I'd obnoxiously removed all my past connections, and I was more alone than I'd ever been in my life. The other students on campus had all left for the winter break at the end of October, because of the pandemic and the University not allowing people to stay on campus. I was one of the only people I knew who had their own apartment off campus. Not like it mattered, though. I'd only been seeing any of them over Zoom.

I did make friends with Pat, my wine dealer at the local wine shop. I went there for human interaction. She was an older woman who told me the story of every wine I bought each week. I was up to six bottles per week, maybe more.

It takes a lot of strength to meet yourself. I wasn't really given the option, and for that I am genuinely grateful. If it weren't for the pandemic, I probably would have continued on with the life I was living. Going to Cornell would have been a very different experience had the campus been open and people been allowed to interact. I bet it would have been a blast, but I wouldn't have become the woman I am now without that forced solitude.

I lived in a basement apartment of a house that stood on a mountainside. The backyard looked out over town, but the side of the mountain was covered with trees so thick, the only visible sights were the beautiful sunsets every evening. I hadn't lived in a northern state for ten years and missed the changing of seasons, but seasonal depression is real, and my depression was bad enough without the darkness. However, I was working on my master's in biomedical engineering at Cornell University. Look at me now!

Blue-Sky Mindset

One of my greatest gifts is being able to see the bigger picture. In my graduate school course, Innovation & Biodesign, that ability is called the *blue-sky mindset*. Everything I say has come from somewhere else. It is my ability to fill in the gaps, create connections, and convey the *blue-sky mindset* across the breadth of knowledge I have acquired in my life that is my unique skill and contribution.

I learned this about myself during the stillness of being alone. I was able to take a step back and see myself for who I really am, when the noise of others ceased surrounding me at all times.

For the first time, in this stillness I learned how it felt to entirely choose myself, and to question everything I thought I knew about myself and who I would choose to be in this world. Who and what I might really want in my relationships. What did the pain of my past really mean? Was I going to hold onto it forever and continue taking it out on those who tried to reach the deeper parts of me?

The man I was seeing at the time when I was living in Ithaca was ethically non-monogamous. *Wonderful!* I thought. *There will be zero expectations from this relationship.* Though I didn't realize how many expectations I put on others, while simultaneously demanding no one put any expectations on me.

I was so alone and in such a dark place mentally at this point. I was blind and unable to acknowledge how I truly felt about certain things. My ego drove every emotion that came out of me.

Sam looked at me and said, "You can be as upset with me as you want, Katie, but I am not your boyfriend. I am also not your keeper. I never made you come over. I never asked you to get someone to take care of your dog or to pay for that. But now, you're mad at me and taking out your frustrations on me for decisions you made. I also told you at the beginning of this relationship, I was not looking for anything monogamous. I have been nothing but honest with you, and I feel as though you might be taking out your frustrations from old relationships on me."

He was right. And for the first time, perhaps ever, I was forced to meet my ego head-on and challenge her. I didn't want to be in a monogamous relationship with this man, but my ego couldn't handle the idea that he did not want a monogamous relationship with me. How ridiculous is that?

I laughed maniacally, my eyes wide open, my body floating right off the dock and that one-hundred-foot-high overlook above Cayuga Lake. I was free!

Finally, someone else had given me the permission I needed to love anybody and everybody I wanted. Not only that, but now jealously no longer needed to exist anymore? Talk about freedom!

We continued as lovers for a few months and slowly turned into platonic friends. There were no conversations about it. There didn't need to be. We were two humans just letting each other be humans in whatever way we each wanted, without ever taking what the other one did personally. It was beautiful. It still is beautiful.

If I hadn't been so cut-off from the world during this time in my life, I don't know if I ever would have developed the stronger connection that I needed with myself to tell me, "*Wait, listen to him. You want the exact same thing. Love and freedom."*

There is no Work Katie versus Home Katie. No professional versus unprofessional. There is Katie. I hope no one ever looks at me and believes they only got a specific version of me, muddled down to appease what feels "appropriate" for the moment. I hope that every person who meets me feels and knows they have met the person I am at heart and can say I am real.

I have formed families everywhere I travel in my life, and this helps create a sense of home base and grounding wherever I go. I know this comes from the lack of safety or love in my familial home. But I have come to learn how the truest safety is in the home I have built within myself. Knowing, wherever I go, there is home. It is within the home of myself that I find the most clarity.

Chapter 4
Settling the Debt of Hustle and Grind

"Look, if you had one shot or one opportunity to seize everything you ever wanted in one moment, would you capture it or just let it slip?"
—Eminem, "Lose Yourself"

DO YOU REALLY WANT IT? Or are you just trying to prove something?

I was out of Havenwyck, and my mom was sleeping in my bed with me every night. How the fuck was I going to escape this?

I had no friends and everyone in my family hated me. I'd had a great job working at a law firm before being sent away, but when they found out what happened to me, I was fired. I was starting from scratch and needed to find people who didn't know about what had happened.

I found a job at a music lesson studio, cleaning and organizing the rooms and passing out flyers and stickers around the neighborhood for free lessons at Guitar Center, who then hired me to be a store "Navigator." I took up cleaning houses when the opportunity arrived.

I was hired by a family to nanny two girls, ages four and six. The older daughter had autism. I also worked as an in-class aid at my high school to a boy with autism. One of my tasks was driving him to his extracurricular activities outside of school.

I put all my energy into these jobs. Having money meant having freedom. The more I made, the more I could save toward moving out. But my car's brakes hadn't worked for over a year, and driving onto people's lawns in order to stop wasn't working anymore. I needed a new car.

My parents gave me an ultimatum. They would pay for me to get a lease on a car, but that meant they controlled when I could and could not use it. Or I could buy my own car and have "freedom." So, I bought my own car, obviously. I was never, ever again going to let them have a say over what I could and could not do in my life.

The car was a lemon, and I had nothing to show for the amount of time I'd worked during my senior year of high school. But the time I spent working taught me the perfect way to avoid anything going on in my life. So long as I was a hard worker, I was useful, and people appreciated me.

I proved my self-worth by working more than I should and giving way more than anyone ever gave back. I went above and beyond again and again. This exhausting work habit did lead to me abruptly ending jobs time and again, once I'd had enough of bosses taking advantage of me.

I didn't understand boundaries. I didn't even know boundaries were allowed.

A year after high school graduation, I found myself working as a cocktail waitress at a strip club in Traverse City, Michigan. They started cutting my hours, trying to push me into becoming a dancer. If only the shame of my Catholic upbringing hadn't weighed on me, I could've flashed my naked body a couple nights a week in Nowheresville and made ten times the amount of money for a quarter of the effort. No one would've ever known I did it, but I still couldn't bring myself to do it.

Eleven years later, and 1,500 miles away in Boynton Beach, Florida, I was in the passenger seat of Coke-Dick Don's car, completely hungover from the night before. This wasn't like a normal hangover, though. Last night while he was behind me, out of nowhere, I flung myself around, screaming, "Get off me! *Get the fuck off me!!*" And I'd rolled to the side of the bed, sobbing.

He didn't do anything wrong. In fact, it had nothing to do with him.

So, sitting in his car the next day, smoking a cigarette to calm this nagging feeling, was the only safety I could get, and I was terrified. Life didn't feel real. I didn't feel real. I couldn't breathe anything but cigarette smoke, and I was supposed to walk into a double shift right then.

Don was the only person who knew what had happened last night, though I was sure he didn't understand it. But I felt better with someone knowing I was not okay and a split-second away from losing my shit.

I had to go. I had to get into work. I'd already called Brie and told her I was running late.

"I need you," she'd said. "We're slammed right now." Had she known the state I was in, though, she would never had made that joke.

I walked in the back door of the brewery and couldn't walk any farther. I opened the door to the tap room and asked Brie to come to the back for a second.

As soon as she walked through the door, I fell to the ground, my body wracked by tremors all over. I couldn't see. I didn't know where I was. I didn't even know who I was.

Three years later and on the other side of Florida, in St. Petersburg, I had only twelve minutes before I had to switch back into corporate-job mode. I was in my weekly L10 with my business partners for a new dating app we are creating called Wing. We used Microsoft Teams, just like my company did, but you can't be logged into two workplace accounts at once. So, I was constantly juggling.

I was presenting my planning screen for our next yearly meeting with my co-founders when they disappeared. My screen went blank and the Wi-Fi went out. It was 12:52 p.m., and I still had the rest of the day filled with meetings. My hotspot wasn't working, either. *How can everything not be working?*

After years of working on myself and taking a step back from over-production, hustling, and bustling, working four jobs at a time while in school full time and breathing alcohol in my free time, this was the moment when I shut it down. This meeting could wait. The meetings for the rest of the day could wait.

I hadn't eaten all day, so this was the moment to put something nutritious in my body, take a fucking step back, and chill. It was hard to feel productive when four jobs didn't involve driving to four different locations anymore. It was hard to feel progress and production when my entire life was spent behind a screen. It was hard to believe the impact four remote positions had on my mental, physical, and emotional wellbeing could be the equivalent of running around like a chicken with my head cut off. Chickens who run around with their heads cut off don't look like someone who sits in front of a computer screen for ten hours, never moving and in complete silence. These two couldn't possibly be similar. But they were, and I would even argue, in some cases, the latter is worse. Especially for a personable person like me.

I work as a product manager at my current company, where my meeting times range between China and California, plus I am a co-founder for Wing, writer of this book, and have stepped into leadership in a local women's group, trying to coordinate sponsorships for St

Petersburg's Pride Parade this year. I moved twice in the past month, which felt more like three or four times, based on how often we went back and forth between storage units and "home."

I also have taken it upon myself to create a new side business, where I am setting up a storage unit as a closet to hold all of my costumes, as a rental service. I am part of a women's entrepreneurship group, which meets twice a week and has two virtual meetings, plus weekly events sprinkled across my calendar. I am also working to finish my master's research, so I can finally publish something scientific.

By the time my partner, Langdon, gets home from work in the evening, I am usually so dissociated, I can't do much more than go on a walk and watch our current binge, *Grey's Anatomy*, from the beginning for the second time. I've had zero sex drive for almost a year at this point. I also travel at least once a month.

At one point this year, I hadn't worked out in three months. This was a problem. Working out keeps me level. Working out balances my routine. Working out gives me energy and happiness and belief in myself. In this moment, I didn't feel very inspired, and I was living by going through the motions.

But despite all of that, I know I have wonderful things going for me. However, I have no ability to enjoy them, because I'm not giving myself the love and attention I deserve and need to feel satisfied and fulfilled. I know all of these things. Yet even in my knowing, it is so terribly difficult to take a step back and say, "Enough is enough."

I got up from my desk and walked into the bathroom. I hadn't showered in three days and was wearing the same clothes from yesterday, just with a flannel button-up overtop, so no one on my work calls could tell I was living in my pajamas. My hair had been up for so long, I couldn't stop itching it over and over again, using my nails to scratch the loose strands up from the base of my neck into my bun.

I pulled out my scrunchie, only to have my hair stay in the exact same position. My face looked empty. Our bathtub had been clogged with my hair for days, failing to drain. This was how much hair I had lost recently. I'd been waiting for a bald spot to appear, and as I was combing through my greasy hair with my fingers, that's when I came upon it.

I have alopecia areata. When I get extremely stressed, I develop a perfectly circular bald spot somewhere on my head. The first time it happened, in 2010, I was twenty-one years old and fresh out of cosmetology school. I had what I had coined as the Mu-Whail (Mohawk-Mullet-Rat Tail): basically, the trendy, shaggy, mullet haircut everyone has these days, but way cooler and with different ways to style it. Anyway, while my boyfriend at the time was cutting my hair, he noticed the first half-dollar sized bald spot, which was perfectly ruining the middle section of the mohawk. I'd had no idea what had happened.

This new bald spot, though, was different than any of the others I had experienced in my past. For the first time ever, the bald spot was on my hairline. No wonder I hadn't noticed it. There was a half-circle-shaped chunk taken right out of the hairline under my temple on the left side. And not just a chunk this time. I could tell I was missing about fifty percent of the hair on the left side of my head. I could see skin through the fine placements of hair at least an inch back past my hairline.

Our body has ways of telling us enough is enough. When I pay attention, I can tell when those first small signs start; about a month prior, the early warning signs began.

For me, they are staying up late, sleeping in but never feeling rested, eating unhealthily, not working out... I knew. But I also knew, after the two moves, I was in survival mode. And to be honest, survival mode is my default; I'm pretty good at it. So, when the shit hits the fan, it can be hard to choose a different method, but I am working on that.

Part of that work is acknowledging how I fall back into survival when I don't necessarily have to. Since I was a teenager, I've prided myself on my ability to be productive, efficient, and useful to the point of pain. Because the ability to take pain like a man is equated with strength. I figured, if I could prove I was able to take pain as much as a man could, or even more, then I was irreplaceable. So, I wore pain and grind as medals of valor.

I wore pain as though my existence wasn't worthy without it. When you can be productive through pain, people look at you like you're a superhero or a machine. But they also begin to treat you like a machine. In these moments, we give other people the opportunity to cross unset boundaries and treat us as though we are less than human. This is because we don't treat ourselves as human.

This is a form of limitations that we fight for, especially in capitalistic societies like ours. We fight so hard for limits on our humanity because we somehow see being human as not enough. Or that being a human is something weak.

Admitting to our humanness has been equated to weakness. A human is the superior being on the planet and in this universe (that we are aware of), yet somehow being human is still not enough. And this is where the competition begins. In the corporate world, I have witnessed how the less humanness you show, the more useful you become, which then means, if any of your colleagues show their humanness, you are now in the running for the top.

When people actively decide to forgo their humanness and actively decide they don't need all the things a normal person needs, such as food, rest, quality time with people, they lose their ability to see the humanity within the people around them.

You treat people different when you are laser-focused in life. Ironically, your personal wants and desires become heightened without the ability to acknowledge anyone else's. Because how could anyone else possibly be doing something as important as you are? Look at the way you have killed yourself over this. If others aren't killing themselves over something, then are they really doing anything of importance in the first place? (Sarcasm)

This is the mentality that is going to eradicate the entire existence of humanity. Self-importance.

So yeah, I had a new bald spot right on my hairline, after spending two years taking Omega oils, biotin, changing my hair products, and doing everything I could to prevent hair loss from happening to me. I'd hoped eventually to grow my hair long enough to cover my nipples for once in my life. Ya know, so I could be like a mermaid. But the joke was on me. I should have just been working on ways to avoid stress.

The years I have spent hustling and grinding have definitely paid off. I work a nice remote job that pays me six figures a year, with health insurance and a match on my 401k. It's not my dream job, but it pays the bills. It keeps me safe financially for the first time in my life. But what did all that stress cost? And is it still costing me?

I spend all my spare time trying to unlearn all these behaviors that got me to where I am. Would I have been capable of making it to this point without almost killing myself due to stress? Might I be happier and healthier had I chosen a different path, one that didn't cause so much turmoil? I can never for sure know the answers to these questions, but I think they are worth asking.

I think they are worth pondering when looking at younger generations and thinking about what our expectations should be of them. I don't have any kids and I may not ever, but if I did, I sure as hell don't want them to have to go through the stress I experienced, only to end up at a job they don't enjoy, with no boundaries and that provokes social anxiety.

Many would look at the position I've made it to at this point in my life and exclaim, "*SUCCESS!*" I think differently. My view of success has changed multiple times over the years, but I think I have finally settled on what it looks like to me. I am sure I'll add more desires in years to come, but my general idea is pretty firm.

Bottom line: Our views on success are stupid. There should be no collective view of what success means or looks like. All that should matter, when it comes to success, is what does it look like to *you*? And to expand on that, does your vision of success include happiness?

I graduated with my master's in biomedical engineering from Cornell University in May 2021. One month before that, I was rejected from every PhD program I applied to. Three months after I graduated, I had applied to over 750 jobs on LinkedIn and was rejected from all of them.

I was kicked out of my first year of college in 2008, because I worked eighty hours a week instead of attending classes, in order to pay my bills. In 2010, during cosmetology school, I was called to the office, mannequin in hand and holding the corn rows I had just learned to do (so proud of myself). In that moment, they tried to expel me. I had applied to represent David Pressley School of Cosmetology in the Real Big Hair Ball and was told, "We can't have someone like you represent our school."

In 2014, after becoming a holistic nutritionist and starting my own company, The Origin of You, I didn't make a single dollar. The first time I was homeless was the day of my high school graduation in 2007, when my parents told me I had two weeks to find a place to live. I moved out that day and never attended my high school graduation. The second time I was homeless was in 2013, and I lived in an abandoned house with no walls, just plastic blowing in the wind. The third time, 2019, and I lived in my car with my dog, Charlie.

I have been rejected and I have failed in every single aspect of my life.

I will be the first to admit my addiction to grind culture. I'm good at it. I always have been. I've been in survival mode my entire life. I've prided myself on my ability to nearly kill myself with a smile on my face while working and going to school since I was thirteen.

That's what I do.

It's what I live for.

Cue Ursula, because we're all poor unfortunate souls who've given in to the garbage that is capitalism. Now, unfortunately, grind culture does pay off. It's not a lie. I don't know that I would be where I am today without first learning how to survive off cigarettes and espresso on the daily, during high school. I blame that time in my life for why I can't handle drinking coffee anymore. I have out-coffee-ed myself. These days, I have to get by on coffee-flavored ice cream. On rare occasions, I think maybe this time will be different, and I order a cappuccino, just to spend the next hour crawling out of my skin before my brain moves so fast and I've dissociated so quickly, I pass out.

Protesting For Joy

It was spring of 2023, and I was driving to a doctor's appointment in Largo from downtown St. Pete. I was driving with one knee, per usual. One phone was on a team's meeting for my corporate job, while the other phone was on a Zoom meeting for Wing, the dating app we are creating. I had a sandwich in the passenger seat of my car that I couldn't stop eying, because I hadn't eaten yet that day, it was almost 2 p.m.

I slammed on the brakes.

Fuck!

My sandwich was on the floor. At the next light, I pulled the seatbelt out as far as it could go, leaned over to pick up the sandwich's scattered pieces, to build it back together. I would have had to rebuild the sandwich before eating it, anyway. I rebuild everything I eat. I ate it.

I get a rush from moments like that, but my body and mind pay for it the next day. I am only thirty-four, and my ability to hustle and grind does not work the same way it used to. When I was in my twenties, I could party until 5 a.m. and show up for work at 7 a.m., happy as a clam. I might actually die if I tried doing that now.

I look back at those moments and wish I could hug myself. Much like the inner-child work I have done, where I pick up my two-year-old self while she cries… "Hold da baby." I look at my teenage and twenty-year-old self and just hug her, telling her to stop doing everything for everyone else and do something for yourself.

Back then, I wanted so badly to belong and be accepted by anyone that I killed myself, offering my time and energy every chance I got to people who never respected or cared about me in the first place.

When I went back to school at twenty-eight, I started to recognize this more.

"Recycle your pain. Use it. Allow it to take you to the next level. Allow it to push you to greatness. Don't quit. You're already in pain. You're already hurt. Get a reward for it. Don't cry to quit, cry to keep going."

I can't count the number of hours I've spent listening to this quote by Eric Thomas on repeat: running at 5 a.m. in Delray Beach, training for my half marathon, driving to and from school during my last semesters, when I was homeless and lost both of my grandparents, walking to visit Carl Sagan's grave in Ithaca every Monday afternoon while attending Cornell, and working out every day in an empty gym with a face mask in downtown Cambridge, while I dealt with mold poisoning, no heat, and a job that wouldn't pay me enough to even afford rent. I cried to keep going through every rep and every step, and I truly don't know where I would be today if it wasn't for Eric Thomas. He taught me to love the hunt.

After I moved back to Florida in September 2022, I kept searching for that same determination. I needed the high off my own pain to keep me moving toward greatness. The problem was, I didn't want to hold on to my pain anymore. I was ready to let it go. Listening to motivational albums wasn't hitting the same way as it used to. I wanted to feel joy. I wanted to listen to music.

This might sound odd, but I spend most of my life in silence. I work in silence, I drive in silence, and I clean in silence. If I am not in silence, I usually have a Black man yelling motivational quotes in my ear. For such a long time, my entire existence was based on how productive I could be, so I never stopped to ask myself what I actually enjoy.

Four years prior to this, in 2018, while living in Delray Beach, Florida, I decided to try out for *The*

Bachelor for the second time. Only this time, I decided to go in person. Casting was being held at a hotel in downtown Fort Lauderdale.

I got there as early as I could, so I could be the first person in line, but I was so early, they wouldn't even let me line up. My only choice was to entertain myself at the hotel bar. So, I drank three Negronis and ordered a piece of toast. I was so nervous, I couldn't eat.

I was wasted by the time I was supposed to go up for casting. I was also late. I walked into a conference room with over a hundred women staring at me, as I held up my ticket that proclaimed I was number one, and the first to arrive that day. Yet, I had showed up thirty minutes late somehow.

They pulled me into a room with four stations set up, each with their own interviewer and camera. I got producer Katie, so we were instantly friends, obvi. I have no idea what most of the questions were she asked me, because I was drunk and barely holding it together. Although, in my drunken state, I assumed I was nailing it.

"What are your hobbies?" the producer asked.

"Tubing and NASA!" I blurted out.

"Cool! So, you have a boat?"

"No, but my uncle in Michigan does, and I like to go tubing when I go back every summer."

"Okay. So, when you say NASA is a hobby, what do you mean by that? Do you go to see launches at Cape Canaveral a lot?"

Laughing to myself, I replied, "No, no, no, I've actually never even seen a launch. I went to Cape Canaveral one time four years ago with my family and boyfriend at the time. I just like NASA."

"Okay, well it looks like we're finished here. It was really nice to meet you. We will call you if you've been selected."

Did I just tell them my hobbies were tubing and NASA? What the fuck is wrong with me? Well, for sure that will get me cast, if nothing else does. Here's the crazy girl who doesn't know what a hobby is. What the hell is a hobby, anyway? Drinking Josh Cellars wine, and doing yoga once a month, when I'm about to lose my mind? At least mine were interesting.

But they weren't interesting. They were sad. I basically admitted to having joy in my life one time four years ago for a day and maybe once every summer for ten minutes. Because that's what hobbies are. They are things or activities that bring you joy, and I didn't have a single ounce of joy. I didn't have time to be worried about this in 2018, but I should have made the time.

I bought a paddleboard around that time, and I only took it out once. It was too wavy for me to even ride that day. My friend Veslemoy invited me to go paddleboarding every week for a year. She was also in school and working. But for some reason, I was the only one who didn't have time.

I didn't allow myself to have time for anything that wasn't what I deemed "productive," yet I spent Saturday nights into early Sunday mornings getting absolutely shit-faced to forget how hard life was, if only for the night.

I'd spend Sundays in my dungeon, ordering Uber Eats three times, paying someone to walk my dog twice, while never leaving my bed. I wasn't allowed to have joy. I hadn't done enough with myself to deserve joy. That's how I treated myself.

Getting a job at a small startup in Cambridge in 2021, after being rejected for over 750 positions I'd applied for after finishing graduate school, was a favor to me. Take what you're given and be grateful, right? Especially when the application process has proven that no one wants you.

I accepted $52,000 a year for a position in Cambridge, Massachusetts, where my rent was $2,000 a month, and I could barely afford to live. I knew my schoolmates from Cornell living in the same area were all making $30,000 or more than I was, but I was just grateful.

I have worried my entire life what might happen when I made it to the "Big Leagues" or whether I would change who I am, now being surrounded by people of stature or fame. Working at a small startup with less than twenty people meant every meeting I took part in involved sitting in the room with the CEO, CSO, CFO, and CMO. The C-suite.

I was grateful for this experience, because it taught me one of the most important things that I ever learned firsthand: the C-suite ain't shit. Remember this, you are usually, if not always, smarter than they are. Learning this meant I would never not use my voice, no matter how scared I am. The hierarchies and levels do not mean anything, especially when it comes to change and progress.

When I moved back to Florida in 2022 and my life started to slow down for the first time, I began protesting for joy. The small glimpses I'd had in the past, advocating for myself at that startup and even at my corporate job, lit a new kind of fire under my ass. Only this time, my fire wasn't one focused on productivity. This fire was pointed toward doing as little as I possibly could while gaining as much as I could. I thought I had been working smarter not harder my entire life, but I'd never done it for me. Now, it was my turn to reap the benefit of working smarter not harder. I was ready to experience joy. And not just *experience* joy but *live* for joy and anything that would bring me happiness.

Healing has a funny way of hurting, and I am not going to lie, I am still healing and hurting. There are some days when I wonder if it might just have been better for me to continue on the way I was going, that's how bad healing can hurt. But I am free in a way I never have been before, which is priceless and I wouldn't give it up for anything.

On the days I am hurting the most, on the days I can't quite let go of the pain inside of me, I go back and listen to Eric Thomas and the rest of my motivational playlist. I recycle my pain and let it fuel my fire again, but this time for joy.

I am learning my balance. I am playing alone on the teeter-totter of life to find my sweet spot. It is exhausting but worth it. And I can tell I am close to settling my debt to hustle and grind every time I choose joy and peace over production and self-sacrifice.

You can cry to keep going, but you can also laugh in the faces of everyone who ever made you cry to keep going. Choosing joy is the currency that pays to get out of the debt that hustle and grind culture creates. And every time you choose joy, there is a White man on the hilltop of capitalism who "suffers."

Chapter 5
You are Not What You Do

"You are not your job, you're not how much money you have in the bank. You are not the car you drive. You're not the contents of your wallet."

—*Fight Club*

SUBJECT: YOUR NEWEST BARTENDER
July 23, 2018

Hi there!
My name is Katie Dickieson. I was told that you are currently looking for a new bartender and should shoot an email this way. I am a full-time student but will only have classes Tues-Thurs starting August 20 and done with class by 4 p.m. on those days.
I worked part-time as a bartender at Pat's Wine Bar in Boca this past year. I have never done "full-bar" bartending (making cocktails) but know that won't be needed here.
I am good friends with Jessie Steele and used to work for him over at CWS in Lake Worth as a server. I also worked at Sons and Daughters farm and winery as a bartender, when they first opened. Copperpoint has been my favorite brewery in Florida since you guys opened, and I

would love to have the chance to become part of your staff! Give me a call if you would like to set up an interview.
 I hope you're having a great day!

My Superpower is Breaking Down Structures

There is a tipping point with structure. It plays a helpful role until it hits a point where our ego takes over, adhering to the structure at the expense of our true selves.

In 2009, when creating my first résumé, I decided I would never adhere to a structure that wouldn't want me exactly as I am. So, against my parents' better judgement, I sent out my purple, green, and orange résumé, and I got my first "real" job in a hair salon.

I lost myself slightly after going back to school, thinking I had to be "professional" in order to move forward in a career of medicine and Ivy League schools. I even deactivated my original Facebook account, to change my entire online presence.

I should have known better. I should never have tried to put myself into another box. I still use the new Facebook page I created while in university, but I also reactivated my old one. I have nothing to hide.

When I sent the email above to Copperpoint Brewery, I knew exactly what I wanted. I wanted a job to work at while in school that would love me just the way I was. I wanted a job that didn't feel like a job, while I worked two others and went to school. And I found it. To this day, Copperpoint Brewery is still the longest position I have ever held, for two years. It would have continued had I not gotten stuck in California on March 13, 2020.

In Summer 2023, I was sitting in the weekly L10 meeting over Teams for Wing, and I was bored to death. I didn't care for the structure of it. I knew it was useful, but I knew where *I* was useful and where I was not, and this was not conducive to the way I work.

My ideas come in spurts. They are explosive, and there is no way to control when and where they happen. Trying to fit creative genius in a box is the exact reason why our society is stuck in a box. All these fucking rules we *made up,* just to make the people who get off on structure more comfortable. *We* didn't make them up. We, as in, the we's like me. We would never do such a thing.

Every time we try to put ourselves in a box, we break the fucking box, and then have to explain why we did this. We aren't given much of an option sometimes. The society we live in has forced decision-making upon us when we would rather not actually have to make a decision, if we don't have to. Why does choosing one thing automatically make you against something else? It's fucking exhausting.

Why isn't, "I don't feel like it," enough of an answer? I think it is one of the most valid answers of all time. I would rather someone tell me they don't feel like it over any other answer. I might pry a bit, because I am a nosy person and fascinated by how individuals work. My prying though isn't in order to change your mind, but to better understand how you work as a human.

Our parents' favorite line, "Because I said so," is basically the same thing, just in a very rude version. Every time my parents said, "Because I said so," I wanted to understand why. If you can teach me the reason, I am more likely to be understanding and willing to give into your wishes. But if you just tell me, "Because I said so…" Well, fuck you, too.

I was still in the meeting and had no idea what anyone was talking about. *Am I an asshole? Or do I just work differently?*

Maybe I am autistic, I thought. I know I am ADHD, have PMDD, and scored very high when I took the online autistic spectrum test. I don't know if there is significant crossover there, but it would make sense that a highly functioning autistic person might be better equipped to understand and work with other autistic people. Because that would be a great explanation of why I excelled at nannying and tutoring autistic kids in high school. Once, the girls for whom I used to nanny asked their parents if I was an adult or was one of them. By age standards, I was an adult, but honestly, how much of being an adult is a twenty-two-year-old capable of?

Hook is my favorite movie. Fat chance you'll ever see me actually "adulting." Whatever the fuck that means.

Why do we even want to be adults? We all know being an adult sucks. I do *love* being able to do whatever I want, whenever I want, hypothetically. Looking at reality retrospectively, I think we are 1000% less free than we were as children.

As we grow up, it seems, every year, we are squeezed smaller and smaller until we can fit into that box society wants to put us in, and then we stay there until we die! But who are you, if you get rid of all the titles?

We give up our passions and hobbies in the name of adulthood, because at some point, some fucking asshole failed in his quest for joy and decided to make everyone else work, as opposed to doing the work on himself. Ya know the stories… the ones from the history books.

Chapter 6
Always Be Advocating

"Speak up, even if your voice shakes."
—*The Color Purple*

I AM NOT FEARLESS. I do everything filled with fear. When I was a child, whether I chose to advocate for myself or not, the outcome seemed to stay the same. So, I decided from a very young age that instead of succumbing to the wishes of everyone else and losing myself, I was going to fight back, and I haven't stopped since.

Remember those pages-long letters I told you about? The ones I printed, stapled, and put on my parents' pillows at night? Well, I keep a memory bin and guess what I found!

The following is from around 2002-2003, when I was thirteen or fourteen years old:

Dear Mom and Dad,
I'm sick of living with you guys, which is obvious. I try to change, to not say anything, or just to try to ignore you, so life is easier... but it doesn't help. It doesn't help because you don't change or care.
You can say you care, but you sure don't act like it. You may act like it for a day and think,

because you cared for one day I'm supposed to praise you for it... That's just stupid and unfair.

I know I'm a brat sometimes, but at least I admit it. Everyone is wrong sometimes, but you guys act like you're some gods who never are wrong and are perfect. At least I fess up and know when what I'm doing is wrong.

You may be the parents, but that gives you no right to act like you are perfect, because you are not. You aren't perfect parents, and I'm no perfect kid. So, don't act like you are or treat me like you are any better.

You wonder why I'm always angry. Well, you're the reason. I never act the way I do at home outside of the house, because I'm not angry or frustrated, because people in the real world are smarter than you. I get stressed from other things, but that's not what counts or gets me upset. It's you blowing every little thing up.

I'm not a stupid person. I know the difference between right and wrong, and I'm not about to let someone who doesn't think for himself or herself control me. Even if you are my parents. That may sound dumb, but it's true, and let me explain.

Both of you have completely different views and state them only when the other is not present. It's not the 1910s anymore, Mom. I know you don't agree with half the things Dad says, but still you keep your mouth shut at any sight of him questioning you. Only God knows why you would do this, but it's dumb.

You constantly tell me I can't do things or tell me not to do something, and no one likes to hear that or listen to it or do it... I wouldn't be so difficult, however, if, for just once in your lives, you could explain yourself without saying "Because I said so..."

You never explain yourself, so why would I listen, if I don't understand? And why would I listen to something I think is stupid, especially when you don't explain yourself. That's why I question so much.

I may not believe in God, but don't pull this crap on me that, because I'm not a Christian, I'm not going to go anywhere good. Because I'm almost sure I'm better than both of you already, because I can think for myself.

You make no difference in this world, when you're always trying to be someone else. You two are the fakest people I've ever met, even in front of each other. I know both of your personalities better than you two know each other, and I wonder every day how you two got married. But then I realized, because you made it easy on yourselves by being fake, so really, neither of you know what each other stands for or really cares about, except maybe God.

But it doesn't seem like either of you really started caring about God until you didn't know the answers to your own questions. It's hard not to dislike each other when you can be completely fake just to make the other person happy. How does that work out? How can you live with the fact of knowing that the opinion of others in your religion is what controls you?

I'm sorry about saying stuff about Christianity, and probably pissing you off, 'cause I understand that's what you base your life on. But I don't. And I don't think for one second, because I'm not like you, I'm a worse person. So, *don't press God on me, because I don't care! And I won't care especially when you constantly push it on me. It's going to make me hate it even more.*

Just like Mr. Sherman told me on the first day I had him, "Teachers always think they're right." And that exact fact shows in you, Mom, and you've got to realize, most of the time, you are not right. Not saying I'm the one who is right, but realize for once there could be a flaw in you.

I've always noticed that quality in you, and I've pointed it out, but you just don't get it, because the fact that you could never be wrong is just impossible to you. The Dickiesons may be a family, but I do not want to be a part of it as long as it is like this.

My friends are more of a family to me, not because I spend so much time with them, but because they understand you have to take into consideration the ideas of other people and not be so closed-minded by the rules of your religion and persecute those who are any different than you. I do not drink, smoke, and I am no slut.

In my entire life, I have not met anyone more oblivious to the world than you two... Even Nana, Papa, and Grandma understand the world more than you two, and they're twenty-some years older than you. It's got to be either you're completely oblivious or you want me, Andy, and Erin to be that way... Which is, again, stupid. You've tried to close us off to the real world and made it seem like such a horrible place.

Things have changed. Not everyone is like you, not even your kids, so get over the fact of trying to make us that way. Or make us want the same things as you, because I, for one, do not. If you just looked at the world for yourselves, or once you realize it wasn't just full of school, responsibility, bad things, and homework. But it's full of life and possibilities that haven't been able to occur yet, because of people like you.

You believe in God so strongly yet have no faith whatsoever, nor trust. You can say as many times as you'd like that you trust us, but what's trust, when you sit at home every night, while we are gone, thinking about and trying to find out something we might possibly be doing wrong, so you can keep us in from the world that you seem to so much despise? That's not trust.

If you're going to trust someone, that means you're always going to have to take chances, even if they're risky. Also realize, when your kids are gone, you could think, "Wow, I can trust my kids I know they're good kids," and feel good about them going out. You believe in God so you should have faith and trust that He will be taking care of me..., if you are such strong believers.

Just because I'm not a Christian does not mean I don't have morals or values or anything else like that. I still have all the same morals I used to. The only thing that's different is that I don't believe in God.

This letter is harsh, I know, but I don't know any other way to get this stuff through your heads without you rejecting every other word that comes out of my mouth. Don't take this personally and act like she said all this stuff, she cannot do that and she has no right, so we have to punish her or yell at her.

If you read this over again with a more open mind, without thinking of the fact that I'm just your daughter and actually think of me as a human being with feelings, maybe you'll begin to realize where I'm coming from and that this isn't some scheme to help me get freedom from parental rule.

I love you guys and everyone in our family, but our family seems a lot more complicated than others. It seems like you guys get upset at the chance that anything in your life may be less than perfect. I'm sick of being the one looked upon as the smartest in the family or the one who can do better. I may not have mental problems, but that doesn't mean I don't have issues that could affect the way I use myself.

You act like the only thing that matters in this world is school. That's the dumbest thing I've ever heard, because, if I was a Christian, I'd see there's no way school relates to how fast I'm going to go to Heaven. School does matter, but some aspects of it do not matter to me. I just do it 'cause I know I have to.

I quit a lot of things, but only to find the one thing I love to do. Passion does not come from something you have to work at or you will begin to dislike it, at the beginning. I think differently than you, and I'd like it if, for once, you respected that.

I understand myself and that's all I need to get through my own life, because I know what I'm doing, even if you guys do not understand. This is my life. You have some control but not total. It may be hard for you to hear that, but it's true.

I'm not a kid who needs her hand held anymore. My decisions come from my brain now, not just a sudden spur-the-moment thing. I'm always going to be the little kid coloring all over the white walls. Of course, I'm going to make mistakes. But so did you guys, and you learned from them on your own.

On the outside, I may not seem like it, but I know for myself that I am a lot more mature than most people my age. I know basic sense that most people look directly over, 'cause their minds are too clogged by what they think is important in life.

Times have changed, and you need to stop living the way your parents did. You think, after decades of people's kids telling them, they'd realize they weren't their parents, and I'm not you. So, stop trying to act like my life is yours to mold. The reason why people get messed up is because of parents like that.

You guys start stupid fights that don't matter and that are just dumb to bring up. Loosen up and realize you shouldn't care about the little things, because, either way, they're going to go away. You guys are going to stop caring about a stupid fight after a couple of minutes, so why blow it up into this huge mess that doesn't matter to anyone?

I laugh at how dumb things in this house are sometimes, because they make no sense. I don't understand your reasoning for anything. It's like you get bored, so you do the things you do. So now, I'm just going to say whatever, because I realize everything I've said in this letter I've said in person, and it has not changed anything.

So, you can ground me, but realize, it will never do anything except piss me off, and you can yell at me, and I'll just laugh more. When I yell back, however, you'll realize now, hopefully, it's for a reason. You'll see that I have always taken the time to explain myself... But in your case, I've never heard anything that establishes the reason why you guys do the things that you do or say the things that you say. All I know is, "Because I said so."

I did believe in God, though. I still do and always have. I say *higher power* or *universe* now, but to me it means the same thing.

This letter came after my mom found out I liked girls. The only way I knew how to make them understand that was possible was if I didn't believe in God. Because there's no way a person who is attracted to the same sex could possibly believe in God! Right?

So, instead of giving up a part of me, I gave up my public relationship with God and put Him in a closet.

Advocate for Yourself

"Katie, I need to talk to you. I found your Myspace, and it says that you like guys and girls. Is this true?"

I was so enraged by her condescending tone, I couldn't think straight. I knew what she had to say would be about the church and God, so I said the only thing I could think of that she would understand and that could explain this to her. The five worst words you can possibly say to a Catholic mother, "I don't believe in God."

Those five words opened the floodgates of my parents' minds, their belief that everything and anything I could ever possibly do was wrong. How could one possibly live a moralistic life without following in the footsteps of Christ?

My relationship with God was/is my relationship with God. I was never going to let her think she was allowed an opinion on what that relationship was, either. I don't like or believe in the possibility of people saying "my God" or "your God." I think it entirely negates the idea of God or a higher power.

No one can say for certain who and what God, higher power, the universe, or whatever you want to call it, is. To say "your" or "my" implies that more than one of these almighty powers exists. Which, unless all the shit we're getting dealt on this Earth is from all our individual higher powers duking it out up there, while we deal with the end results, then I'm just going to call bullshit.

There are literally colors we cannot even see and microbes between your eyes and on this page right now that are invisible to you. There is an entire universe living in the air we walk through during our daily lives. We don't know shit.

I am a scientist, and I believe in science. I also recognize that we invented science and math based on patterns we've studied in the universe, and I believe it is fucking magical. Nothing gets me off more than solving puzzles, patterns, and enigmas. But there is not a single person on this planet who can prove God to me or to anyone, for that matter.

In the famous words of John Mulaney, the great prophet, "There are no experts on this topic!"

At the end of the day, your prayer is just as good as your pastor's, rabbi's, shaman's, or whomever you look to for salvation, lack of salvation, or whatever it is you believe in. At the end of the day, what is the relationship you have with the universe by yourself? You spend enough time alone, you spend enough time within, and I promise you none of these religions are going to make any sense to you.

In this world, we do not practice what we preach, so why the fuck would I want to be part of a church stained with hypocrisy? That is why I believe my first and biggest act of advocacy for the self was cutting my family and everyone else in this world out of my relationship with God. No one is ever going to control me based on what their definition of God is.

Are you an advocate for yourself?

Me, Too.

I hate that.

I hate that it is the truth. And I also hate that it has the tendency to minimize what each woman has gone through, individually. That instead of going through their experience and being able to heal their trauma, we are diminished by "Me, Too," because that's just how normal of an experience it is.

Brian and I were no longer together, but I had won the friend group in the divorce. Gina's mom was going out of town for the weekend, and we were planning to have a party. Nothing outrageous, just our group of friends.

JJ was new to our school and quickly became friends with our group. He was our school's Eminem minus any talent. He had a lot more life experience than any of us did, which I found attractive.

I don't even know how JJ and I started to take an interest in each other. I had a mouth on me, though, and so did he, so I can only imagine it started with us making fun of each other, since I flirt like a five-year-old.

It's weird writing this and feeling all the feelings of shame come up for me in the moment. Not wanting to say I was attracted to JJ. Not wanting to admit we were seeing each other. Not wanting to admit any positive thing about this person, in fear that saying I was interested is an admission to "wanting it" or "asking for it."

At that point in my life, I was still planning on saving myself for marriage. Just because I'd left the church and lied to my parents about believing in God didn't mean that was the truth. The truth, my truth, was that my relationship with God was my relationship with God, and no one had any business trying to nose their way in it. Just like JJ had no business nosing his dick into my vagina without any consent.

I walked upstairs with JJ and we went into Gina's sister's bedroom. We were making out pretty heavily, but then it shifted so quickly, I couldn't even try to stop what was going to happen next. It was like he was already fucking me, and I didn't even have my clothes off yet. It was like he thought his dick was going to stab straight through my pants and do the work for him, but when it didn't, he took matters into his own hands.

I didn't know his pants were off. It was pitch-black, and he was twice my size. I had all of my clothes on, and I kept saying no. I kept pushing back. I never knew I didn't have a choice. I never knew that he would take his hand between my legs and under my back to pull the back of my pants down just enough, with my legs over my head, so I was pinned, and he could shove his dick inside me.

I didn't know I didn't have a choice. He only got a second before I kicked as hard as I fucking could and rolled off the side of the bed to run out of the room. I used to tell people the reason I always win in a fight is because I won't ever hit someone first, but the second I am hit, I black out and immediately go into survival mode.

I'd never stopped to think about why that was true about me, until now. It was this moment that taught me it was true. The moment JJ stuck his dick inside of me, it created the trigger in my mind. Not until after this moment did I ever get into fights. When I did, they got everything I wished I had done to JJ that night.

When I ran out the door of the bedroom, Jessica was standing there. She knew. She knew exactly what had happened without me even needing to tell her. She immediately slapped JJ across the face as he ran out behind me.

All the girls left and were supposed to go back to Jessica's for the night. I didn't tell anyone else what happened. Jessica was the only one who knew. It sounds moronic now, but at the time, JJ was best friends with everyone in the group. What was I going to do, ruin that for everyone? Create drama, by telling everyone JJ had just raped me? Go to the cops? Admit to my Catholic parents I had just been raped and I *wasn't a virgin anymore*? No way. I wasn't going to live my life dealing with all the backlash that would have come from it.

Everyone wanted to go back to Gina's. Everyone's boyfriends were there, and now, by default, JJ was mine. We went back to Gina's and stayed the night. I slept with JJ in the freezing-cold cement basement that felt like a torture chamber. I had sex with him.

I continued to date him and continued to allow him to do this to me for months. The only time I tried to tell someone what actually happened that night, I was met with the retort, "We all heard you. We could tell you were enjoying it. Don't lie."

So, I stopped telling anyone what really happened. Even today, as I write, I anticipate I'll be met with those same words.

You Have the Face of Someone Who Would Go Missing On the News

"You have the face of someone who would go missing on the news," my sister randomly said to me in the kitchen one day.

Why would she say something like that?

In April 2007, I was on my senior-year spring break in the Bahamas. We were at Senor Frogs, and they'd just announced an ass-shaking competition.

I had spent every school dance I'd ever attended in the Black girls' dance circle, training and preparing for this moment. I already knew I had won before it started, because every single contestant was White, and I had one up on them.

I won.

The DJ had me follow him to a POS system near the doors to the kitchen. I was to wait with him while he ordered the free drink I had won. Something was wrong with the POS, so he had me follow him into the kitchen. There was a long hallway before it opened up to dishwashers and the rest of the BOH. Then there was another doorway with another long hallway.

I continued to follow him but was becoming increasingly more suspicious.

"Where are we going?"

"This is where the real party is at!"

We walked through another set of double swinging doors that opened up to the back alley of a hotel and the bar.

"You're not going to want to miss this, girl."

Before I could ask another question, I was thrown into the sliding side door of a dumpster. Without thinking twice, I jumped up out of the top lid, over the DJ's head, and sprinted back to the swinging door. I had never run so fast in my life.

Down the hallway, just before the kitchen, a man was standing with his arms crossed, as though he was waiting, ready for me to try to run. I ran so fast, I ran straight through him, throwing him to the side as though I somehow had just become the Hulk.

Back through the kitchen and down the first long hallway, I made it back to the POS system. The bar was packed, and I couldn't see anyone I'd come there with. So, I jumped on the stage and started dancing.

If I am on the stage and people can see me, nothing can happen to me.

That's when I felt a hand slip around my waist.

"Babygirl, why did you leave me?"

It was the DJ.

I turned around to dance with him, trying to do anything I could to make him believe I wanted him, so nothing would happen to me. I kept dancing but moving closer and closer to the edge of the stage, inch by inch until, at a distance I could see my friends. So, I jumped down and ran as fast as I could to get to them, grabbing them and begging them to leave that very moment. And they did.

I have no idea what that man was trying to do to me, but I am grateful I got out of it. It terrifies me to wonder, had anyone else been in that situation, what might have happened. But it also makes me wonder if maybe I'm the only one dumb enough to get myself into a situation like that.

That is bullshit, though, because, as women, we should have the ability to have fun and shake our asses without fear of being abducted or raped. I wanted to believe there was a cooler party to go to. People will blame me for being naive but also berate me for being a bitch, when situations like this happen and cause me to become more cautious or "difficult."

Anytime you find yourself thinking or wondering if you're being too difficult, that is the exact moment you double down on what you're doing. That's advocating for yourself. Until you do it enough, you will always second-guess and question if you should, because as women, our worth has been denied throughout history. We're taking it back without asking.

I have been raped by six different men in my life. Three of them, I dated for a time. Two of them, I woke up to them having sex with me. And the last one was someone I worked with. All of them, I considered friends at one time and someone I could trust. I have slept with other men when I had no place to sleep or ways of getting home, thinking I owed them my body for giving me a place to rest my head. I've slept with other guys because I felt bad and didn't know how to say no, guilty if I didn't put out after a guy took me out.

Even after I found my voice and learned how to say no enough times, when I was strong enough for a man to accept that I meant it, then came the counter, "You'll sleep with everyone else, but you won't sleep with me?" Those type of comments and ridicule.

My story is not unique, I am just willing to tell it.

We need to do better than "Me, Too." The psychology behind men believing they have a right to women's bodies is so bad and systemically ingrained that self-declared male feminists don't even realize how ignorant they are in their behavior and self-righteousness. A lot of men believe, if a woman does not adhere to their feelings even in partnership, it means the woman doesn't respect them or the relationship. They believe the woman has decided it is a partnership only under their terms and based on their emotions and guidelines.

Moreover, many men still don't understand what it means to be emotionally abusive and controlling. So, they misinterpret a woman's freedom as her being disobedient to them and the relationship, or she doesn't care about the man's feelings.

Gentlemen, here it is: your "feelings" in these situations are misguided, toxic, emotionally abusive, and controlling. Our society has led men to believe this behavior is acceptable and part of the social norm, but it is not. And although I can see this being terribly uncomfortable for you to accept, we're done coddling your feelings about all the shit you put us through. We're going to need you to woman-up, accept that times have changed, recognize and apologize for your behavior, and then we can start to move forward.

As women, it seems as though we all have that one partner about whom we vow "never again." Seth was mine.

It was 2011. I spent the first three months after moving to Florida saving my paychecks in my locker at work, so I could move out and escape the situation I was in.

Seth was eighteen years older than me, on the sex offenders' list, and my free ticket out of Michigan. I did love him at one point. Even now as I write this, I want to list all of my excuses for being with him and all of the ways I defended him to everyone else. But now, looking back after twelve years, it is very clear to me.

Just as I was about to storm through the back door, vowing never to speak to him again, I heard my name being called. This time, it was not in the tone of someone screaming at me. I could hear in his voice that he needed my help.

I turned back and walked through the kitchen, annoyed for even giving him the time of day *again*. As I crossed the threshold from the dining room to the living, I saw it. As if someone had spilled a bucket of reddish-black paint all over the floor, thick enough to spread to every corner of the house with ease.

I didn't know blood could be this thick.

I didn't know, when it comes out that quickly, it is coagulated and in chunks. But even worse than the horrific scene I had just walked into was I didn't know what was coming next.

He had already smashed both of our phones. We'd only moved here a few months before. I didn't know anyone or anywhere I could go. The last time I went to the cops, they were discussing details about a woman all of them had fucked at different times, while hovering over me as they watched and waited for me to pack some things and get out. They shined a flashlight over my throat where he had strangled me and claimed they didn't notice any markings. The next day, my coworkers could see the choke marks and fat lip, though, even through my makeup.

The time before that, I was blamed for going back when I had nowhere else to live or stay. But the first time I called the police on Seth, they didn't even show up to arrest him.

There I was again, though, and this time I wasn't sure if it would be my blood on the floor next. But he fell to the ground, sobbing, as blood poured out of both his arms. He appeared to be realizing he had underestimated the sharpness of his chef's knives.

I grabbed the knives, knowing he was too weak to do anything about it, ran outside, and hid them under the deck, as far back as possible, hoping no one would ever be able to see or reach them. I ran back inside, and I pulled him into the bathroom shower, running the water to clear away as much blood as I could, in order to see how big the wounds were. I had no medical training and no first aid kit. Just Neosporin, towels, and tape.

I knew I had to somehow stop the bleeding. I knew the wounds needed stitches, but I also knew, if I left, he would finish the job. I became his nurse. I applied the pressure, covered the towels with Neosporin, and wrapped the tape as tightly as I could around each wound. I made him believe that I loved him.

I got him cleaned up and into bed, then I held him until he fell asleep. At that point, I walked the block away to my new apartment. (I had somehow been able to keep a secret from him, despite my not having a car or being able to live farther away from where I worked.) I had also gotten smarter: I knew he would break my phone again, so I had a back-up at my place, just in case. I called his mom.

"I can't be there for him anymore. I can't lie, I can't do this. I am sorry, but he needs help. He needs help I am not capable of giving him."

"Please stay away from him forever, Katie," his mom said. "Take care of yourself. Thank you for letting me know."

Past Trauma

My entire relationship with Seth was traumatic. Having a DJ throw me in a dumpster was traumatic. Being raped by JJ was traumatic. Being sent to Havenwyck was traumatic. Having so many people in my life die at such a young age was traumatic. My childhood home, to me, was traumatic.

People who don't understand trauma don't believe the extended effects it has on a person, even when trauma could very well be affecting them, and most likely is. I don't claim to be an expert in this field, but I am aware of the traumatic events that have happened in my life, and I have tried to become self-aware enough to acknowledge the long-term effects and what I need to do in order to learn and grow from these experience's.

A problem I have only recently come to acknowledge is how much I lean on comedy as a crutch. My life has had a lot of dramatic events, which people love to hear. I have used my trauma as a comedy routine, as a means of coping. For some time, I thought that meant I was fine and possibly healed, because I was able to talk about it with such ease.

That is not the truth. It only comes easily as a joke. I don't want to be looked at as the victim of my story. I don't wish these things happened to me so that I could have a good story to tell. I know that, if I were to meet myself, I would not believe me (like I said before) or feel bad for me. So, it is with this knowledge I try to tread very lightly when meeting people who seem to have similar stories. We can so easily pass judgment on others, especially when they are going through something we have never been though ourselves.

This part of my story is disturbing though, and at the time I was going through it, I made big jokes about the situation. Looking back, though, it really wasn't funny at all.

I knew Bradley Baxter from high school. He was my "high-school sweetheart's" best friend. I put that in quotes only because I don't know how sweet your first abusive relationship can really be.

I had known Bradley since middle school but never really talked to him until about tenth grade. Along with Brian, the high school sweetheart, Bradley was part of the skater boy stoner group. Bradley and Brian's houses were both places we were allowed to freely smoke weed and drink without any real parental supervision. Bradley was always pretty weird. I should have noticed it more back then, but I was just a kid smoking weed and drinking in someone's basement, because I could. I didn't think to check his mental health history. Plus, the other guys who hung out in that group were all pretty great people, some of whom I still talk to today.

Bradley was very quiet. I always attributed that to his being shy. I have always been intrigued by shy people, because I am so socially anxiety-ridden, I don't even know how to be shy. I always wanted to understand the shy ones.

I don't remember Bradley ever having a girlfriend. The closest we got to that was when Jamie Kessler had a crush on him one summer; I think they held hands walking back from Beverly Park one time.

His home dynamic was very strange, as well. His dad was never there and supposedly lived between Michigan and Florida for work. His mom never said hello or goodbye when we walked in. I don't know that she ever really noticed we were there, until a random occasion where she had an episode, and we all had to run out of there, high out of our minds, with no place to go. Bradley's mom was a schizophrenic, but again, I didn't know that back then. If I did, I certainly didn't understand what it meant.

While we were in high school, we had quite a few traumatic events occur. One of our good friends, Janis, died of a fentanyl-laced heroin overdose (which I wrote about earlier), and my high school sweetheart, Brian's mom also passed.

Brian's mom had gone in for a routine surgery, to have her gallbladder removed. It was a typical procedure, and we'd had no reason for worry. I went to the hospital with Brian after her surgery. He was terrified of hospitals and doctors and was shaking and crying before we even made it to her room. He couldn't handle seeing her in the hospital and couldn't stay there any longer. In the moment, she was fine, or so it seemed. A little weak after surgery, yes, but awake and talking.

For some reason, Brian's mom was not checking out well, and the hospital wouldn't let her leave. She became increasingly weak, and an infection was spreading the doctors didn't understand. They kept waiting to see if she would just pull through, but what they failed to realize was that, during surgery, the surgeon had left a sponge inside her body. This was causing an infection to spread throughout her entire body.

Once they came to this realization, they made it seem like everything was okay. It was a simple mistake, and they would schedule a new surgery for her right away, to remove the sponge. Right away turned into a day, two, three days, until they said they no longer could perform surgery on her, because she was too weak. She was too weak because, the day before surgery, you are not allowed to eat. Every day she was in the hospital, awaiting her new surgery, she was not eating. She also had that major internal infection, all causing her to be too weak by the time they decided finally to do surgery, on the woman, inside of whom they had left a sponge. They killed her. If Brian wasn't fucked up already and angry enough, he sure as shit was after that happened.

I remember Bradley not being at her funeral. This was a huge issue for Brian. He was really upset about his best friend from childhood not being at his mom's funeral. That's all I remember about that, though.

Throughout high school, Bradley became increasingly more reclusive until one day, he was just gone. I was sent away the summer of our junior year, going into senior year, and I don't remember seeing him senior year at all. Supposedly, he had fled the States with his mom, who was also a Canadian citizen, and no one really heard from him again. That would have been 2006-2007.

Fast forward to May 2011. I moved to Delray Beach, Florida on Cinco de Mayo. I left Michigan at 3 a.m. on May 4 and arrived at 3 a.m. May 5.

I wrote this story because I think it is important to see how much needs to happen before this system is willing to do anything. I know I am not alone in this type of encounter.

Bradley reached out to me via Facebook when I first moved to Delray Beach. He just so happened to live there, as well. At first, what seemed like a friendly blast from the past quickly turned to something a lot less friendly.

8/3/11, 3:24 PM

Bradley:
hey, how's it going katie?

my number is ********** if you ever need help, I am in an appartement in the same town, my cat has been sick, just took her to the vet. how are your cats?

8/3/11, 3:44 PM

I mean, maybe we can hang out soon! or I'll suprise you to cut my hair!

8/4/11, 11:23 PM

ok, didn't mean to affend you (i'm the one who needs help). wasn't even a friend too you, at all. but. anyway's. god bless you. if i run into you i'll just say hi katie! been a long time, and sorry to weird you out, i'm just visiting my dad and cousins, i'm still recovering from my mom getting extremely sick.. with septic shock. life is weird enough as it is... i'll leave you alone if you want, i was just excited to know your in delray too.!! anyways, your missing out, if you want to ingnore me. facebook is not really for me, don't ask me why i'm on it!

REMEMBER WHO THE FUCK YOU ARE

8/6/11, 8:11 PM

i am i the same town as you. i'll be around for a long time! maybe we can get together and talk about the old days.. take care for now.. i'm determined to find you soon!

8/8/11, 3:58 AM

hey! please message me your number# A

8/10/11, 12:18 AM
we should hang out this week!

we probably on opossite side's of delray. don't know though. we can be on the same street.

well my car isn't working, my computer keeps fucking up.. i feel like an idiot, trying to find a job these next couple of weeks

if you want to check out my dad's appartement in delray, we have 2 bikes to ride around on, and a nice belcony if you want to take it off! lol. take care..

8/24/11, 7:03 PM

HEY ☺ i am in Delray too, YOU. at least befriend be once again. i deleted you cause you weren't messaging me back.. but i don't care. will leave you alone. just want to still be friends!..

10/15/11, 3:55 PM

Hey, i have 2 bikes if you guys want to borrow, and a scouter. i've been stayin at my dads appartment in Delray . havn't been able to track you down.. i see you in Alantic Ave. Magazine!! looks like it might be rainy for jessicas visit.. you guys have fun though!!

KATIE DICKIESON

10/15/11, 4:14 PM

--****

2/7/12, 1:32 PM

Would you ever meet up with Mr. Eggslave BB GUN in Delray?
http://en.wikipedia.org/wiki/Humpty_Dumpty
http://en.wikipedia.org/wiki/Green_eggs_and_ham

BREAKFAST AT BRADLEY'S? o well maybe next time..

2/7/12, 4:00 PM

http://www.findwaldo.com/playaround.html

4/4/12, 7:51 PM

hi katiee, looks like naked hair is awesome yo.. 😉. if you want to start over. and meet up. that would be insane... 😉 i know your protesting something with that pic. come on now.

can i meet you in the abandoned trailer park next to mcdonalds..?

naww.. i would love to take you out sometime, sports bars? i've been to that duffys. have you been to gizzy's coffee shop?

4/4/12, 8:31 PM

i thought that video was cool how they all play the same guitar.. 🙂

4/6/12, 8:06 PM

(***)-***-****

[address given]

please explain to me how to meet up with you.. show up at O' Connors? maybe (I would).. ahh.. this is killing me. 😕 *anyways message me back. if you don't i totally understand. YET you don't undertand what i've been though either..*

give me your number. i'm about to go pic up some bud tonight, i have a connection from my old next door friend, no joke.. or call me for some if you want to get high..

problem is i don't know my away around Fort Laderdale i may have to though. i can't drink by myself.

4/6/12, 9:16 PM

sorry.. i've gone mad rabbit.. lookin good hun. 😊

4/6/12, 9:35 PM

gunna find some new friends someday.. but you are one to never forget, i must say.. i'd hang out with you over scott grinder any day.. lol.

4/6/12, 10:03 PM

gunna bee writing music again for now on, i got some many new ideas just need to record them... will be sending you my new music soon. 😊

KATIE DICKIESON

4/7/12, 6:17 PM

WUT, you think i'm not long tall and cool, you may be suprised.. katie i need a ride to get some pot in fort laderdale ASAP!

4/7/12, 6:33 PM

i'll get some very nice buds, soon... and we will get together to watch titanic... lol.. i'm not going to hunt you down though, like i said before. sorry.. if you really must know, i'm am about to work for comcast.. and am not a creep!

4/7/12, 6:50 PM

what the heck? is your number?

4/7/12, 7:31 PM

hope you get your cock problem figured out, them roaches will cause both sinus infections, ear infections, they are just the worst for both you and your cat...(just want the best for you) Florida has them in all apartments this time of year... it is not cool. you gotta get traps and stuff or you will get sick.

4/7/12, 8:22 PM

I am going to be moving back to canada for the summer so don't be confused, was just interested in meeting up for oldtime sake of some kind of friendship we used to have, if you don't give a funk i don't either.. best wishes. BB!

REMEMBER WHO THE FUCK YOU ARE

4/7/12, 8:38 PM

Dear: kathryn marie.. you are amazing to me, please send me a message..anything..

i take that back i'm probably staying in town, so just keep on doing great things, and hope to see you in a magazine again. P.M. salon was a great experience for you, i am happy about naked hair looks so much better!

hey i ended up geting drunk. so just forget for i typed.. peace.

have a nice easter sunday! please don't think of anthing to do with the name eggslave cuz that was a stupid band name. and please send me a message..

4/7/12, 10:19 PM

i tried going downtown, man is it packed. can't find o connor's. bye

4/7/12, 10:52 PM

you are out of my mind, i'm done thinking about you, there is no chance, c ya never again.. you should of kept that other profile pic katie. i'm pissed... i'm stuck in delray with no friends right now.. and it just made my life, even more pointless. bye.

4/8/12, 12:27 AM

full moons give me a mentaly breakdown.. sorry.

4/8/12, 11:43 AM

happy easter! i'm going to my uncles house today. hope you have a nice one 😊

4/8/12, 2:05 PM

hey, we have our own belcony (nice day) what are you up too?

well, hope you have a really nice and wonderful day, the beach is probably crowded, hope you have good friends to be with if not any family around.. bye

This went on for eight years. I never responded to him.

I was very careful not to put my personal information online after the first time Bradley talked about showing up at O'Connor's (my home pub at the time). The problem is the Internet. It's true: when something is out there, it's out there forever.

A lot of people have asked me over the years why I didn't just block him from the beginning. Honestly, I thought it was smarter not to block him. If I'd blocked him, I would have had no way of knowing if he was still looking for me. He clearly had no shame about letting me know that he was, so I really thought it was safest to know what he was up to, instead of having him show up at my house unannounced one day.

After the original messages about showing up at O'Connor's, I began to tell people about this, especially my boyfriend at the time, Langdon, who was also the bartender. I showed all the guys I trusted in my life pictures of Bradley, just in case he ever showed up.

Though I didn't have much faith, due to the issues involving Seth, I went to the police anyway, to see what could be done. Not surprisingly, they proved to be just as useless in this case, too. Bradley wasn't an ex-boyfriend, he hadn't done anything physical to me, and all I had was to prove he was stalking me was the record of his messages. The police claimed that wasn't enough.

Today, I know that it *was* enough. Cops just don't want to take the time to write reports or give you any useful advice. So, I let it be. For eight years! For eight years this went on. This man stalked me, got a job where I had a job a week after I left (he didn't know that, when he started), drove by my work, showed up to places I went, saw me in public places, told me about it, and never said a word to me.

I did send him a text message one time, but inadvertently. I got a call from an unknown number, and I assumed it was my manager from work, but in typical millennial fashion, instead of calling him back, I texted. I am grateful for this lazy decision to this day, because it created proof. Bradley had gotten my phone number from the employer at the job I left when he started working there as well, which, heads-up, is illegal for employers to do.

In January 2019, I got a call from one of my friends in high school who was friends with the same stoner-skater group back then. When this harassment started in 2011, I reached out to some of these boys, to see if they still had contact with Bradley and noticed anything unusual. Even they said to me things like, "He's lonely, don't be mean to him. He just wants friends," and so on. They didn't believe me, and frankly, they thought I was being a judgmental bitch. That was, until 2019.

Bradley had reached out to our mutual friend, Enrique. He called him to gloat about how he'd just been arrested for assault. He thought it was cool and that his high school buddy, whom he used to smoke weed and go garage hopping with, would find it impressive. Enrique didn't. He called me to tell me about it, to say that he believed me and also to inform me, I was not the only girl Bradley was doing this to. I just so happened to be the only one who lived in the same area as him.

I went to the courthouse. I waited as long as I needed to in order to talk to someone about what steps to take to obtain a restraining order. I still cared about Bradley's wellbeing, though, and realized this was more of a mental health issue, and I didn't want this to ruin his life.

It turns out, with a restraining order, the biggest thing is, aside from the person not being allowed near the filer, is this person is no longer allowed to purchase or carry a gun. Cool. I didn't think he should be able to have a weapon anyway. The restraining order also would not affect future employment applications, and this made me feel better about serving him.

The court-appointed attorney and I spent five hours reading over the entirety of the messages with Bradley, pulling out the most damning lines and creating a report for the judge. Considering nothing physical had ever happened, I needed sufficient evidence of a reason to fear this man based on words alone.

The report was filed, and a week later I had a response. I didn't have enough information for an immediate restraining order, but I had enough for a court date to state my case. However, this also meant Bradley was allowed to state his. Everything in my body did not want to do this. I wanted to brush it off and tell myself he was harmless, it was just messages and not a big deal. If not for the friends I'd shared this information with, I probably would have done just that. Brush it off.

But I'd shared the details with my coworker and manager, Brie. Thank God for this woman. She immediately offered to take me there and be in the courtroom with me. I know for certain I never would have shown up that day, had it not been for her.

She took me to lunch before the court hearing. I couldn't even eat, so I downed two beers quickly instead. She knew what I needed. Despite being my manager and also knowing we both had to go back to work after this, she put that aside and was my friend and family that day.

We made it to the courthouse in West Palm Beach only to find out we were in the wrong location, my hearing was in Delray, a twenty-minute drive away. We would miss it. And Bradley already knew I'd filed a restraining order. But now it would not be put in place if I missed my hearing.

Brie was not allowing this to happen. She had the clerk call the Delray courthouse and inform them of the mistake. We accepted the last place of the day, since we'd missed being the first case.

We drove to the Delray courthouse and had to sit in a huge hallway, alongside everyone else who was there for court hearings that day. While we checked in, I noticed an older gentleman who seemed oddly familiar; he was standing way too close for comfort. After we finished and walked to find a bench to sit on, I looked back to see the older gentleman walking directly toward Bradley, who was sitting down about fifty feet away from us on a bench.

It was his dad. Bradley sat across the room from us. I could feel him staring at me for six hours as we waited for my turn. At one point, after three hours, I turned to Brie and said, "Hey, you can go. I realize this is boring, just sitting here, and I don't want to take up your day."

She told me she would stay and that it was no problem. We sat in silence for hours, because my anxiety was so high, I couldn't even think about talking. Why did I feel like I was in trouble? The answer is obvious to me now. The justice system had never worked in my favor in the past, so my faith was lacking.

Finally, it was my turn. We walked through the glass doors into the courtroom. Brie sat behind me in a crowd of fifty people all who lived in Delray Beach, a tiny little beach town where everyone knows everyone. I don't know who was in the courtroom that day, but I definitely wasn't comfortable about it.

Why was I embarrassed about the actions of someone else? As though what they had done was a direct reflection of who I was? I was starting to believe it myself. I could hear my mother's words: "What did you do to deserve this?"

I was seated facing the judge, my court-appointed lawyer to my right, while Bradley sat no more than five feet to my left. He didn't have any representation, and his father had left him to fend for himself. I was shaking, and my mind was blank.

The judge opened by asking me to give my side of the story. I didn't know how to recount everything, so I started to tell the story in different snippets from throughout the years. My story wasn't cohesive; I was just rambling. To this day, I have never felt like that or reacted to being in the presence of someone the way I did in that courtroom.

After a few moments, the judge interrupted me.

"Miss Dickieson, I read the report."

"The whole thing?" I asked.

"The entire report, including the messages transcript. I am more concerned with how this made you feel. I want you to give us as much information about that as you're comfortable sharing."

I couldn't believe it. It had taken me and the court-appointed attorney five hours to read through and digest the messages from Bradley. It wasn't the judge's job to read all of that, but he had. The moment this realization hit me, I knew he was not like all the other judges and police officers I'd had dealt with in the past.

I proceeded to share my side of the story. Afterward, the judge asked Bradley to do the same. That was when I realized how bad the situation actually was. Bradley had not only been stalking me all these years, he had been stalking Langdon, as well.

The judge asked me the first question. "Miss Dickieson, what is your relationship to Bradley Baxter?"

"We were part of the same friend group in high school," I replied. "More than twelve years ago."

"Have you and Bradley ever had a romantic relationship together?"

"No. I dated his best friend in high school."

I don't remember everything that was said next, but this is what I recall:

Bradley said, "I ended the relationship with Kathryn (Ed: *he has never known me as Kathryn*) after a few years and took a break from our relationship, when I realized she and Langdon seemed happy together. I also was really mad at her, so I thought we should take a break anyway."

The judge asked Bradley, "Why were you angry with Katie?"

He answered, "My mom had died, and she was supposed to be there for me. She was supposed to be there for me the same way she was there for me in high school. She wasn't there for me, and that wasn't right."

Then the judge asked me, "Do you know what Bradley is referring to in regards to high school?"

(This was the moment I realized Bradley thought he was Brian, or so it seemed. He thought I was *his* girlfriend in high school.)

I said, "My boyfriend in high school was Bradley's best friend, Brian. *His* mom died while we were in school. I was there for Brian's family. I don't know what he means by being there for him in high school.

"How do you know Katie's boyfriend?" the judge asked Bradley.

"I went to Hurricane's a few times to see if Kathryn was there. The bar he works at," Bradley added.

"How did you know Katie was pregnant?" the judge asked.

"I saw them together, and they seemed pretty happy together, so I just assumed she must be pregnant."

The judge said, "Why did you think it was appropriate to invite Katie to the abandoned trailer park?"

"I had found a family of stray cats that needed to be taken care of," Bradley replied. "I thought Kathryn would want to help take care of them with me."

"You didn't think to tell her about the stray cats?" the judge continued. "Don't you think that comes off as strange, to invite someone to an abandoned trailer park? Can you see how this woman next to you is physically distressed? How this makes her extremely uncomfortable?"

Bradley motioned his hand my way as he looked over at me. "She looks great to me! She's dressed really nice, seems to have a lot going for her. She seems really great to me."

I was visibly shaking and staring at the floor when he said this.

Next, the judge asked, "If you and Katie are such close friends, why wouldn't you have acknowledged her at the Trader Joe's, when you saw her in public?

"I didn't want to scare her," he replied. "I didn't want to weird her out by saying hi in public."

"If you two were as close as you claim to be, it doesn't make sense to me as to why you think she would be scared for you to say hi, unless she had some reason to be afraid that you were aware of."

This went on for over an hour. Mainly because, whenever the judge asked Bradley a question, he rambled on for minutes at a time, digging himself deeper and deeper. He could have walked in there and responded, after I gave my testimony, saying something along the lines of, "I am sorry I made you uncomfortable, Katie. I realize my actions were wrong, and you don't have to worry about me continuing in the future."

But he couldn't do that! At one point in the middle of one of his ramblings, the attorney turned to me and whispered, "How much time do you want?" The case was done. She knew, within the first five minutes of Bradley opening his mouth, that I would be granted the restraining order. Typical time for a restraining order is six to twelve months. I told her twelve.

I asked her if I could say anything to the judge. She was very puzzled by this and suggested to me that I not, so I bit my tongue. I wanted to address Bradley and the judge. I wanted to tell Bradley I cared for him and he was my friend, that I just wanted him to get help. Looking back, I realize why that wasn't a good idea. There was no reasoning with Bradley, and the chance of his taking my words the wrong way was far too great.

At the end, the judge asked, "Do you have anything final you would like to say, Bradley?"

He said, "I just want the courtroom to know how well I have been doing. I am trying to make friends here. I planted an entire tomato patch a couple of months ago and even have taken in a family of stray kittens..."

He went on like this for a few minutes before the judge interrupted him.

Looking at my attorney, he asked, "How much time are we asking for?"

My attorney replied, "Twelve months, Your Honor."

Gavel drop.

He announced, "Restraining order granted for twelve months with ability to renew every year indefinitely. Bradley, please stay here. Miss Dickieson, we will give you ten minutes to exit the building safely before we will allow Mr. Baxter to leave."

Brie and I ran skipping down the hallway, telling all the officers we passed that we were going to get celebratory shots. We ran down the street to El Camino, my favorite spot for tacos and the best watermelon jalapeno margaritas, took two shots of espresso tequila, and headed back to work.

The adrenaline quickly wore off, and I immediately started to wonder, *but now what?*

What happens to someone who's just been given a restraining order? Is there any mandatory therapy? Is there any mental health evaluation? What happens next? I wanted to know.

Nothing.

Nothing happens after a restraining order is granted. I didn't know that. *How is there not a process set in place after a restraining order is granted?* I am pretty sure all parties on both sides would very much have benefitted from mental health counseling. How is that not a thing? I didn't understand. I still don't understand.

A year went by before I got my next message. (I have left this message in its original format as I feel it tells a lot about the state this person was in.)

> *hey katie..! i am sorry i had to see you in court last year... i pray for better. i wasn't really stalking you, but you have a right to be concerned*

i know. i was arrested by my neighbor who hurt my feelings...., and i ended up yelling at her and getting arrested. but i was drunk also. PLEASE FOR GIVE ME for over messaging all that crap. and i just wanted to beg to drop the charges. or i hope it goes away after a year, because it is starting to affect my work, as i can't get a background check to cater pizza party at boca elementary school. I HAVE BEEN DOING GOOD. and since my mom passed in delray i was only desparatly looking for a friend and i saw you in atlantic ave. magazine on scouter. and also saw you on puppy mill rescue news... ONCE AGAIN. i made a mistake to scare. you and this is the last message of maybe dropping the charges early so i can go on with my work and be successful. i never wanted to be negative or bother people i swear... GOD bless you. and i will never talk to you again now.....! PEACE.

Bradley had violated the restraining order. Sure, it wasn't a terrible violation. He'd only sent me a message, but he had only ever sent me messages before, too. Or so I had thought.

I was walking out of one of my classes at FAU when I got that message, and I decided immediately to act on it. I couldn't allow him to think this was acceptable. I needed to advocate for myself.

I assumed having a restraining order would make things easier this time. Call the police, let them know he violated, and they would pick him up. Yeah, right.

I was sent on a wild goose chase, calling and contacting over six police stations. I couldn't help but wonder what would have happened if Bradley actually showed up in person.

"Excuse me, Bradley. Please give me a moment. I am trying to ask the police what I am supposed to do, since you have violated your restraining order, and they just can't seem to get it together, so I am going to need you to wait."

It's a fucking joke.

Finally, I decided to drive to the county sheriff's department. There, only when I refused to leave and asked to see an officer did they finally make it happen. I informed the officer of the situation and asked what the next steps were.

"Well, I can file a report, I guess, if you really want to."

"If I really want to? I already have a restraining order! Why do I have to file a report? He has violated a restraining order already granted by a judge! But yes, if this is the process, yes. I want to file a report."

Reluctantly, the cop filled out the report. I was told the cops would go to his house and contact me about further developments.

Weeks went by, and I never heard anything. It wasn't until I was studying with my physical chemistry partner (who just happened to also be an attorney) that I found out, without a lawyer, nothing would be done.

What is the fucking point of our judicial system, if it only works for those who have money?

Getting a lawyer to help you with something like this isn't cheap. At least a thousand dollars just for them to send a letter to the court, to act on the violation. Luckily, my friend, the lab partner, was kind enough to do this for me.

I tend to meet humans like this in my life, and for that I am eternally grateful. I know such luck is not common for all who need help. Not only did he write the letter to the court, but when a court date was set, he showed up in my place and asked what I wanted done on my behalf. I didn't even know there were options. This was my moment!

I had him request that Bradley be assigned court-mandated therapy, and if he ever violated the restraining order again, he would go to jail. In my opinion, it should have been that way from the beginning, but at least we got it in the end.

I haven't heard from Bradley since. Every once in a while, I will check his Facebook just to see how he's doing, although you can never really tell with that sort of thing.

Back when I got out of Havenwyck, I had every intention of suing them and the doctor who'd had me placed there. But I was too damaged. I'd lost my voice. Being Baker Acted was the single most traumatizing thing that has ever happened in my life. Even today, I live with the constant fear that anything I might do or say could get me institutionalized again.

So, I kept putting it off. The statute of limitations for something like this is about seven years, but I thought about it constantly. I held on to the pain and shame of being sent away for so long. To this day, I am disappointed in myself for never suing them. I didn't advocate for myself the way I should have. The reasons I didn't were out of fear. So many layers of fear.

Would anyone believe anything I have to say?
They'll just lock me up again...
What if I am crazy?
What if there is something the matter with me?
I don't want to see that woman ever again.
I can't handle what seeing that woman again would do to me.

Finally filing for a restraining order against Bradley taught me this lesson. I have to thank Brie Friese, because without her, I would never have made it to that courtroom. I told her she could go and that I would be fine on my own and how thankful I was she waited seven hours for my hearing. She knew better, though. She knew I would have left. She saw through the face I put on that tells everyone I can do everything on my own.

I am grateful to have someone like her in my life, because I don't know very many people who would do that kind of thing. She believed me. She believed me enough to force me to see it through to the end. I'm not used to people believing me. It's hard for people to believe me, but when they do and also stand up for me, that is something I hold very close to my heart. That is something that makes me feel seen and cared for more than anything.

Becoming a Champion of Health

Advocating for yourself is the single most important tool a person can learn. When you are capable of advocating for yourself, you are capable of keeping your voice and your knowing. The more we are capable of keeping those intact, the more we are reminded exactly who the fuck we are.

Advocating for your health is one of the most difficult things to advocate for in a country with commercialized healthcare and a system that makes you jump through hoops and climb ladders just to get a referral, even when you have *good* health insurance!

In 2021, I was in the living room of my apartment in Ithaca, New York. I read a text from my mother and heard her loud and clear. For the first time in my life, my mom was telling me something that made sense. Not only did it make sense, but it showed she had actually been listening to me.

I clicked on Safari and typed in *PMDD symptoms.* There it was: a list of everything I had been experiencing since before I can remember. There was a name for it. I was not crazy. Well, I guess this showed I was actually a little crazy, but not crazy for recognizing a pattern inside my body all this time that I couldn't define.

I was thirty-one years old and learning this information for the first time. I felt like I had been fucking life completely raw with no condom on for all these years, when I could have been using protection, but I didn't even know there was something I needed protection from. As I read through the list of symptoms, it punched me in the gut so hard, I burst into tears. Suicidal ideation quickly came next, but for the first time in my life, I realized it was not really me who wanted to kill myself.

I spent the next two years obsessively trying to figure out how to cure my PMDD. Only problem with that: there is no cure. Not only is there no cure, but there isn't even a full understanding of the disorder. The more answers I found, the more questions I had and the further I went down a rabbit hole of frustration. I had become my own greatest science experiment.

For the first time since Havenwyck, I felt safe enough to talk to a psychiatrist about what was happening and to vocalize my fears from my past. The doctor explained to me that people with PMDD are prescribed an SSRI. But for people who have ADHD and take SSRIs, it can lead to increased suicidal ideation and depression, which makes sense as to why I was so negatively impacted by the drugs they'd put me on when I was sent away.

So, the doctor had me try bupropion, which is better known as Wellbutrin. The first month was great. The second month? Well, I became so carefree, I could have laid on my couch for the rest of my life and not given one shit about anything or anyone ever again. I knew this was not me. I was not okay with this being me, and so I stopped taking it.

Back to square one.

Six months later, I was lying on my green futon in my apartment in Cambridge, Massachusetts. It had been a year and a half since the initial Covid shutdown, and only now was I living somewhere that was starting to lift restrictions. We still had to wear masks everywhere in Cambridge, but bars and restaurants were allowing inside dining again.

I had started a new job as a research associate at a small biotech startup, purifying proteins to later glycosylate small molecules. Which is really just fancy speak for adding sugars to drugs in order to make them more easily absorbed into the body.

I should have been at the lab, but I couldn't be around people when I felt like that, so I went to work late at night or before the sun even rose, to avoid being dissociated in front of coworkers. I couldn't let them know there was something wrong with me.

I was scrolling Instagram when I came across a girl with ADHD and PMDD who'd been researching seemingly her entire life, trying to cope with her situation. The work she had put into understanding her body's reaction to every single day of her cycle was really overwhelming. I could feel the tears start to pour down my face. I couldn't help but feel completely defeated. I DMed her a couple of questions. I just wanted someone to give me the answers to fix me.

What days do you take Adderall?
What days don't you take Adderall?
What is famotidine, and where do I get it? How often do you take it, and on what days?

I didn't have the patience or focus to try to understand all the science she had posted. I just needed her to tell me what to do, but she couldn't. She told me to take the famotidine during my luteal phase, and I chucked my phone against the wall.

"*What the fuck is a luteal phase?*" I screamed out loud.

I contemplated suicide, but I couldn't even move off the couch, so instead, I allowed myself to just be a dungeon dog. I got my period a week and a half later, and suddenly, I was human again.

I created a note in my iPhone for tracking my symptoms. I did the research and found out that a luteal phase happens in the second part of your menstrual cycle. It begins around day fifteen of a twenty-eight-day cycle and ends when you get your period. The luteal phase prepares your uterus for pregnancy by thickening your uterine lining. A disorder involving your luteal phase can affect getting and staying pregnant. The fact I didn't already know what a luteal phase was before my thirty-third birthday is maddening and proof that there isn't enough sexual education in this country.

Day one of a menstrual cycle is the day a person gets her period. So, I started tracking for the next several months.

> Day 10- depressed, no care to do anything, exhausted, insomnia (haven't worked out in a week, though) / symptoms are starting around day 10 now again (June 10, 2022) / cramping nausea exhaustion dry eyes.
> Day 11- not taking Adderall, took famotidine, exhausted midday, dry eyes (6/11/22) / Nauseated, noises driving me crazy, rageish (10/20/22)
> Day 13- exhausted (8/31/22)
> Day 15- irritated, headache, maybe not take Adderall? / Wake up with headache. had a migraine now for three days, took mushrooms yesterday

Day 16- woke up with dry eyes, exhausted, very negative self-image, thinking I'm not good enough or pretty enough, scared that I'm not good enough to deserve what I want in life and the changes I am looking for. / Can't look at social media without wishing I were someone else and that I'll never make it or be what I want to be. Walked first thing in the morning, which has been good, nauseous but forcing myself to hit my macros to see how it changes my reactions (8/6/22)

Day 17- Exhausted, can't focus / exhausted but feeling peace. / Took famotidine did not take Adderall immediately. / took habanero gummy when I woke up and famotidine, drank matcha afternoon! (great decision, still exhausted but positive and able to get stuff done)

Day 18- Did not take Adderal. (3/10/22) (Insomnia that night) / had a great day and felt amazing / RAGE DAY / RAGE DAY (7/14/22) / so exhausted extremely nauseous (8/8/22) / Woke up exhausted, nauseous, dry eyes, but ate eggs and bacon that Lang made. / Went to gym, had a minor panic attack, got on Stairmaster, and got through it, then finished workout (9/5/22)

Day 19- woke up 3 a.m., wrote blogs then crashed at 8 a.m., exhaustion, very bloated, dry eyes; nauseous, no Adderall, exhausted, bloated, depressed, suicidal ideation, might have Covid (7/15) / nauseous not eating much, walking every morning and having collagen greens and powders to keep me replenished but no gym (8/9/2022)

Day 20- no Adderall / feeling good, not 100%, but made it to the gym, not as bad nausea (8/10/22)

Day 21- So exhausted don't want to leave the house, dissociations. / Super-dry eyes at wake-up, MOST EXHAUSTED, no Adderall, took Adderall later and got the spicy edibles (6/21/22) / extreme suicidal ideation

Day 23- Can't sleep well

Day 24- Can't sleep well, woke up with headache, super-dehydrated, complete exhaustion, forgot to do morning routine, not taking Adderall today / feel GREAT! Feel like fire!

In September 2022, I moved back to Florida to live with Langdon in St. Petersburg, after almost a year of our long-distance relationship. I'd been working remotely for my company since March, and my manager wanted me to move to the middle of fucking nowhere on Long Island, New York, to work in person.

My manager did not like me. She hadn't liked me from the first virtual interview she watched of me. I knew, because she commented to a friend of mine, who vouched for me at the company, that she feared I would not be a team player and that I came off as a "strong" personality on my interview.

She is the type of person who has worked in the same position for thirty years and never broken a rule, especially if the rule makes no sense and is actually a detriment to progress for the company.

For the first time in my life, I applied for disability accommodations through work, so I could remain a remote employee, something my manager was extremely opposed to. I had to meet with her to discuss these accommodations.

When I hit "join call," a woman other than my manager, Karen, was on the screen.

Karen began by saying, "Katie, this is Debra from HR. She is going to be witnessing our conversation today."

This fucking bitch blindsided me. I was going to play nice, but now I am going to let her see the real me.

I asked, "What happens when I don't show up to work in Bohemia on October 18?"

Karen replied, "You mean, what happens when you cannot fulfill the requirements of the position?"

Ha! She thinks she can get me to slip up on that comment.

I said, "No, what I mean is, what happens when I do not show up due to a disability? It is then your job to find me another position within your company, since that is what you are legally required to do, right?"

The HR woman jumped in at that point and said, "Okay Katie, you and I will continue this conversation later, just us."

Within the next three weeks, I found another position at the company. I was promoted, given a raise, and instantly paid my bonus at 100%.

If I'd needed any sign or reason for just how important it is to advocate for yourself, this was definitely it.

All the Small Things

On May 9, 2023, I was ten feet from Tom DeLonge in the pit at Little Caesars Arena in Detroit, Michigan. This was home. This was church.

I closed my eyes and felt the music of Stay together for the Kids pulse through my body. 22,000 broken hearts of emotionally damaged adults pounded all around me, and suddenly, I was twelve years old again. Tears poured down my face.

When I opened my eyes, the graphic on the screen depicted a child's stages in life, as he channeled all of his pain into guitar, while his parents fought on different levels of the house, until the day the house finally burned to the ground. The child was now Tom DeLonge, ripping a guitar solo in front of 22,000 hearts, who were empathizing and relating to all the pain it took to make it to this point.

We all made it. We all were that child, and somehow, some way, we made it that far in life, coming full circle just to scream at the top of our lungs in camaraderie against the emotional baggage our parents had stranded us with.

My parents never got divorced, but I wished for most of my childhood that they would. I don't wish that anymore, but that doesn't erase the pain I felt back then. It doesn't erase the pain I feel right now.

"Why is there so much pain?"

This moment wasn't just me at twelve years old. This moment and this pain are universal. Right now, there are kids at home experiencing this exact moment. Right now, the cycle is continuing, and all anyone wants to talk about is the cost of gas, inflation, and tax hikes.

22,000 people took out their phones to shine their flashlights like lighters, and I could see faces up into the rafters. In that moment, the individual human experience was overwhelming. Why could we come together and scream for our freedom from emotional baggage on that night and not do the same in our everyday lives? Why don't we fight for ourselves the way we fight to experience the people who inspire us?

This book in itself is a form of self-advocacy.

During my senior year of high school, I got a job at a music store called Axis Music Academy in Southfield, Michigan. It was in the same plaza as a Guitar Center, so I spent a lot of my time stickering the beginner Stratocaster boxes with an offer of free lessons over at our studio.

The term *grooming* is used when an adult builds a relationship, trust, and emotional connection with a child or young person, so they can manipulate, exploit, and abuse the child. I was groomed by many of the men who worked at this Guitar Center. I didn't know it at the time. I honestly didn't even know it was something that had affected me the way it did, until recently, after watching the television drama, *A Million Little Things*.

I finally realized that the narrative I'd told myself all these years was my way of protecting myself from the truth of what happened to me. For all these years, I took responsibility for my actions, as though I wasn't targeted as a seventeen-year-old girl who was just about to turn eighteen and become legal to all the guys. The men who groomed me would later slut-shame and make fun of me. Instead of advocating for myself, I blamed myself for how these twenty-eight-year-old men abused me.

I have never found it difficult to be an advocate for other people. It has always been something that comes naturally to me. I don't know if this was my way of standing up for myself by doing it for someone else, or whether, by standing up for someone else, I felt as though I was making up for the times when I hadn't stuck up for myself.

Advocating for yourself is an entirely different story. Usually, when someone has to advocate for themselves, it is because they have endured a wrongdoing. Unfortunately, we all have past traumas that have made us who we are today. My past traumas had a huge impact on my self-worth, allowing many instances when I should have been advocating for myself or have an automatic response to protect myself. Instead, my first instinct was to feel guilty, ashamed, or not want to make a big deal of something.

I'd think, *It's fine, I can handle this. It would hurt them more than this is hurting me now* (...if I were to stand up for myself).

I more often than not feel bad for my abuser, whether because I understand why they are acting the way they are or just because I was taught from a young age, because of my parents and my sister, to make things easier for the people having tantrums. I tend to put abusers ahead of myself, and this makes advocating for myself hard.

What makes advocating for yourself scary is the fear of loss. The fear that, if you advocate for yourself against a parent/friend/partner, they will walk out on you. If you advocate for yourself against your boss, you will be fired. If you advocate for your freedoms, you will lose what little freedoms you already have.

Advocating for yourself feels like the scariest gamble you've ever made, but in gambling for yourself, you can lose a lot more than money. Advocating for yourself is also exhausting because, if you succeed once, I guarantee you will have to continue to advocate for the same thing over and over again, until your side becomes the majority.

For a person who already suffers from self-worth issues, it is incredibly difficult and scary to continuously talk yourself into why you're worth it. Advocating for yourself is scary because, at some point, no matter what, you will question your own sanity in the process. And if you don't have a support system in place, that can be exponentially more detrimental to our mental health. Advocating for yourself is scary because it is never the easier option, but if you continue to advocate, life on the other side will be easier.

Advocating for myself has taught me self-worth. Or I should say it has *reminded* me of my worth. Once you start advocating for yourself and the whole world doesn't blow up in flames, you realize you should've always been advocating for yourself.

No one is going to do it for you, though, and even if they do, most likely it's a one-time thing. When it comes to advocating, it's an ongoing process. It's a practice, and you get better and better at it the more you do it.

It teaches us boundaries and what those boundaries are for you. You begin to recognize what you are and are not okay with. You learn what things you were pretending to be okay with, just to avoid conflict. Advocating for yourself helps you to see who respects you and who doesn't.

Advocating for yourself gives you more information about the people who surround you, and information is everything. The information you collect from advocating for yourself sets you up to be better equipped to continue the practice in more constructive and less energy-draining ways. When other people witness how you show up for yourself, it inspires them to do the same. It's these small but major acts that move the needle toward a world where people's boundaries will be more respected and where people will have a better chance of not being taken advantage of. Advocating for yourself doesn't make you a difficult person. Advocating for yourself opens doors to allow the most authentic version of yourself shine.

Privilege

"Privilege is not in and of itself bad; what matters is what we do with privilege."

—Bell Hooks

After cutting off my hair in middle school, the only people who accepted me at their lunch table were the Black girls. I didn't recognize the truth until many years later. Right then, I could only see myself.

When people gave looks and were judgmental, all I could think was the rest of the world couldn't understand why all these girls would accept me and be friends with the crazy girl who'd cut off all her hair. When really, they were not used to seeing a White girl sit with the Black girls. It had nothing to do with me. I was so self-absorbed in my own shit, I couldn't see that anyone else's shit existed. I can see now, though.

Since then, I have always felt safer amongst Black women than White women. The Black community has never othered me or cast me out. When I am attending an event where I don't know anyone, the first thing I do is look for Black women, if there even are any. I am still a White woman, though. Regardless of if I feel safe or not, I am safe because of my skin color. My fears are rooted in the anxiety of being ousted, not in the fear of someone wanting me dead.

It's an infuriating feeling, after educating yourself, working on yourself, and doing everything you can to become a better, more capable person, just to feel inadequate and incapable because the world is run by a bunch of power-hungry, selfish morons. Just writing that sentence made me have to take a pause to face palm and scream.

I get why we give up the fight. I get why we work so hard for causes we believe in until we get to a place of comfort, and at some point, it becomes too exhausting to try anymore. Which is a luxury and privilege we have, as White women. While contemplating about people who "don't see color" or people I know voted for Trump for "financial reasons," I thought about how, if I wanted to, I could ignore all of the causes I care to fight for. I could ignore them, and if I chose to ignore them, it would give me the ability to fully focus on me and furthering myself to become more successful.

I could toe the line just enough and talk about the things I "care about," to make people see I am a "good person," but, in private, never donate to any charities, never give any of my time to causes that are important and just live my simple, easy life, because I am a White woman and, in a racist world fighting for equality, the

White woman gets next in line. And oh, what a wonderful thing that is for the White woman.

    I could be that White woman, if I wanted to. I have sat in those spaces. Rooms of the ultra-wealthy, White, old-money people of the world, where I was looked at as the entertainment. The jester to their castle. But also as a pet to show off, because of my brilliant mind and persevering will power. How easy it would be to become their next pet project, so that, one day, they could claim my success for themselves. Which would be fair, because sitting in those spaces and accepting that position would be selling myself to the devil.

    I don't understand the people who can comfortably keep their seat in those spaces, who claim not to hold the same beliefs. You can tell me it's the money, and you can tell me it's the power. You can even tell me it is blatant hate and greed, and I will still never understand.

    I don't know how to have empathy for hate. I can't feel it. I don't fucking get it. I don't understand how, with this one life, people want to play like it's actually a game of war from back when we were five years old. It doesn't make sense to me that this is the world we've chosen to live in. Where, somehow, we have become okay with getting ahead and watching those behind us suffer. A world where White women will cross a bridge built from the bodies of Black women and praise ourselves for how hard we've worked to get there, while our stiletto stabs into another woman's back.

    There are always exceptions to the rule. We're not here to debate each individual contribution made by every White woman, so we can pat ourselves on the back and tell ourselves we're not as bad as the last woman. It's not about comparing ourselves to the evil of this world, just so we can say, "Well, I am not as bad as they are." It's never been about comparing ourselves to others. In any aspect of life, it is never about how we measure up to the person next to us. It is how we measure up to who we were yesterday.

I'm so fucking tired, but I don't know how to stop. I can't be that woman. Having the option to stop, though. That is a privilege. As White women, we have had the privilege to be courageous without the fear of death. There are plenty of fears that do exist for us, but none of them even come close to fearing we will be murdered because of the way we look.

Being courageous as a White woman versus being courageous as a Black woman is a very different thing. The things we have to be courageous about are very different. As White women, it takes courage for us to speak up in meetings, ask for raises, start new businesses, speak in public—ya know, the things that "terrify" us.

As a Black woman, it takes courage to leave the house in the morning. It takes courage to let your children leave the house and tell them to have a good time. It takes courage to teach your children from a very young age how to respond in the presence of police. It takes courage to go for a jog or run before the sun rises or after the sun sets (the only time I am willing to go for a run). It takes courage to simply exist as a Black woman, as a Black person. How is it that a Black woman is then expected to have the courage to push any further in life, the way we White women do, when their mere existence can be what gets them murdered? To not recognize this, to pretend Black women have the same opportunities, allowances, and space to act on their courageous wants and needs, is complete and utter bullshit and fucking racist.

I am not perfect. I more than likely have not articulated this topic perfectly, but I am willing to learn. I am willing to be wrong. I am willing to be corrected. I am willing to change and look at things from a different perspective. Because, though those things might be uncomfortable and take courage, I won't die. But Black people will continue to, if we don't recognize that we can be courageous in fighting for the lives of Black people while simultaneously being courageous for ourselves. I just don't understand what is so hard to understand about equality or, better yet, being willing to recognize the inequalities that exist. How is it so easy for us to turn off our brains to the billions of people who are underprivileged and just trying to survive? Why are we okay with watching the world crumble? Why are we comfortable, knowing others are in pain?

If you are not one of these people who have turned off your brain, it is important to remember that working to ensure Black people have equal rights does not mean we deserve a pat on the back or congratulations. We're not doing anything special by fighting for equal rights for others. We are doing what is right and what is the bare minimum. We're not fighting to become the wokest of woke White people. We're not fighting for who is the best advocate. We are fighting for people's right to equality. That's it. It's not for us. This space does not have room for us to have egos.

Furthermore, this space does not have room for our feelings. It is not the job of a Black person to make us feel better about White supremacy, colonialism, systemic racism, or how sad we are about how Black people have been treated. It is depressing, horrifying, and enraging. And it is our job to process those feelings and emotions without the help of a Black person to make us feel better about ourselves. It is important for us to feel those emotions, we should feel those emotions, but the weight of processing those emotions does not lie on Black people.

You'll get to a point in your process when things will all of a sudden become a little bit easier. It's in this moment you might lose yourself again, because you don't know life without being in survival mode. When life was between living or dying, you had it, because you're a badass and you are resilient. Resilience doesn't know how to comprehend ease, because it's never met it before.

This ease also comes to test you. Okay, you've proven you can fight the world, you can fight back against those who have come to take you out, but when and where did you learn to fight yourself? Not in your confidence; not in your procrastination. When have you learned to fight yourself in complacency?

You haven't. This is the moment, and it's harder than any of the other tests you've passed before, because your privilege can keep you here, and for most people, it does.

Chapter 7

Revealing Magnifies Healing

"It's not until you talk about it that you realize how you really feel."
— Sean Maguire, *Good Will Hunting*

HIDING EVEN THE TINIEST PIECE of who you are causes damage you are not aware of until you free yourself.

Back at Havenwyck, a case worker met me after my first appointment with Dr. S and walked me out into the courtyard. This was a twenty-by-twenty-foot, U-shaped brick encasing with a twelve-foot fence at the open end, to stop anyone from coming or going.

We sat down on a bench and she started to ask me questions:

Name?

Date of Birth?

Gender?

I thought, *Gender? Why would she ask me my gender? Can't she tell I'm a girl?*

Sexual Orientation?

Am I allowed to answer this question truthfully? Or is it going to be used against me? The last time anyone found out I liked girls, I was thirteen and grounded, after my mom saw I had ticked "guys and girls" on my Myspace profile for who I was into.

"Who is this for?"

Case Worker: This is just for your file. No one is ever going to see this. It is confidential.

Am I even gay enough to admit this?

"I think I would say I am bisexual"

Does she think I want her now, because I admitted to liking girls? I mean, she is really hot, but she probably thinks I am disgusting now. Does she know what I'm thinking?

Case Worker: Okay! And when did you first start liking women and men? Or have you always liked both?

What is going on here? Am I allowed to talk about this? Is this some kind of trick?

I finished answering her questions.

This was the first time I had ever told anyone I liked girls and nothing bad had come from it. I mean, I was already in the worst situation I could imagine, but it didn't get any worse. I didn't know I could feel safe to talk about my sexuality. I didn't know it could be that easy. She just accepted everything I said without batting an eye. She didn't question my belief in God, and she didn't try to belittle me by saying I just liked girls for attention. I was allowed to say that I liked girls, and that was it.

It would take fourteen more years before I would publicly announce my sexuality to the world on social media. Looking back at that moment with the social worker, in a place I felt more unsafe than any time or place in my entire life, she gave me the sense of safety I had no idea I needed more than anything. She offered me the safety to be myself. After fourteen years, I finally gave myself the permission to honor that safety and publicly come out, a step I never knew I needed, in order to allow myself to be the person I needed me to be. And in a Facebook post two days after National Coming-Out Day, I did just that.

October 13, 2020

I've been late for everything else this week, so I decided I might as well keep up the pattern...

I don't want to wait until next year, and I am done pretending I'm not who I am just to make others around me feel more comfortable.

For those of you close to me, it should come as no surprise. Here are a bunch of pictures of me being Queer, because I am.

Also, my dog is gay.

So happy coming out day to both of us, although I think he just came out of a rainbow the day he was born!

#ComingOut

192 likes and 39 comments on FB. 134 likes and 24 comments on IG.

Not a single acknowledgment from my parents. Not online, not in person, not over the phone, not ever, until I brought it to their attention.

It's been three years since I publicly came out and to this day, I still have yet to have a conversation with anyone in my family about my sexuality. Not because I don't want to, but because they still have yet to actually acknowledge it. Being in a relationship with a cis man automatically makes me straight again, right? I assume that's what they think, or maybe even hope.

I've liked girls for as long as I can remember. I've always liked guys, too, but that's not the interesting part here. I was always very interested in sex from a young age. Putting socks in my shirt to pretend I had big boobs, humping the handle pole of our treadmill in the basement because it felt good, making out with a face I drew on the wall—ya know, that kind of thing.

As a kid, I kept one of those Christmas cookie tins under my bed to safely store away my secrets. I still believed in the tooth fairy, but I also believed I could trick her. So, whenever I lost a tooth, I told my parents and showed them, but then I would hide the tooth in my tin, to keep and reuse at a later date, in order to con the tooth fairy out of more money, which worked. The tooth fairy didn't pay much attention to me.

The other thing I kept in my treasure tin was a ripped-out magazine ad for Viagra. It was a picture of an old man and woman in robes, looking out the window, and her leg was coming through the bottom of the robe, I think. There was nothing very sexual about it, but it was the *idea* of the ad that drew me in. My imagination was endless, and that Viagra ad continued to be my only form of porn until I stumbled across *About Last Night* with Rob Lowe and Demi Moore on tv one day.

That was one of the most exciting Saturday afternoons I can remember. After that came Cinemax and late-night HBO.

On a Sunday morning before church, I got caught watching online porn the first time I ever tried. Porn was not like porn today. The only free thing I could get to was a slide show of a woman who looked very much like Dolly Parton in the back of a limo, taking off one more piece of clothing with every click. I didn't know what pop-ups or a browsing history were back then, so when my mom snuck up on me, there was no time to exit out of the 50-100 pop-ups and viruses that had invaded our computer.

I blamed it on my brother; I had just so happened to stumble across it, left up on the screen. I was not believed, but there was also no conversation after the incident.

I was obsessed with sex scenes in movies, and my two favorites, ironically, both starred Sean Young in similar roles and storylines. That's right ladies, gentlemen. Those of you guessed it, the two movies that got me off most as a kid were *Ace Ventura: Pet Detective* and *Dr. Jekyll and Ms. Hyde*. In both films, Sean Young "transitions" from being a man into a woman. Ironic? Maybe not so much.

I thought she was the hottest thing on Earth, but I'm just realizing that now. When I was young, I didn't understand the concept of being allowed to like girls.

When my friends and I would practice kissing and I would get turned on, I believed I was just getting turned on by the idea of what could happen with a guy. That I was imagining I was doing that with a guy. But I was never doing that. I was always moving as though I was the guy, and that's what turned me on.

When Ms. Hyde gets naked in front of her boss and her boobs deflate as she turns back into a man, I wasn't turned on looking at Stephen Tobolowsky. I was turned on looking at her! Oh, boy did I also want to be her though! She was so strong and dominant. She was so much smarter than all the men in both movies. Granted, in the end, she does not come out on top. Spoiler Alert.

But honestly, that's just because, in the nineties, there was no way Hollywood would have allowed a trans person to win. In fact, *Ace Ventura* and *Dr. Jekyll and Ms. Hyde* were both extremely transphobic movies. I didn't understand transgender as being a thing that really existed, when I was a kid. *Dr. Jekyll and Ms. Hyde* was a complete fantasy. Honestly, it's still one of my fantasies today.

It can be very tricky in this world to navigate being a female scientist, who is also sexy. This is very evident in that movie. Sean Young plays a sexy scientist who is depicted as evil, so as a kid, that was my only reference for what a female scientist could be. She is faking it, first of all, because she's not even the *real* scientist. The only reason why she is there is *because* of her sex appeal. But her sex appeal means that no one will ever take her seriously. By sleeping with multiple men, she is automatically deemed a slut and a disturbance in the workplace. Look at the turmoil and turbulence that happens when men can't handle a strong, smart woman having consensual sex with her coworkers. While men have been doing this and boasting about their ability to do so across time.

This is why I was over the moon when I came across Dr. Korie Grayson and the Instagram hashtag she created, #ThisIsWhatAScientistLooksLike. Not only is this woman a brilliant scientist who has her PhD in biomedical engineering from Cornell University, but she is *hot*, sexy, beautiful, gorgeous, and flaunting all of it right out on her public social media accounts. What a fucking badass.

Dr. Korie gave me the permission I needed to fully embrace not only my sexuality but my sex appeal and to stand firm knowing I can still be taken seriously as a scientist with a master's degree in biomedical engineering from Cornell. Dr. Korie is known as an advocate for diversity and inclusion in the STEM (science, technology, engineering, and mathematics) fields and shares her experiences as a Black woman in science. #ThisIsWhatAScientistLooksLike has been used over the years to challenge and expand traditional stereotypes of what scientists "should" look like.

The purpose behind such a hashtag is to highlight the diverse backgrounds, genders, ethnicities, and other identities that exist within the scientific community, thereby dispelling the narrow and often inaccurate stereotype of scientists. Thank you, Dr. Korie.

Though Dr. Korie gave me this newfound permission, I still find myself shrinking into my guilt and shame about how I was raised to believe what was and was not acceptable from a woman. I hid so much of myself. It wasn't until I came out that I realized just how much I hid behind the "bigness" I present to the world on a daily basis. My entire life, I have spent endless amounts of energy trying to prove who I am, only to have so many of the people I meet call me a liar. And hey, maybe they were right. Maybe I have been lying about who I am. But not in the way I think they might believe.

The truth is, I am actually bigger than I portray. I am expansive and innovative. I am the alpha wolf of the pack, leading from the back to make sure none are left behind. Never the leader, but always leading.

I am terrified to be seen. Which might seem pretty ironic, if you've ever met me. I am loud and expressive, I put myself out there, and I am obtusely steadfast in my beliefs and morals. I will be the first person to spontaneously take action or show up at the last minute, and when I show up, I show up hard.

Rarely will you find me making commitments, though. Making commitments is defining. Making commitments doesn't leave room to change your mind without scrutiny. I learned early that if I just never commit to doing something, people can't get mad at me when I don't show up. Planning is terrifying and annoying to me. I am much better at watching everyone else plan, then, with organized chaos, I come in to put the pieces together as I go.

Stepping into leadership is terrifying. Because what happens when people actually start to follow you? It's easier to fix the mess others make than it is to deal with the fallout of your own mistakes.

When you allow yourself the opportunity to fall, though, you end up learning how to fly. Even better, when you give yourself permission to step into the bigness of who you really are and always have been, *and then* running toward that fall, you take off like a rocket, baby!

My final piece of advice on this topic, not only for you but for myself as well: go back to being the dumbest person in the room. Ask all the questions that come to your head, and don't even think to turn your head to see who's looking.

Chapter 8

The People Who Make Us

"The effect you have on others is the most valuable currency there is."

—Jim Carrey

YOU NEVER THINK SOMEONE close to you is going to die. You think, especially as a teenager, that kind of thing only happens in the movies. It couldn't possibly ever happen to you or someone you know. Well, it did.

I hold a vivid image in my mind, though I'm not sure if it is a memory or only a dream. I felt exhausted, walking up Beverly Hill. The grass was emerald-green and lush. I climbed toward the top, and as I looked up, I could only see the sunlight illuminating Ann's curly, golden locks. She was at the top, waiting for Joan and me to make it...

I met my oldest friend, Joan, when I was almost two years old. My mom was pregnant with my sister at the time, and we were having a garage sale. Ann walked over to our house with Joan in a stroller, and the rest is history.

I owe my imagination to Ann. The way I dream and believe. The way I love. Ann is the first person who ever saw me for who I really was, even as a child. She was the first person to teach me about yoga and reiki. Joan and I might have laughed at Ann, the first time she tried to teach us how to be trees, but now I can't get into tree pose during a yoga class without thinking of her.

Ann bought me my first sketchbook on a Saturday afternoon, when she'd allowed me to tag along for Joan's Irish dancing class and errands. I was one of those kids who never wanted to go home. So, I will never forget days like the one when I was allowed to come along, because they provided what I so desperately craved, to feel included and wanted. Ann also took us to the French bakery and we got loaves of fish bread. (I still have no idea why we called it that.) It did not taste like fish. It was delicious, light and flakey.

Ann taught me about gardening and introduced me to chives for the first time, directly from her garden. I'll never forget how spicy that first taste of a chive was. I don't even know if I actually liked it, but I have been obsessed with them ever since. I feel the need to tell all these little details about Ann because they are the majority of the memories I have as a child. I have a very good memory for the most part, but unfortunately, much of my childhood is blank, except for Ann.

Ann had a large costume collection with the most gorgeous dresses I had ever seen. Specifically, there was one orange, long-sleeved chiffon dress I will never forget. We spent hundreds of hours playing "olden days" in the Smyths' basement, hanging sheets from the push-up ceilings, creating our own worlds, guided by candlelight. Just like the girls in *Little Women*.

On weekends, all the kids would gather at my house to play in the basement and be watched by the older kids in the neighborhood, while all our parents got drunk and stoned down at the Smyths'. Once it was dark, all the kids met their parents back down at the Smyths', to walk home together.

But Joan was my best friend, which meant we were always going to have a sleepover. I always wanted to stay at their house, because Pat and Ann would both scoop me up and drag me around the house, dancing to Irish music. I lived for that. I would laugh uncomfortably and even act like I didn't like it, all while they were the happiest moments of my life.

Ann is the kind of person who changes your life. Not because of the big moments, but because of the little ones. She made everyone around her feel seen and included. My entire life, I have lived with the mentality of "What Would Ann Do?" Because I know, if I could make half the impact on people that Ann did, my life would be worth something.

Ann died September 2, 2001. She was forty-three. She had battled breast cancer and gone into remission. When the cancer came back after five years, it quickly spread to her bone marrow, and there was no coming back.

My mom told me recently that Pat had asked whether Joan could stay over at our house on the night before Ann passed. I have no memory of any of this. My mom had to wake up Joan and walk her home in the morning, knowing her mom was gone.

I was too young to understand what was happening or why the entire Smyth family seemed to cut us out of their lives. To me, they were my family. Living in a home where I never felt accepted, I would flee to their house to be free and escape the pain I was living within my own home, through imagination and creating worlds and places that only existed in my mind. When Ann died, that was all gone. It was over. Life became real, and only the painful parts seemed to exist anymore.

I didn't know how to understand the pain I was going through, and I didn't know how to understand the abandonment I felt by the Smyths. I understand better now, as an adult, that they'd lost their mother and it was just too hard. As a child, though, I just wanted to be with them and grieve with them, because I had no one to grieve with or teach me how to do it. My family didn't talk about it. No one talked about it.

I still remember Ann's funeral, although I was not quite aware of what was going on. I can still see her in the casket and how illuminated she appeared, even in death. Like her angel was still right there with us, eternal. Ann was my first real experience with death. Her death affects me to this day.

Pretty soon thereafter, the Smyths moved from Eldridge Lane, USA. Their house was abandoned for a while thereafter, except for a leather Lazy Boy that had been left in their front room. I would break into their house every day for a while, sit on the ground against that Lazy Boy, and cry for hours.

I refused to go to their new house for years. I was so stubborn and mad, as though their moving away was a personal attack on me. I realize how childish and selfish this was. My birthday gift to Joan one year was finally going to their house and decorating her room while she was gone, to surprise her. It sounds so ridiculous and petty, but I didn't know how else to deal with my emotions back then. I was a very emotional and dramatic child, so things tended to be pretty extra from me. I wouldn't say being extra ever really stopped, though.

I got my first period on Jan. 3, 2001. Just so you guys can understand at what point I was in my life. I will never forget it (as I am assuming most girls don't).

I was in our downstairs bathroom before school one morning, and when I went to wipe, I saw a spot of blood. It wasn't much, but it was apparent.

I asked my mom, "If there is even just a spot of blood, does that mean I am having my period?"

I remember her looking at me, stressed, almost as if she were annoyed. She sighed and then said something along the lines of, "Why? Do you have your period?" as if I were an inconvenience to her.

So, I lied and said, "No, just wondering," and went along with my day, asking a girl at school for a pad during lunch and what I was supposed to do with it. Anyway, welcome to middle school, Katie.

I think the people I have met along the way in my life are the story here. The spectacular humans who were capable of seeing me, the real me. Who were not led astray by other people's views. They're the real MVP. If it weren't for them, I know I wouldn't be alive today.

They have been able to see in me things I couldn't see in myself. They're capable of believing in me when I can't/couldn't believe in myself. That is a miracle to me. I feel conceited saying it, but the truth is, I have a fucking army of people behind me who love me. I know this because so many of them show me on a daily basis.

I have been mostly alone for the better part of the past two years, yet I have never felt more filled with love and encouragement in my life. They say it takes a village to raise a child. Well, it's taken an army to grow the powerful woman I am today, and there is absolutely no way in hell I would be anywhere near where I am in my life without those people. I wrote a list of all the people I could remember having major impacts on my life. I feel guilty, because I could go even further, but it's blowing my mind that I can name so many whom I still reach out to, even to this day, to catch up with.

It's hard to believe in something that most people do not. It takes courage and a sense of confidence a lot of people don't have. That's what I see in these people. They're the real heroes, the ones who think out of the box and accept what isn't the norm. They accepted me. Not only did they accept me, they cheered for me. They held my hand when I had no one else and made sure I would stay alive. Whether or not they knew it, they literally kept me alive simply by being amazing people.

I've told a few people I was writing this book. All of them asked the same questions: what is it about? Is it a memoir? About your life? And every time I hear the questions, I hear my own demons coming at me.

Who cares what you have to say? Who are you to anybody else? What makes you think you're so important?

But then I remember. They do.

Chapter 9

Seeking Your Own Attention

"You're only given a little spark of madness. You mustn't lose it."

—Robin Williams

6/04/2020

>Dear Young Katie,
>
>I want you to know you were right. Everything you stood for and believed in, whether it had to do with family, friends, or society, it was right.
>
>You definitely made multiple mistakes. Quite a few were pretty bad, too. A few, I'm sure, were from lack of guidance and the understanding you needed, because, looking back at you now, you were far ahead of your time. I am proud of you. In fact, I wish I could be more like you.
>
>There's something that happens when you become an adult where, somehow, it all of a sudden is unacceptable to be who you actually are, even though you've spent your entire adolescence fighting for the ability to be exactly who you want to be. Then we go to school, get jobs, and wake up every day, thinking, how did I get here? And, this is not what I planned or expected for my life.

Here lies the problem. The same problem in bad relationships, lost dreams, and unused talent. Expectations of any situation without work put in is the sad story, put on repeat, for most the people we know. Your dreams are beautiful, your expectations of life are divine, but it is your character development that will create the person you were meant to be and the direction you should follow.

The journey will not be perfect; it will not come anywhere near a straight path. Sometimes, your path will put you where you were five years ago, and everything you've done up to that point will feel absolutely worthless. That's the point. Sometimes, you will need to learn and then relearn the lessons of your life repeatedly before permanent change can occur.

Don't lose sight. Don't be too hard on yourself, and whatever you do, do not give up. Light is not only at the end of the tunnel; there are cracks along the way, made by the people who've come before you and who worked so hard to break that tunnel open, that so tightly tries to hold us in. Those cracks show us glimmers of hope. It is in those cracks that you will find the strength you need to keep moving forward.

Become the adult whom the child in you always needed, because they still exist and they need you to show them the way.

06/04/2020

I finally made it
I lost my words for years
In a love that only knew tears
A love made of fear

Something I forever held dear
It was that clasp that overtook me
Swallowed me whole
And changed everything I really would be
It's that circle
That circles once again
Remember? The one that'd be my friend
The one until the end
It was me
It always was
I just had to remember
I love me
I love everything I'll be
And I am only just me
I love the way I love
I love the person I've become
Because, in the end,
I am my best friend
And I would do it all again
Because I did win
And I am the fire
The fire you never will devour
I am smarter
And I do work harder
You can't put me down
Because I'll do nothing but tower
And not to put you down
But to put you in your place
Because you never did anything
But try to hide my face
What you mistook for weakness
Is my greatness
And in everything you took
I never lost my grace
Because no matter how hard you ever tried

REMEMBER WHO THE FUCK YOU ARE

You'll never erase this face
I won because I cared
Not because I hurt
I won because I love
And always kept alert
Let them laugh
Let them play games
Let all the people you lie to
Play dead and stay the same
Because I won't
And you know that
Because of that
I ain't your doormat
Because I am smarter
And I do work harder
Because I never want to end
Going back to another barter
There's no bargaining when it comes to life
I got what I got
For not knowing how
To deal with strife
But now I do
And you know what I learned?
It was never you
Who would determine what I earned

Who Am I?

My best friend left me today
She makes her rounds you see
And it's when she leaves
That I am no longer me

She is confident and secure
Happy and unreserved

With a childlike heart
Could never be unnerved

She loves without fear
Forgives in total faith
Cares about every soul
Incompetent in knowing wraith

Without her

I become numb
I lose my light
That feels the way
That leads me to what's right

A pathetic shell of a human I become
In a sullen state of apathy
I fade into the darkness
Into a world of only agony

This world I do not know
This world I do not understand
This world ruins everything I believe in
In this world no one holds my hand

It's when my best friend leaves
That I forget how to fight
I forget what once was beautiful
I forget that everything will be alright

I forget the man inside my heads a liar
That he likes to fill my head and heart with lead
That he's there to make me fail
To create another walking dead

I need her back
In order to win this never-ending battle
I need my best friend
Because I cannot win with only just one paddle

Because my best friend is one of a kind you see
And sometimes I forget
That my best friend is actually me

I was back in Delray Beach, visiting friends, and stopped by 3rd & 3rd. I go there every time I'm back in town. Nowadays, it feels as though I am walking through a dream. I'm not sure if I ever really lived there.

I stepped out the back door with a Narragansett in one hand and my pack of American Spirits, light blue, in the other. I've had this pack of cigarettes for three years now. I bought it in Ithaca, New York while attending graduate school at Cornell. I have lived in two different states since that time. And I kept it with me for moments exactly like this. The moments when I wanted to remember where I came from. The moments when I wanted to remember who I was, who I am, and everything that paved the way just to bring me right back here, to bask in the glorious nostalgia.

A cigarette brings me to the places of my past. I don't know anyone else who would refer to having a cigarette and a beer as self-care, but I do. This is the attention I give myself. This is the space I give myself, the recognition that, other times, I am unable to give.

It was in this space I wrote my admissions essay to Cornell. It was in this space I spent countless nights up until 6 a.m., dancing and singing the night away with the other misfits of Delray who became my family. It was here where Langdon told me for the first time he loves me. It's also the space I spent countless nights crying over Langdon leaving me, and my misfit family helping me pick up the pieces and remind me of who I am.

Nostalgia is the attention I give myself. The moments when I allow myself to deeply feel all life has offered me. To recognize just how interconnected my entire life has been from the beginning, bringing me all the way to the present moment.

Who am I? Who am I without all the titles? Who am I as a human being? Who am I when I am just being? I am kind, compassionate, magnetic, energetic, creative, smart, intense, caring, and wild.

We all have a being inside of us. We all are someone who exists before the noise tries to tell us who we are, and if we're lucky, we have the clit to stand our ground when people try to tell us who we are. Advocating for yourself is self-love. Advocating for yourself is needed attention.

There are some people in this world who give us more attention than we want. This is both good and bad. A lot of times, it is these people who like to believe they know everything about you, and for a time being, they might. But we're always evolving.

I used to be a lot of things I no longer am. I used to be a lot of different people I would never associate myself with now, and my past selves would very harshly judge the person I am now. Should a time machine exist and I had the chance to go back to steer myself on a different path, do I think I would believe myself? What would it take for me to actually listen to my future self?

Older people love to talk about all the mistakes they've made, in hopes younger generations will take their word for it and not have to learn how life works on their own. More often than not, though, that isn't how people work. We need to learn from our own mistakes, and people are very afraid to make mistakes. So, many people never really learn or ever really grow.

There are so many things I would tell myself. I would tell myself that you survive no matter what and against all odds, because your biggest enemy in survival is yourself. I would promise myself I won't kill myself and to stop thinking and fantasizing about it, because I won't and it isn't going to happen.

I would say, be single as long as you possibly can, until you find the person who matches your energy and beliefs in this world. The longer you stay in relationships where you are not respected or loved the way you deserve, the more time you are losing to love yourself fully. You love yourself. You really do. You just haven't given yourself a chance to shine unapologetically yet.

You already don't listen to anyone who tells you no, but to take it even a step further, don't ever second-guess that first instinct to drown out all the naysayers. You are beautiful just the way you are: now, back then, in the future, and always.

You don't need anyone, but you love everyone, and there is nothing wrong with that. Embrace things that are new, and don't make automatic opinions about something you've never tried. Keep an open mind.

Papa was right when he told you that you're not the marrying kind, but that only applies to what the marrying kind was in his time. You get to define your entire world, and you always have. Stop wasting your time caring for others who never care for you. You think you dream big, but you don't even know how limitless the possibilities are. Take the guardrails off of every single aspect of your life, and see what happens.

I want to take the guardrails off of every single aspect of my life so badly, but I have allowed other people to get in the way of that happening. Other people tend to take our attention away from ourselves. Especially when you're a people-pleaser. Even more especially when you're a people-pleaser who has decided to get back into a relationship with someone you were on-again, off-again with for years, and now, you have to entirely re-meet each other.

Langdon is my partner. We have been back together for almost two years now. And a few months ago, I found him to be distracting. Even if he didn't mean to be. I didn't know if I could be with someone whom I constantly had to worry about, before I make any decisions. That may sound selfish, because it is. It's also called being codependent.

I thought maybe I was distracting myself with Langdon for all those years, when we were together before. Maybe he was my excuse that entire time. Maybe I chose to be heartbroken instead of move on because I could use it as an excuse for my place in the world.

I thought what I wanted was more than he can give me. At least that's how it felt in the moment. Like maybe we had outgrown each other. Or maybe we were just getting started. I honestly couldn't tell the difference then.

I was bored. Or maybe I was content. I wanted more. I always want more. I was happy, but I couldn't help feel like there was something else I was supposed to be doing. I heard one time that, after things have gone missing for a long time and then randomly reappear, it is a sign you hopped timelines in the multiverse. That had been happening a lot.

I felt like I broke the matrix, because I wasn't sure where I existed in the world. I guess I never really felt there was a place where I exist in this world. The older I get, though, the more I am seeing most of us, if not all of us, feel this way.

Before Langdon and I got back together, I had spent the years we were apart giving myself all the attention. I was in immense pain for the majority of that time, but close to the end, I started to really find who I was, what I wanted, and who I wanted to be in the world.

I was free in a way I had never been before. Allowing myself to practice ethical non-monogamy unapologetically and dating whomever I wanted, whenever I wanted. I didn't answer to anyone but myself and my dog, and every day developed organically yet with intention. It's difficult at times for me to be in a monogamous relationship. There is a part of my soul that feels as though it has been cut off from the universe since the day Langdon and I decided to close off our relationship. I stopped fully giving myself the attention I need to be the human I am at my fullest. I have taken responsibility for that decision. I chose to be in this relationship, and now, I have chosen to put in the work it takes to fully understand both of our wants and desires, not just my own. I love him and the way we have grown since putting in the work from both ends, which has enhanced our relationship in ways I have never felt with someone before.

When I was living in Cambridge from September 2021 to September 2022, there was a house at the end of my street that had been under construction since the first day I moved in. When I first moved in, it had its foundation and everything was pretty much there; all that needed to be built was the outside. Construction came almost to a halt during the winter.

Every day, I would walk Charlie past this house, and I couldn't help but feel we were on similar journeys together. Throughout the winter, it was really hard for both of us and not much got done, but the foundation was always there. The foundation of my life was all of the work and attention I had been giving myself during the time I was single. More than that, during the time I was in solitude. This time taught me to love myself and to enjoy the moments I was creating *for me*. No one else.

As it got warmer, things started to happen faster. I felt like this house was a very good omen for my life. Somehow, I knew from the beginning I would never see that house finished, because I was not finished being built.

I have this recurring feeling. I won't say it's a dream, because it's always been more than that. A smell, a scent, a feeling of serenity and excitement all at once. I imagine it's where I go in the deepest core of a meditation. Somewhere only I am able to access. My safe space. My foundation. It holds me when I feel it coming on, and it's my own universe, one I have created full of such lush life and stillness.

There is nothing but greenery and a gray brick wall. It extends to infinity in all directions. There is no escaping this space, even though I would never want to. I have been waiting for something to happen in this space my entire life, but I am beginning to think the entire point is that nothing will ever happen to it. It is my sacred space, and no matter how much I try to explain this, no one will ever know, because it is the only one true thing I have that is all my own.

No one can ever take it from me. No one can manipulate it. It's me. It's my essence. It's that common feeling in every place I have ever lived. I put it in each space I have been, in hopes the next person will feel it, too, and create their own universe. The universe inside them that makes them unbreakable. The space where they attend to themselves. It is my job, no one else's, to never stop attending to myself.

Triple Point

I live in the triple point.
There is a space where liquid, gas and solid all meet and I am the mediator.
A combination of Bowie, Dali, Curie and Robin Williams.
I see you smiling Robin.
I see you laugh as I figure out there is nothing to figure out but only to explore.
To live would be an awfully great adventure.
And here we are worried about starting a sentence with and.
I've never been like the rest.
I never chose if I were to be a solid, liquid or gas.
There have been times when I was more solid than the rest, at times even more liquid and gas.
But when I am living at my full expression I am the triple point.
I am where the glacier meets the ocean and sky.
The exact spot where a droplet forms on an ice cube greeted by air.
The mediator of elements physical states.
Do you know this place?
You might be able to feel it when you're in a trance.
We are the ribosomes in a cell of the universe.
Can you feel them looking at us under their microscope?

My constant change in form is how I manage to never get caught.
I don't want to worry about getting caught anymore though.
I want to shine.
And I shine when I am the triple point.

Chapter 10
We're All Somebody's Bad Guy

"Life's tough. Get a helmet."
—Eric in *Boy Meets World*

H I, IT'S ME. I'm the problem.
You know that scene from *Romy and Michelle's High School Reunion*, when Janine Garafolo is at the reunion and Tobi addresses her about signing her yearbook, since she never did in high school?

Just as Tobi is about to finish asking Heather (Garafolo) to sign her yearbook, Tobi cuts herself off to add, "And please don't tell me to fuck off, because it really hurt my feelings."

To which Heather's response is, "I hurt your feelings? Tremendous! That's tremendous! Go get your stupid yearbook. I would be happy to sign it!"

Heather's pain throughout high school prevented her from acknowledging she could be a person with enough power to hurt someone else.

This happens all the time in real life. Underestimating our own power doesn't only stop us from acknowledging what our greatest strengths could be. Underestimating our own power also stops us from acknowledging our power is great enough to actually hurt someone else. Sometimes, we think so little of ourselves, we can't imagine anyone else caring about our actions. Because who are we, anyway?

But the truth is, we are all nobodies who are somebodies, for better or worse. It's easy to believe we're the good guy in the story, because to us it's "our" story. It's our movie. What's hard to recognize is, at some points in our lives, we are all the bad guy. Recognizing the pain we are capable of causing in others is of utmost importance to keeping our humanity. I've been the mistress, I've been the cheater. I've been the fighter and the verbal abuser. I've even been the physical abuser.

I think owning the moments when we have played the bad guy in our stories is important. It's important not just because I think it's honest, but because it recognizes the dark side of humanity in even the best of us.

We are all capable of being the good guy, just as much as we are capable of being the bad guy. I think good guys are just bad guys who own their shit, take it as a lesson, and work to be a better person than they've been in the past. Because, at the end of the day, we all fuck up, we all make mistakes. We are all young, in love, and naive at some point.

I can't do anything about my past. I can only admit to my wrongdoings. Recognize when I have been the bad guy, do the work to make sure I don't make the same decisions I have in the past, and grow from these experiences.

To those whom I have hurt in the past:

I will not name you, because I wouldn't put you on blast unknowingly like that. Unless you want some sort of public apology, I have no problem in doing so. Just let me know. Otherwise, I am sorry.

I do my best to reach out to those I think I may have hurt and to apologize no matter how much time has passed or how silly the situation might seem now. If you're reading this right now and thinking I am writing about you, I probably am, and I want you to know, I apologize for anything I have put you through in the past.

In most cases, when I look back on where I recognize my wrongdoings, I realize the person I usually had problems with would have most likely been a good friend of mine, had the storyline played out differently.

I just hope that those of you who take the time to read this recognize nothing I have done has been intentional. Stupid, misguided, or out of pain, yes. But I would never truly want to hurt someone else, and I hope you can forgive me, if you haven't already.

Homewrecker

I met Seth when I first started working at The Salon in Birmingham, Michigan, right after hair school in 2010. There was an immediate attraction between us, but he was eighteen years my senior, in a long-term relationship with a women who had kids, who also happened to work at the salon with us. Also, I was still with Benjamin.

I was twenty, which was prime time for me to make all the mistakes I would come to shake my head at, later in life. Seth was very charming and completely fed into my fresh-graduate spunk of wanting to become a master stylist for the stars. He buttered me up and fed into my ego. Quickly, we started to fall into an infatuation. It began with eye contact in the mirrors while working. Our little secret and innocent.

Benjamin was planning to join the Border Patrol and couldn't tell me we would stay together in the process, so I ended things with him amicably. I am not proud of most things that happened in my relationship with Seth. I learned many lessons through this relationship. Lessons can be very difficult for many of us to learn, if we don't know how to stop the patterns when we first see them happening. Unfortunately, a lot of abusive relationships tend to bleed into your future relationships, if you are not careful.

Seth and I left work early one day and went to the pub next door, Dick O'Dows, for some beers. We got hammered—typical. There was no reason for him to drive me to my car, as it might as well have been parked in the same lot, but it happened, because we both wanted to spend more time together.

Right as we were saying goodbye and I was reaching for the handle to step out of the car, he grabbed my face, spun it around, and started kissing me. Like, full-blown total make-out session, movie-style, to the point where he put the car in drive while we were still making out, drove his car to the top of the parking structure, and we had sex right there in the front seat of his car. Bad guys. Afterward, we spent the next few months meeting for secret rendezvous.

I worked at a tanning salon during this time, as well. On my morning shifts, Seth would make lunch and bring it to work for me. He was a chef in training at the time, as well, and his food was incredible... and anyone who knows me knows I am a sucker for a chef. Seth might have been the person who started that trend.

We would have sex in the laundry room of the tanning salon. I am pretty sure that is what led to me getting fired from there. I showed up one day and my boss was there. This was not normal. She told me they didn't need me anymore, that they were overstaffed. I didn't ask questions. She was either telling the truth, knew about me sleeping in her business, or found out I had been telling her customers it was actually the most expensive beds that cause cancer, while the lower-grade beds, which just had burning rays, were less likely to cause cancer. I learned this reading a book I'd found in the tanning salon while working one day, about the difference between UVA and UVB sun rays. Either way, I didn't care enough to battle that one out.

Seth would sneak me kisses in the back room at work when no one was looking. We weren't good at hiding it. I am pretty sure everyone knew from the beginning what was going on. I was staying at my parents' house for a few months at the time. My apartment had been foreclosed on after my landlord stopped paying his mortgage, so it was not like Seth could ever come to my place. I would leave my parents' house and meet him at one of the elementary schools near his house, on the playground where he took the family dog for walks and came to fuck me. Due to Seth's being on the sex offender list (I was not aware of this at the time), other than the obvious, this was one of the dumbest ideas ever.

Gerry, Seth's girlfriend of eleven years, became suspicious, but she didn't know for sure. The receptionist for our salon was getting married, and the entire staff was invited. I wasn't going to attend, because the thought of being around Gerry and Seth together in a setting like that terrified me. He wanted me to go, though, so I did.

I had to sit with everyone from work, directly across the table from Seth and Gerry. I couldn't lift my head. Every time I went to look up, Seth was staring dead at me, and texting me the entire time he was sitting next to her. It was so painfully obvious.

Gerry kicked him out night. Seth moved in to his parents' house temporarily, as well. We basically lived out of hotels after this, considering we couldn't stay at our parents' places together. I still hadn't gotten my cosmetology license and was waiting to take the board exams.

One Saturday morning, Seth waited for me in the car while I took my practical and written exams for my license. I was out by 11 a.m., and we were going to celebrate.

We went to my favorite bar, Hi-Tops, which I frequented for lunch during hair school. It was right across the street from the Detroit Zoo. We got shitfaced, like usual.

I always drove, because the car he'd used to drive was Gerry's. He didn't have his own car. I'm sure you see just how blatant all the red flags were. We got so drunk. We were at the bar from 11 a.m. to 9pm., but, honestly, I believed I'd only had two beers to drink. There was no way.

So, like any moron twenty-year-old in a pre-Uber world, I made the wonderful decision to drive home. Except we weren't going home. We were driving to a friend of mine's apartment across town who would let us sleep on their floor, when we had nowhere else to go.

Driving north up Woodward from Royal Oak, I was trying to make my way to West Bloomfield, more than a half-hour drive away. Woodward is a large road with three to four lanes on each side and a divider down the middle. It has openings every so often for people to do Michigan lefts, since U-turns are illegal. Most of the strip malls that line the side of the road don't have full parking lots, just parking spaces lined diagonally in front, one way in and one way out.

I made it to Birmingham and was driving perfectly when I got flicked. I couldn't hear anything, because I had two twelve-inch subwoofers in the trunk of my Chevy

Aveo hatchback roller skate of a car, and I was blasting music. But I saw the lights and my heart sank.

I pulled into one of the one-way parking line-ups but did not pull into a space. The officer came to my window.

"License and registration. Where are you coming from tonight, and where are you going?"

I am great with cops. I always have been. I have gotten myself out of a lot of situations. I used to think I was lucky and smart. Now, I realize that I am a White woman who is good at playing dumb. But mainly, it's the fact that I am a White woman. I know this.

"We are coming from Hi-Tops in Royal Oak."

"How much have you have to drink?"

"Two beers."

At no point did this officer have me turn off my car or step out of my vehicle. He knew I had been drinking. I'd just told him I had.

He went back to his car to run my information and returned back with a breathalyzer. He stuck the breathalyzer in through my window. My car was still running and in park, blocking in cars that were parked in front of this strip mall. If you know Birmingham, I was near the Little Caesars in Woodward.

I blew.

".18. That's way more than two beers! What about you over there?" he asked, looking at Seth in the passenger seat. "Can you do any better?"

The cop walked over to Seth's side of the car and asked him to step out of the vehicle. As he stepped out, he put his hands up in a way I could tell that he had been arrested before.

"Don't do that!" the cop yelled as he grabbed one of Seth's arms to pull it down. "I'm not arresting you. You're embarrassing yourself."

This cop is so weird, I thought to myself.

".23," he said. "You're even worse than she is! Get back in the car."

The cop went back to his vehicle for a moment before coming back to my window.

"Do you have anyone you can call that could be here in five minutes? I am not talking ten or fifteen. They must be here in five minutes."

"Yes, yes, yes."

"Call them now."

I scrambled to think of who I could call. Seth starts calling his sister and brother, who lived thirty minutes away. I had never been more annoyed at how stupid he was.

I reached a coworker from the salon on the phone. It just so happened her husband was at the Papa Joe's down the street and could be to us in less than five minutes. I hung up.

The officer looked at Seth. "All right, Seth, please get out of the car."

I started to fume at the idea that Seth would be let go and I would be the person to pay in this situation I would have never been in had he had his own car. I have zero ownership over my own actions in this moment.

When the cop came back to my window, he asked me to put my car into reverse, back up, and then pull into the empty parking spot to my right. He stepped back from the window without breaking eye contact with me.

I put my car into reverse.

SMASH! I slammed my car directly into the officer's car.

Immediately filled with adrenaline, rage, and through tears, I screamed, "YOU TOLD ME TO DRIVE MY CAR! YOU KNOW I'M DRUNK! YOU KNOW I SHOULDN'T BE DRIVING, AND YOU TOLD ME TO DO THIS!"

"Calm down, calm down, *shh, shh, shh...*," he said, moving his hands up and down in mini bows, as though I was a queen.

"Put the car into drive and just pull right into that spot."

I did, successfully.

The cop came back to my window. At this point, Seth and my coworker's husband were sitting in the minivan next to us, not sure what to do next.

"I am giving you a ticket for expired registration, and a warning for the headlight you have out."

It was the headlight that got me pulled over.

"My registration isn't expired."

What is wrong with me?

I had accidentally given him two different registrations. One of them was the correct and up-to-date copy, and the other was an outdated copy. He put them next to each other to show me he was aware of this.

"This is the only way I can take your license from you, let you go home with you friend over here for the night, and have you come pick up your keys at the station tomorrow with this proof of your up-to-date registration."

What the fuck just happened?

The next morning, I was dropped off at the cop shop in downtown Birmingham to pick up my car keys and show my registration. They handed me a ticket with all the information about what had happened the previous night, and that's when I saw it. I was so drunk the previous night, I hadn't realized.

The cop who had just saved me from ruining my life was the same cop who, a year before, had helped me during a time a friend of mine was kicked out of her house. I was letting her live with me, but she was in high school, and I lived too far for her to get there every day. We knew it was illegal for her mom to kick her out, so we broke into her mom's house, stole all the weed plants she was growing, and took them to the cop shop in Birmingham.

The cop had laughed at us and told us that without any budding on the plants, they are still considered weeds under the law, so there was nothing to charge.

If a cop pulls me over and finds all the seeds and dirt from sixteen weed plants falling over in my car, would they have the same thing to say about that? I'd wondered.

The cop called her mom into the station and got my friend back into her house. Then, he thanked me for taking care of her and said to let him know in the future, if anything ever should arise again.

It was him. The same cop. It's hard not to feel like the universe was protecting me in that moment I got pulled over by the same guy. He remembered me, and he gave me a break.

I never should have been driving that night. I was a bad guy to everyone on the road around me.

After going through this event together, Seth and I needed to have a conversation about what was going to happen moving forward. We could not continue to live the way we were living.

I learned he had a son who lived in Florida, and also that he was a sex offender. The story was he had slept with a girl who was eighteen when he was in his early twenties. Michigan law at the time stated, if someone under the age of twenty-one and under the influence of alcohol had sex with someone, it could be considered rape, because that person was not old enough to be drinking.

Seth was never incarcerated for this or charged for anything. The girl's parents blackmailed his family for $25,000 and said they would press charges, if they were not paid. Or so I was told. So, his family paid it to avoid prison, but somehow Seth was still put on the sex offender list. I decided to believe the story.

In May 2011, Seth and I moved to Delray Beach, Florida. Laws in Florida were quite different than laws in Michigan when it came to the charges Seth had on his record. In Michigan, it is illegal to take the information about someone who has a record and post flyers with that information to the public, in these cases. In Florida, the law states that flyers *be* posted and police officers go door to door, informing the public about who their new neighbor is. Seth lost his job and the situation made it very difficult for him to find another for a while. He was a recovering heroin/opioid addict and at this point began using again. That is when the physical abuse began, which ended with him cutting his wrists in front of me.

Lab Rats

I wasn't originally going to put this next story in the book; I hadn't properly processed everything that happened yet. I was still in the cyclical pattern of shame that people who have been abused go into, where it's easier to blame oneself than it is to recognize just how wrong it was, what someone else did to you.

This story has two bad guys: me and the man who broke my heart. But isn't that how it always works? No one is ever completely innocent in relationships. But that mindset can make it hard to recognize the pain that comes from being taken advantage of. I blame myself because, at some point, I made the choice to stay. Or I allowed a person to treat me in a way I was not okay with. However, it's never that black and white.

It was September, 2020. My first semester at Cornell University, at the height of the pandemic. On Wednesdays, we had lab meetings over Zoom, since none of us could meet in person yet. Either way, for me, it wouldn't have mattered. I was in Ithaca, and my lab was in New York City.

I was in the Master's of Engineering for Biomedical Engineering program at Cornell. Most people who join that program spend the year working with a team to develop some type of medical device. But there was an option X. Option X was for anyone who didn't want to do what everyone else was doing. Option X was for the people who already had an in with a Principal Investigator (PI) and could work on a project in a specific lab with that person.

I picked option X. I made up my own master's program with the help of Dr. Scott McAuliffe and Christina Suarez. Christina's first presentation on perchlorate and microbes fascinated me. Christina also terrified me. She was so professional. She seemed to know everything and not in an annoying way. In a way that was intimidating and inspiring at the same time.

You know the kind of person you don't want to seem stupid around, but also aspire to be just like? Quick word of advice: always follow that girl. Always follow the Christinas. Do everything you can to stay under their wing and learn everything you possibly can, Christinas will not lead you in the wrong direction.

I was in love with Bill from the first time I saw him over Zoom, during the first lab meeting I ever took part in. Later, other people in the lab would joke they thought they should keep us separated and worried about what might happen, if he and I were to meet. Recognizing both of our fiery, magnetic tendencies was easy, even through a screen.

I was first invited to New York City to work on an Covid testing competition, where we were testing rapid Covid-testing protocols. I went for two weeks during the height of winter.

The days were grueling. I would get to the lab by 7-8 a.m. and wouldn't leave some days until 11 p.m. I loved every second of it. Being in the lab makes me come alive. I have limitless energy, when I am in my "sciencing" groove.

That's probably why it was so easy for me to be blinded. I was living out my passion, doing my dream job, while working alongside someone I loved spending time with. Bill immediately took me under his wing.

On the first morning, we both had to get vaccinated before working directly with Covid samples. He made it a point to buy me breakfast on the way, saying it was what he would do for any new lab member. The banter between us flowed effortlessly. So effortlessly that, as we waited in line to get vaccinated, we were mistaken for boyfriend and girlfriend multiple times. In a hospital in the middle of Manhattan during the peak of the pandemic, where everyone was still six feet apart and wearing masks, including us, strangers were acknowledging our connection. It was impossible to ignore.

And I didn't want to ignore it. Bill and I talked about polyamory and the relationships we had been in, both having experienced ethical nonmonogamy. He was also bisexual; I found both of these qualities incredibly attractive. *This is what I've been looking for in a partner,* I thought.

It was days before I found out he had a girlfriend whom he lived with. And they were monogamous. How does that not come up, when you're spending every day with a person, talking for hours? When I finally did learn about his girlfriend, I tried to shut my feelings down. I knew they still existed, but I wasn't going to let them impact our friendship/work relationship.

To me, he already meant so much more, and if that meant only being able to be his friend, I was okay with it. Just so long as I got to keep him in my life and enjoy his company.

He told me a lot about his girlfriend, and he told me a lot about their relationship. He told me a lot more than any girl would want the girl who is in love with their boyfriend to know. He told me about her insecurities around infidelity, and how every time he left the house for more than six hours, she automatically assumed he was cheating on her. He told me about all of the different medications she was taking and why she was taking them. He told me about her premenstrual cycle, and I tried to give him advice about PMDD, because it sounded like that was what she was experiencing, which I empathized with. We talked in depth about their relationship.

It felt as though I was becoming somewhat of a therapist to his relationship, at that point. I was invested in the friendship and I was in love with him, but I was not interested in trying to break up a relationship. If anything, I wanted to try to help.

He would explain to me how she craved more attention and to be seen more in their relationship, so I gave him advice, very specific advice that I would think, if someone was trying to help their relationship, they would act on.

For example, there was a flower shop on the walk to the subway when leaving work, so I would tell him he should buy her flowers, to remind her, even though he was working long hours, he was still thinking of her. This was something that bothered her: the long hours and lack of response she got from him, while he was working.

He never bought her flowers. He never took my advice on ways to show her attention and remind her he was thinking of her. Instead, he stayed for hours after work to play cribbage with me. He entered a screenplay-writing competition and used my Celtx software account to write. We would take walks outside the lab to discuss all of the ideas he was writing about. On my birthday, he took me out for dessert. When I asked if they were thinking of getting married anytime soon, his response to me was, "How does one buy a ring for someone who doesn't like or wear rings or jewelry?"

Personally, if I'm in a monogamous relationship, I would rather my partner have sex with someone else than emotionally cheat.

Bill offered to help me with my master's thesis. I had never been through this kind of project before, so I assumed the person mentoring me in the lab would know what they were doing and what I was supposed to do.

Bill didn't know what he was doing. Whether he did this as a way of getting my attention or to get out of the work he was supposed to be doing in the lab, it doesn't matter to me, because either way, he was using me. I recognize this now. I did not recognize this back then. I finished what I could on my master's project, presented, and graduated without ever publishing once. I didn't know how any of that worked. My mentor did not teach me that I was supposed to do that or how to go about it, but I didn't recognize that. I blamed myself.

It was on me. Bill did everything he could to help me. Didn't he?

The lab was planning the first in-person get together toward the end of May 2021, so I invited the guy I was seeing at the time, Jim, to join me for the trip from Ithaca. I also invited my friend Omar, whom I had been telling about Bill for months now. He wanted to see what was happening with his own eyes.

The night was a mess and ended with me, Omar, Bill, and Jim out at a bar together. Omar and I couldn't tell whether Bill and Jim wanted to fuck or fight each other. And at some point, Bill and I did an exchange of hats, with a handshake and pinky promise there would never be any trade-backs allowed.

Jim ended the night puking at every corner on the way home and slept on the toilet, once we got back to Omar's. I was fine with that. After he'd spent the night trying to talk the computational biology and physiology lab from Weill Cornell University out of the Covid-19 vaccine, I was over him. Let him puke. He'd made me look like a moron.

But he definitely did bring out a side in Bill I hadn't seen before: jealousy.

I spent the summer in New York City, working in the lab. Bill offered to teach me air sampling one day throughout the city. When I arrived, he very quickly taught me how to air sample, then he gave me a map of Manhattan to show me every stop I would need to take a sample at.

He was not going with me; again, he was not teaching me anything, just putting his work on me. But I did it happily, because I was an excited student who wanted to do anything I could to be in their good graces so, when the end of summer came, I could get hired into the McAuliffe Lab and continue my research from my master's.

Dr. McAuliffe wanted to hire me. The only problem was there were no openings and no budget for another employee in the lab. He told me not to worry, though; we would work something out.

The process of getting hired at a university is very difficult and time-consuming. It doesn't work the same way other jobs work, where you can have an interview one day and be on the payroll the next. You can get hired at a university in one day, but it can take sometimes three months or more to finalize paperwork for HR and payroll.

I couldn't afford to live in New York for three months without a paycheck. I had spent the last year scraping by on student loans and unemployment, both of which had ended.

The end of July was nearing, and Bill and I started discussing plans for his thirtieth birthday in August. We made a list of Airbnbs for him to rent in upstate New York with all of his friends. It never happened. He did something with his girlfriend, instead.

Why would he talk about and plan something like that with me?

After applying to over 750 jobs over the summer, I found a promising small startup in Cambridge, Massachusetts. Prism Biosciences. I was heartbroken to leave New York City, though. This wasn't my plan. It wasn't supposed to happen. I was supposed to continue my work in the McAuliffe Lab.

Bill knew how heartbroken I was. He knew how much I wanted to stay. He understood how much working in that lab meant to me and to my future and everything it was I wanted to accomplish.

Then he said to me, "Katie, I was hired by another company this week. It will be my last week in the McAuliffe Lab."

Wait, what?

"You were hired by another company? How many interviews have you had with them?"

"Three."

"So, you knew you were planning to leave the McAuliffe Lab?"

"Well, I didn't know if I would get the job, and I wanted to be sure before I said anything, but yes. I have been interviewing with other companies now for the past month or so. Oh, I also proposed to Kaylin. We're getting married."

Okay, let's just throw that in there.

He knew he was leaving the lab and he knew, with him leaving, there would be a spot opening up for me to take. He knew I wanted that position. He knew I had been waiting for that position. He knew he could have told McAuliffe, and it would have been fine. He knew he could have prepped me to take over his position and helped the lab not have to struggle to fill the position, if he had just told us he was looking for other positions. But he chose not to tell anyone.

It was too difficult to be mad at a person who was so good at coming up with excuses for every reason why he did or did not do certain things. And I have never been good at showing or experiencing my anger. So, I chose to be sad for me but also happy for him, at the same time.

The day before I moved to Cambridge, we planned to get together. He met me at a restaurant and then surprised me by taking me to a speakeasy that served hot dogs and martinis. Two of my favorite things. It felt like a date. I think it was a date.

We moved on to another spot with margaritas. We ordered a pitcher while sitting outside. I got drunk enough to start asking him questions I wouldn't ever normally have asked him. I wanted to understand why he would sell out to corporate America and why he would marry a person he couldn't effectively communicate with. Why didn't using his privilege to better the world matter to him?

"I am a privileged White man, and I enjoy having higher status. I don't want to lose that. And I like what I have to gain with the family I am marrying into."

And there it was. Honesty. Honesty that I didn't want to believe. And, for the first time, I didn't have respect for someone's honesty.

He can't be serious.

Our other lab mate, Meredith, joined us, and he spent the remainder of the night belittling and talking down to me, as if I were a peasant. And just like that, every single insecurity I'd kept bottled up about my self-worth being based on my class and monetary status began to drown me. I became the size of an ant. I felt so small that, when he began to cry and apologize for not giving anyone a heads-up that he was leaving the lab, instead of being able to see through the performance, Meredith and I embraced him, hoping to comfort and make him feel better on the ground in the middle of the night, surrounded by rats in New York City.

It was one of the most disgusting and lowest points in my life. At some point, we finally got up from the gutter and went our separate ways. But I needed to say goodbye in my own way, so I called him to come back, and he did.

When people tell you who they are, you should listen. I didn't. I had been watching way too much *Sex and the City* and was far too drunk for my own good. So, instead of allowing myself to watch him leave and be done with it all, I decided to call him back to let him read the love letter I had written him in February, after the very first time I met him in person. I am not proud of this action, though grateful for what it taught me.

My Dearest William,

If I am reading this to you, it is safe to say we made it. We are together now. Otherwise, if that is not the case and somehow you are reading this, well, this is very awkward.

I have loved you from the first moment I saw you on Zoom during a McAuliffe Lab meeting. When people say they knew their partner was it immediately, I believe them, because I believed in you and me from day one.

When I came to the City to work on the Covid testing protocol competition, meeting you in person solidified everything I already knew. I was so scared to meet you in person. Terrified of making a fool of myself and looking like an idiot. But that wasn't even close to what actually happened. Meeting you was like being introduced to the other part of my soul, which I didn't even know was missing.

I have never laughed so hard with anyone as I do with you on a daily basis. I have never felt so comfortable baring my soul or confident about someone protecting it. You see me and everything I am, without ever questioning my sincerity. You did things to make me feel special and seen as a human being, not even as someone you were pursuing.

The thing is, you were in a relationship when we first met, but our connection was undeniable. I had never felt so confident about my feelings for someone or their feelings for me without ever once talking about it. I tried to avoid eye contact with you as much as possible, because, when we did make eye contact, it was as if all the conversations we weren't allowed to have were out in the open.

As much as I wanted that, I wanted it to be right. It would ruin any chance for us, if I didn't let your current relationship run its course. I cannot wait for the day when our timing is right. The past two weeks have been torture while also being extremely beautiful at the same time.

With you, all of my walls crumble and all that is left is my childhood innocence in love. I am soft and fear nothing. Bill, you are my partner, and I already love you with my whole heart. You are kind, witty, the goofiest coolest nerd, incredibly handsome, charming, endearing, compassionate, insanely intelligent, and poised enough for the both of us. But I swear I'll pick up my slack in that department, because, with you, I no longer need my defense mechanisms. I want to live this life with you. I want you as my partner. I want to collect our passions and color the world with our imaginations. I want to know the insanity of the monsters we will have as children. I want my family to be you. I want to pursue all our goals without hesitation and create the most magical life in an impossible world by making things more possible for others, as we carve new paths.

I want you to be my best friend forever.

After he finished, he looked up and said, "I can understand why you feel that way and what would make you write that. I can't say the feelings haven't been reciprocated. Hopefully, what you learned about me earlier tonight will make it easier for you to move on from this and change the way you see me. You know I will have to tell Kaylin about this. She always told me you had feelings for me."

This was a very big lesson for me to learn. I do not doubt the feelings between Bill and me were mutual, but he cared more about carving out a material, easy life for himself. He was proud of being privileged and White, but not in a way through which he could help the world. Only in a way that meant he didn't have to care about the world. Ew.

Chapter 11
Get to Know Yourself Enough to Love Yourself

"If you can't love yourself, how in the hell are you gonna love somebody else?"
—RuPaul, *RuPaul's Drag Race*

Hi Mom and Dad,

I am going to try to do this in the least emotional way I can, because maybe it might get through.

I am upset and honestly don't feel very comfortable about coming to Christmas, but I am coming because I want to see my cousins and niece and nephews.

I know that you both know I came out on social media a few months ago, because Dad commented on one of the pictures, not even acknowledging what the post said, and Mom, you stalk me all the time, so I know you saw it.

I also, in a very distressed moment, outright told Dad last week, with no response yet again.

My entire life, I have felt ignored. It's the reason I wrote all the letters I did as a kid. It's probably why "hold the baby" started, and it is definitely why I told you I don't believe in God as a teenager, in hopes that you might just listen to what I have to say.

I don't understand how Uncle Harold, a ninety-five-year-old man, can reach out to me on Facebook, commending my actions, but my parents can't.

I understand the past is the past, and there is nothing we can do to change it, which is why I moved on from holding on to being sent away. But this is different. When I was a teenager, you saw on my MySpace that I liked girls and guys. I'm not going to say what you should or shouldn't have done, because, again, we can't change it. I can only tell you how it made me feel and what I experienced through that.

I have been ashamed and hiding who I am from our entire family for my whole life because of moments like that. I lied to you about not believing in God, because I didn't want you telling me how I was supposed to believe in God or what my relationship with God was supposed to look like, because it was my relationship, and funny enough, it carries on to all my relationships.

I was never arrested as a kid, never got in trouble, had pretty good grades, and, overall, all my teachers liked me. I might have been difficult to you guys, but you never took the time to actually know who I was.

I love my family, and that is why this has been so hard for me. Because, for years, I've had to change my life to align with yours, in order to make you all feel comfortable, when I have been dying inside since I can remember. Yet my ability to have been comfortable would have had no impact on yours. The lack of consideration for my *comfort in this family is omnipresent. It took me doing something with my life big enough for you to gloat to your friends for you to even remotely start listening to me.*

Well, here I am, thirty-one years old, and I still feel the same way. I can't continue to have these fake conversations, where you guys reach out, asking if I am okay and getting through school well enough, while you completely ignore me, when I blatantly tell you what actually hurts me. And I'll let you know again, it's not school.

It's been three years since I sent that email to my parents. I just spent the last hour taking quizzes to find out what kind of makeup I should be wearing. I usually don't wear makeup unless I am wearing a costume. I have no business taking these quizzes, because I already know I will not be buying what they are selling. I am doing this to waste time.

My manuscript is due in three days, to hand off to editing, and I have a dozen or more stories left to write, plus the book isn't yet even organized properly. But that is not the real problem. The real problem is that I have this fear of being seen.

I have been taught my entire life that wanting to be seen or asking for attention is a bad thing. It invalidates your emotions. Because, for some reason, seeking attention has become a negative quality to have, as though needing attention from other humans isn't something we inherently need as human beings. So, what I have craved my entire life has become my largest fear. And I don't know what life would be like, if I actually had the attention I need and want.

Asking for what you want and need as a human is a very vulnerable place to be, because it always comes with the option of someone turning you down. Which is okay, because someone or something turning you down is just information, and information is everything. The more information you have, the more capable you will be in making decisions and figuring out what your next steps are.

You'd think the over 750 no's I got after my master's program would have taught me how to handle rejection, but no, this feels different. I would not be being rejected. I am rejecting all of the wrong that has been done to me throughout my life. I am rejecting the people who have harmed me and will try to continue to harm me, after I publish this book. I am making the choice to take the first step in closing doors this time. Because I know myself well enough to love myself. Which means I come first now.

I am over explaining what my sexuality is based on my upbringing, because my sexuality exists without my upbringing. It was just stunted by the life I was thrown into. So, I would like to explain my sexuality without borders or constraints.

The best way to describe my sexuality would be pansexual. I am attracted to individuals regardless of their sex or gender. I am ethically non-monogamous. Currently, I am in a monogamous relationship and trying to figure it out.

I, at the core of my being, am not monogamous. I am finding myself in a frustrating position with my sexuality at this moment in my life. I love Langdon dearly. We want all the same things out of life, except for one thing: having an open relationship.

He doesn't understand how me having sex with someone else has no effect on how much I love him. I understand people want different things out of their relationships, and he is allowed to have what he wants, as well. This makes things so tricky. Especially when two people have completely different definitions of what it means to cheat, be disrespectful, or disloyal. To me, having sex with another person is not defined as cheating. Cheating is way more complicated than that. Are you lying to me? Are you hiding things from me? Was having sex with someone else an intentional move to hurt me?

At its very center, the idea of having an open relationship seems like it should be simple. The same way I view how our society works. Like, quality healthcare, food, school, and housing should be accessible to everyone, right? That seems like a simple idea, but over the years, decades, and centuries, the way we have built the foundation of our society has made it incredibly difficult to make that possible for us. It's infuriating.

That is how I view my sexuality and even that of most heterosexuals. As a country founded in Christian roots, we have been preconditioned to believe there is a right and wrong way of living/being. This is how relationships have been done for hundreds of years, so this is the way they are supposed to be, traditionally.

Then that person cheats on their wife or husband but claims they still love them. While their partner can't possibly believe that, because they have stood strong in their belief that if you sleep with another person that means you can't possibly love your partner. *But that's not always true.* My partner and I have been together on and off now for twelve years. He has had sex with other women while we were together. I have slept with many people outside of our relationship, when we were separated, and I've loved him the entire time.

I recently thought I had to end this relationship, because it was not meeting the wants I have for a relationship in my life. I hadn't felt like my sexuality was seen properly, therefore I was not seen properly. I also had been feeling caged by monogamy. When the conversation finally came up, there was the roadblock: I want to have sex with other people. A man is usually more than fine bringing a women into bed with his woman, but anything beyond that seems to be unfathomable.

So, I asked him, "When you cheated on me, did that mean you didn't love me? Or did you still love me, even though you did that?"

It's funny, because I feel like a lot of women my age are very concerned about their aging, because they want to get married, have a family, and have kids. My personal fear was, by the time my partner is comfortable having an open relationship, I wouldn't be as hot as I am now and therefore wouldn't be able to hook up with all the people in whom I would be interested. Although that is a very ageist mindset.

I was made to feel so ashamed and guilty about all the sex I had throughout my whole life. Though it never stopped me from having as much sex as I did, I do believe it stopped me from feeling allowed to enjoy it. Sex came with a price. Whether I was slut-shamed by men and women, or not taken seriously in relationships, or used and thrown away like trash, my sexuality was never respected. My body wasn't respected. I was not respected.

I was told I wasn't respected because I didn't have any respect for myself, which is a total crock of shit. People have been offended that I am okay with being the way I am, so they have done everything in their power to try to make me feel not okay with the way I am. And unfortunately, for a long time it worked. Until it didn't.

To those who've thought of me as too much before this, just wait. There is so much more. I actually like myself now, and I'm the only person who's ever held me back.

I talk to many couples about sex and communication. Whenever I have a problem in my relationship, it seems the consensus is to say, "Oh, that's normal," and then let it be. Luckily for me, my partner does not just let these conversations be. We have them, as difficult as they might be, and we work through them.

It is depressing for me to hear that and hard for me to accept. I don't want to be in a relationship with a nonexistent sex life and lack of communication. I want to communicate clearly and fuck consistently. What is this shit we've allowed ourselves to believe about marriage and a lifetime of happiness? It's a joke. It's not real connection. You don't marry someone and suddenly become attracted only to that person for the rest of your life. But this is unbearable for the ego to comprehend, despite knowing that our fantasies, and those of our partner, for other people never stop. Where our wants and needs aren't met sexually and romantically, instead of having honest conversations about these things, people turn to cheating.

According to Arianne Resnick, CNC, in "What is Ethical Monogamy" at verywellmind.com:

> *Ethical non-monogamy (ENM) is the practice of taking part in romantic relationships that are not completely exclusive between two people. This involves very open communication between all parties involved. The most important part of ENM, everyone involved consents to the situation without coercion, deception, or guilt-tripping.*
>
> *The idea that monogamy is the only ethical relationship model and that all others must be*

qualified with the term, ethical, to denote their morality stems from colonialism.

Nonmonogamy has always existed in indigenous cultures. However, Western conquerors changed this when church-sanctioned marriages between one man and one woman became considered the only acceptable relationship format in order to force indigenous societies into Christianity and behave in more "civilized" ways. (15 Mar 2023)

Inside the non-monogamy community, I have found more safety than outside of it. Communication and consent are two of the most important aspects to non-monogamy. This leads to an increase in honesty and respect for one another. Funny how that works.

Chapter 12
When the Way you Love is Different

"People call these things imperfections, but they're not. Aww, that's the good stuff. And then we get to choose who we let in to our weird little worlds."
—Sean Maguire in *Good Will Hunting*

IT'S HARD TO GET ADVICE from people who are willing to accept a level of love you are not.

What is your definition of love? What were you taught love was as a child? Is that real love? Or was it meant as a way to control you? What things have been pressed upon you in the name of love that you aren't actually sure would be deemed love? Have you ever questioned what love actually is and not just accepted what you were taught to believe it is? As Bell Hook's says in *All About Love,* "We accept the love that we've learned as our definition of love."

This concept and belief of love is just as debatable as the existence of God. As children, we learn in the church that God is love and that love is God. But if that is true, then for a lot of us, God is also pain, which means that love is also synonymous with pain. I don't believe that can be considered true love, and I do still believe in true love. Even though I have been taught to believe for a very long time that love is synonymous with pain, I don't want to be a person who loses hope in the possibility of love, because, if I don't believe in love, then I don't know what I am doing here.

I was driving down 13 Mile Road, passing Southfield, going west toward Woodward, and my phone rang. Unknown number, so I declined. A few moments later, the phone vibrated. It as a voicemail, telling me to call back, my test results were in.

I had been out of Havenwyck for two weeks and was wracking my brain to figure out what test I had taken that I would need results for. My brain was mush after the medical lobotomy they'd put me through, and I couldn't think straight. So, I called back.

"You have been diagnosed with gonorrhea..."

I already thought my life was over. How could this get any worse? Now, I have an STD!

I was drowning in shame and embarrassment. Then, I came halfway to my senses and realized that Brian gave this to me. Meaning he'd gotten it from someone else, meaning he'd cheated on me, again. But this time, it was while I was imprisoned.

How fucking dare he?

At that point though, my insecurity and loneliness were through the roof. I had no one but Brian still telling me he loved me and wanted to be with me, so I held on to the last person I had on this Earth who could keep me afloat. High school love is forever, when it's all you've ever known, and I needed an escape mentally, so I'd settled for the only thing I had: day-dreaming of running away from my family forever and being with my mentally and emotionally abusive boyfriend, because even if all he ever told were lies, they still felt better than what I felt at home.

So, I sat on the phone after confronting him about giving me an STD and allowed him to call me a whore. I allowed him to blame this on me. I allowed him to tell me I'd fucked someone inside Havenwyck and that he would never trust me again after this.

Then, I begged and pleaded for him to forgive me for something I never did, just so I wouldn't have to lose the only person I felt a connection to in this world.

Had non-monogamy and the acceptance of being queer been something on my radar back then, there's a very good chance I might have been in a throuple by the age of seventeen. But that wasn't my reality back then. It's been seventeen years since I got out of Havenwyck. Today, I am twice as old as I was then, and only now am I finally comfortable with celebrating my sexuality and asking for what I want in relationships, even if other people don't understand or accept it.

In 2021 and 2022, I was at the height of my exploration in my sexuality and on my journey to define my perfect relationship. I had never felt freer to be myself. Langdon and I got back together in December of 2021 and decided to begin an open relationship for multiple reasons. I still lived in Cambridge, while he lived in St. Petersburg, and both of us were uncertain about a fully committed relationship. I believe he thought I only offered the option at the time as a way to keep him in my life, as he had never tried anything like this before, but what he didn't understand was that this is what I had always wanted. I don't think I communicated that clearly enough or even the extent and details of what an open relationship meant to me. I am certain they differed from what Langdon thought of or envisioned the concept of an open relationship to be. Neither of us anticipated how the meaning of an open relationship would change, once we moved in together.

Very quickly, jealously got the best of both of us. We decided to close our relationship in February, 2022. I think we would both agree that decision was made too quickly, and without giving non-monogamy much of a chance. Neither of us dated other people during our open time, but the *thought* of it was enough to drive us both mad.

Truly, though, we hadn't yet done the work to fully forgive and move on from our relationship in the past. We stayed long-distance for almost a year. That summer, I took my yearly pilgrimage back to Michigan...

Fourth of July used to be my favorite holiday. Not because I was an overtly patriotic person, but because it was always a great time to come together with friends and family. To spend time camping, drinking, eating good food, and playing games. Always a fun time. Always a time that felt like everyone was celebrating the same thing, when people were really united.

I decided to spend July 4, 2022 driving eleven hours across the country, with a shortcut through Canada, alone, because I would have done anything to avoid watching ignorant, drunk assholes celebrate a country that had done nothing for its people lately. I decided to spend Independence Day sharing my abortion story as a gift to these here "United" States on my blog.

It was during this month in 2012 when I got pregnant. Langdon had cheated on me, then broke up with me. I decided break-up sex was the answer.

I had just come off the Depo-Provera shot a year prior and hadn't had a period in years. I still had yet to have one, so that was normal for me. September came around, and I noticed my boobs had gotten huge. So big, they looked and felt like fake boobs.

I was very excited about this but also very confused. I hadn't really had a period since middle school, so I had never really experienced the symptoms of PMS or anything like that. The thought of being pregnant didn't even cross my mind, until a friend suggested the idea.

I bought a few pregnancy tests. I drew a bath, lit candles, and opened a bottle of wine. I took one test. Two lines came up, but not exactly like the box said it should look, so for all I knew, I was clear! I was twenty-three at the time and proceeded to get blackout drunk, like ya do.

Another week went by and my boobs had become painful to the touch. I finally did the math and realized it had been over a year since getting off birth control, and I should have already had my period by then. I took another pregnancy test. The lines came up the same way. I took a picture and sent it to my friend.

"Pregnant is what that means," she responded.

I stayed up all night, contemplating what I was going to do. Langdon was working at O'Connor's until 2 a.m., and I couldn't tell anyone else. You see, I was raised in a Catholic home. I was always against abortion. For myself, not for anyone else, but all of a sudden, I was in this position I'd never thought I would be in.

Langdon didn't want kids, I was brand-new to the city where I lived, and I had no family around or friends I knew very well. I had never felt so alone. I knew I wanted to keep the baby, but I also knew what that would mean, if I did.

I texted Langdon and waited for him to get off work. I met him outside his job and went back to his place, where I told him. His initial reaction was to question whether it was his, which I am sure doesn't really surprise anyone.

I knew I couldn't take care of a baby on my own. I also knew it would have killed me to move back to Michigan and in with my parents, if I told them the truth. My ex didn't want a kid, and I didn't expect him to. I even let him off the hook, in case I decided to have the baby, giving him the choice of whether or not to be in the kid's life.

I wanted to have the baby. I needed time to make this decision. By the time I learned I was pregnant, I was already seven weeks. I could barely take care of myself at the time. I didn't even own a car. I had to ask a friend to take me to Planned Parenthood. They gave me the Mifepristone and Misoprostol, and my friend dropped me off at Langdon's. He was going to a football game out of town that weekend, but he let me stay at his house while I went through the medically-induced abortion alone.

Two weeks later, I went in for my post-abortion check-up. The baby was still there. There is a one-percent chance of that happening. That is what it tells you on the paperwork you sign. I had to meet with the doctor to discuss all of the dangers in keeping a baby that survives a medical abortion. It was extremely difficult for me not to think of this as a sign I was meant to have this child. So, I decided I was going to keep it.

Over the next month, I was told I was lying about being pregnant and lying about who the father was. Not just by Langdon, but by a lot of people in the town where I lived. In fact, it was people who didn't even know me who told me Langdon was lying about both of those things, along with a "friend" of mine.

It was so bad, I had to force him to come to Planned Parenthood with me, so he could see the ultrasound himself, to know for sure I wasn't lying. I was also still unable to tell anyone close to me, at this point, in fear of my family finding out.

One of the only people I did confide in was a guy I had previously dated. After telling him everything I was going through, he proceeded to try to force me to have sex with him. When I refused to do that, he went to Langdon's bar the next day and told him I tried to sleep with him while pregnant with his baby. I realize how much this sounds like a soap opera and too insane to be true, because why the fuck would anyone care enough to be this involved in someone else's life? But as we can all see from the decision made by the Supreme Court in 2022, people love to insert themselves into other people's business constantly.

This wasn't the first time the people in this town tried to bully and harass me, and it certainly wouldn't be the last time. Why they did it? No fucking clue. I have my theories, but at this point, it doesn't matter to me anymore. They tried to break me for whatever bullshit excuse they had, but ya know what? Look at me now.

I decided to set a date for a surgical abortion on the last day possible for me to get the procedure done. I had no intention of going, but just in case I changed my mind.

I did it. I am not going to go into all the nitty-gritty details of what I do and don't believe in right now, but I will tell you that, during this time, I started to attend group reiki sessions on a weekly basis. Two days before the abortion was scheduled, I went to a reiki session. During the session, I saw the baby inside of me with a rainbow in its heart and a rainbow in my heart; the rainbows connected through an umbilical cord made of white light. In the moment, and shortly after, all I could make of it was that the baby and I had connected and it was happening. I was going to have this baby.

I went home and went to sleep. The next morning, I woke up and had the strangest feeling. I don't know how to explain what or how I knew it, but it felt as though this huge weight had been lifted off of my shoulders. As though the baby had told me: *It is okay. We have made our connection, and I can go now.*

The next day, I called Langdon and asked him to take me to Planned Parenthood. I brought my Bible with me to hold as I walked into the office, while protesters stood outside. I was further along than the rest of the girls who were there, so I had to be dilated further, and it was going to take longer. So, I was the first one in the office and the last to leave that day.

The room they put you in is filled with Lazy-Boys all set in a circle, so you can look at every girl about to get an abortion and then watch her after it is completed. By the time it was my turn, I had been sitting in my Lazy-Boy for over five hours and watched eight women go in for their abortions.

By the time it was my turn, the conscious sedation medication had kicked in, and I wasn't holding anything back. I was enraged, scared, sad, and alone. The nurses set me up, one on each side, holding my arms and legs. When the doctor came in, I started yelling at him as he picked up different utensils. I called him a murderer of babies and said, "I bet you like this. I bet you get off on the idea of murdering babies every day."

So, he stopped. He told everyone to stop and step away, and he sat down next to me. He told me, "I don't want to be here anymore than you want to be here. However, the only way you can make it through this process is with the help of me and these nurses today. I am here for you. I am here to do the part no one wants to do, and I am doing this for you."

I wish I knew the name of that doctor. I wish I could tell him how grateful I am to him for everything he did and said to me that day and just how much his words have stuck with me over the past eleven years. How the grace and care he showed me changed me forever.

The nurses took their places again, and with my eased mind and plenty of drugs in my system, the procedure began. I told him he "was like a dentist of my vagina with all that suction." He said he was going to get a coffee mug that said that.

I used humor like I always do to get through a hard situation, so we all were laughing and crying by the end of it. I am grateful I was awake for the procedure and able to have closure in that regard. After it was over, I went back to my Lazy-Boy and cried. I couldn't stop crying. Langdon took me to get my favorite pizza, Jet's, and we went back to his house and watched movies.

Two weeks later, I went back to reiki. Normally, at the end of our sessions, the woman would ask people about their experiences and invite them to share with the group. Instead, before everyone opened their eyes, she came to me and whispered in my ear, "I have a message they want me to give you. The soul wasn't ready yet, and you can't blame yourself."

I would have a ten-year-old today, had I not had those two abortions. I told my family later that I had gotten pregnant and had a miscarriage, because I didn't know how to hide my sadness, when I came home for Christmas that year. I have never shared the truth with them, and if they are reading this, it will be the first time they are hearing it.

I made a choice. I wasn't raped. I decided to have unprotected break-up sex with an ex, when I was twenty-three years old and alone. I did not want to have an abortion, but I made the difficult decision that was right for me. That is all that matters, and that is all that should matter. Maybe I would have had the baby had I known I would have been taken care of as a single mother, or that my child would have been taken care of, if I was unable to adequately provide for my child. But this country has shown it does not care about a child outside of the womb, and nor does it care for single mothers. So, as an almost-mother, I did what was best for my child. That is love.

Almost a year after I shared that blog post depicting my abortion story, I was visiting my friend Gina. You know: the one who fucked my boyfriend Brian in high school? Yeah, we're still friends.

Gina and I were sitting on her couch while she breastfed her newborn. Her one-year-old napped next to the baby monitor. It was May 2023, and I was back in Detroit for a quick trip to see Blink-182, staying at her new home in Grosse Pointe while in town.

It had been eleven years since my abortion. I could have had a ten-year-old child, but I didn't, and honestly, I was grateful that I didn't. I never would have been capable of being the kind of mother Gina was being for her children. Before the second abortion, my greatest fear was that I would never know how to experience happiness again in my life, if I were to go through with it. As I sat there, eleven years later, I was grateful I did not allow that one moment in my life define everything else.

I allowed myself the space to grieve and go through the pain of choosing not to have a child, so that I could be confident enough in my choice from the past and could experience the joy my friends' children bring them and me, without any regret. I was so excited and happy for this life she had created, for the family she was the matriarch of. So proud of her and everything she had become.

Gina is one of my closest and longest-term friends. We can't offend each other at this point in our relationship. We know each other's tones for every emotion and have been through everything together. I've always loved to reminisce about the past with her, finding connections and understandings in who we once were and why it had such an impact on who we've become. I do this with everyone, not just her. But she and I have always loved looking more into the details, trying to figure out why we are the way we are.

This started in middle school, when we first read our horoscopes in *Cosmopolitan* magazine in the library at school. And right then, I wanted her to explain myself to me. I wanted her to help me understand why I don't work the same way everyone else does. Like somehow, after all these years, she would have the answers for me. But she didn't. All she had were more clarifying questions for me, and maybe that's what we all need in our closest friends. Someone who's going to help us get down to the bottom of ourselves.

I had been questioning my relationship with Langdon for months now. Not because I don't love him, but because I wanted something I didn't think he was' capable of giving me. I told him before we got back together that there were three things I would not live without. I want to get married, I want to have kids, and I want an open relationship.

Since we have gotten back together, though, my strong feelings have waned on those three things. He has been my greatest weakness for eleven years now, and for some reason, still I don't know how to draw the line with him. I would not even be in a relationship right now if he didn't know all three of those things were on the table.

But he still doesn't understand what an open relationship means to me. He doesn't understand it doesn't mean my feelings and wants for him are any less. I can't blame him, though, because this society isn't built to help people be okay with alternative forms of love and living. And right then, as I sat in front of Gina, my best friend, who I believe knows me better than anyone else in the world, she questioned my desires.

"You don't actually want that, Katie?"

"Yes, I do. The way I love is different, Gina."

"Look at how heartbroken you were all those times he cheated on you."

"I was never upset that he slept with someone else. I was upset that he lied to me and kept things from me. I didn't know that was the reality until I learned that being ethically non-monogamous was a thing. If I had known about this from a younger age, I think my love life would have been drastically different and so much healthier."

"I just can't see myself ever being okay with something like that. And I don't blame him for not being okay with it, either."

"I know," I said. "And I understand that, which is what makes all of this so incredibly difficult. But I just don't see love the same way most people I know do. If I did, then there would be no way you and I would still be friends, because I would have never been able to forgive you."

"Well, I am very grateful you did."

"This is why I am able to forgive Langdon, too. This is why I am able to be in a relationship with him again after all of that pain. I don't want to be possessive or jealous of another person. I want everyone to experience all life has to offer them, which includes love and connection with all people."

It is through conversations like this one I had with Gina that I have begun to understand myself and my desires better. I somewhat lost my sex drive this year. There are many things that have caused this but I believe a small portion could be because, just as I finally became comfortable being open about my sexuality, I entered into a monogamous relationship with a cisgendered heterosexual man. I felt like I was unable to truly be myself again, because I didn't want to hurt him. So, just as I was finally coming out of my self-inscribed imaginary cage of shame, I put myself right back in. I want to be very clear here, Langdon never did anything to make me feel this way.

I was so afraid to lose him that I was unwilling to fully admit that what I wanted in our relationship was necessary to my happiness. The story has changed from when I was seventeen years old. I am no longer with a mentally and emotionally abusive boyfriend. This time, I am with an incredible man whom I have watched grow and evolve over the past eleven years into everything I always knew he already was.

Now, we communicate and we heal, we explore and evolve, we disagree but discuss, and we are an incredible team together. We have the same goals and aspirations for our lives, and we plan for them together. But still, I don't know if he wants the same kind of love. The way I want to love.

My craving to be understood my entire life has left me at these crossroads all too often, and if the world has taught me anything, it is that there might never be anyone who actually understands me. So, do I accept what I have, because it's closer to what I've wanted than anything else I have ever experienced? Or am I misunderstood because the people whom I am surrounded by aren't very much like me? Can I have faith in the universe and put it all out there? Or should I stay safe where I am?

If you've learned anything about me by this point in the story, you know the latter is the most unlikely choice for me. Yet when it comes to my sexuality, it has been ever-present. Only since starting to write this book has it become clearer and clearer just how much I have "stayed safe" in this area of my life. Even as I write this, I can feel my shoulders tensing up and my throat swell, as I fight back the tears and rage from knowing just how much easier life would have been had my family accepted me for who I was. Just how much easier and more joyful life would be if the world would let us all love who we want to love and be who we want to be.

The thought that telling Langdon what I wanted in a relationship could've meant losing the person I love most, because he might not love me for who I am, was terrifying. But I would never have had to be in that position, if we all were allowed to be who we are without being shamed from the beginning. However, I know now that he is willing to have these conversations. I bit the bullet, and in expressing these very big emotions, I have learned just how accepting and loving this man truly is. We may not want the same things (still to be determined) but he has never once shamed me for vocalizing the way I feel.

One of the major reasons I want to be ethically non-monogamous is because of my love for meeting strangers. The invigorating feeling that I get when meeting friendly strangers is one of my favorite highs. Without knowing any backgrounds, beliefs, or ideals, you are just kind to one another.

I often think about the strangers I have met in my life and wonder where they are now. A lot of times, while walking on a street, I will think to myself about how this might be the only time I'll come in contact with a person for my entire life. All I will ever know about them is as a face walking past on the street. Like I have FOMO of not being able to meet and know everyone on this Earth, as though that would be possible.

I love connecting. There is nothing like the rush of a new connection. Just to fall in love, even if only for the night. It makes me feel free. It makes me feel alive. It makes me feel like I am sixteen with my best friend, staying up until the sunrise, talking about life and the universe.

I don't think our love should be tamed. I don't think our love is meant to be for only one person our entire lives, and maybe that's the problem. As a society, we have been taming our love for centuries, and it is making us sick as a whole. It hurts when you can't love the way you want to. It's not even a want; it is necessary for a healthy human life, to experience love and human interaction. We see what happens when children are deprived of love, or Queer people are closeted for so long. The love we have to give and the space we have to receive become dark and blocked off.

I want all of us to find a way to love everyone for their differences, yet I constantly feel myself boiling over in fumes of anger on a day-to-day basis, due to people who are completely different than me. I have tried looking at this from so many different angles, attempting to understand. Sometimes, the people who are so different than I am have really frightening beliefs, so I wonder if I must be in the wrong.

Is it possible that the definitions humanity has created for pain, suffering, hate, and bigotry are so far off, we're the ones in the wrong? Have I gone absolutely mad? This isn't the first time I have found myself questioning such things.

I am a person who likes to understand all sides of an issue. I want to understand everyone's feelings, because most of the time, an issue can easily be talked out, when you have someone who understands what both people are saying. When it comes to emotions, it's hard, because emotions can be read, heard, and taken so many wrong ways before there is even a chance to come to understanding, and by then, it's too late, and everyone has already blown up. I have come to this reckoning of sorts, for when my mind wanders into wondering if we're all supposed to be racist, misogynistic, homophobes: if, somehow, that is the truth, it is not a truth I want to be part of.

Anthony Bourdain said, "Eat at a local restaurant tonight. Get the cream sauce. Have a cold pint at 4 o'clock in a mostly empty bar. Go somewhere you've never been. Listen to someone you think may have nothing in common with you. Order the steak rare. Eat an oyster. Have a Negroni. Have two. Be open to a world where you may not understand or agree with the person next to you, but have a drink with them anyways. Eat slowly. Tip your server. Check in on your friends. Check in on yourself. Enjoy the ride."

I have forgotten to enjoy the ride. I used to live for the ride. I used to burn the candle at both ends plus in the middle, but now I feel as though I have become a shell of myself. I want to enjoy the ride. I want to feel free. I don't want to live by someone else's clock. I don't want to live by any clock. I want to be wild. I want to be untamed. And I only want people who love me that way to be part of my life.

This year of healing has been my hardest yet. I think that is because I am on the verge of my biggest breakthrough. Freedom is scary when you've never known what true freedom looks like.

I wish he could understand that my wanting relationships with other people has nothing to do with how much I love him and just because I want to experience something with someone else doesn't mean he isn't fulfilling me. This does not pertain to just sex.

At different times and spaces in our lives, we need and want different things from various people. I don't think we should have to suffer in those times when we are not capable of being "perfect" or in a monogamous relationship.

I think the normal thought process behind what defines a healthy relationship has fucked up our ability to want and desire what brings us joy. We deprive ourselves of joy in the name of satisfying another person's ego.

Right now, I don't enjoy sex. Or I can't enjoy sex. It's hard for me to get horny, and honestly, I wish my partner would just go have sex with someone else sometimes, so it would take the pressure off of me to have sex.

I don't know exactly why my sex drive has completely diminished. But I don't think it is due to just one thing.

I have been reexamining the times when I was raped over this past year, and I noticed that has made it uncomfortable for me to have the type of sex I used to enjoy, without feeling like I am being forced, even when it is consensual. Most sex feels nonconsensual right now, because the only sex I can handle having is with myself, and that is usually just to make myself cum as fast as I can to get a release or fall asleep. It's not sexy at all.

These conversations with my partner are extremely difficult and understandably so. How do you explain to the person you love that you want to have an open relationship while not being very active sexually in the relationship you already have? Navigating my sexual trauma, while simultaneously trying to figure out exactly what I want in a relationship, has been extremely difficult. I am so grateful to my partner for his willingness to have these conversations and hold space for me.

I love my partner. I want to be with him. We have conversations about this. He knows I am pansexual, and he knows my relationships during our breakups were ethically non-monogamous. But our individual ideas of what an open relationship is, are not something we necessarily agree on. There is nothing wrong with either preference. That's what makes this so difficult and what makes these conversations so difficult. This is when the movies that say, "sometimes love isn't enough," start to make more sense.

I honestly don't know what will happen with Langdon and me. For now, I know that I love him, and he loves me. I know that we have goals and aspirations, together and separately. We talk about getting a second dog, getting married, having kids, buying a house in Detroit, buying an RV or building a Skoolie, and becoming snowbirds who travel the world yearlong. I want all of those things with him, and I can see our life so clearly and beautifully. I always have. I have been able to see our future together since the first time he kissed me on that picnic bench at O'Connors.

But I want more. I want to share my love with more than him. I want to love women and men and everyone in between and outside the box. I want to flirt freely and be wild, and I want that for my partner, as well. I want the entire life with Langdon I describe above plus the freedom to explore relationships with other people. I want commitment without constraint. I want devotion without a cage. I want for people to recognize that not everything is as black and white as we have made it out to be. There is no universal definition of love.

> *Our nation is equally driven by sexual obsession. There's no aspect of sexuality that's not studied, talked about, or demonstrated. How-to classes exist for every dimension of sexuality, even masturbation. Yet schools for love do not exist. Everyone assumes that we'll be able to love instinctively. Despite overwhelming evidence to*

the contrary, we still accept that the family is the primary school for love. Those of us who do not learn how to love among family are expected to experience love in romantic relationships. However, this love often eludes us. And we spend a lifetime undoing the damage caused by cruelty, neglect, and all matter of lovelessness experienced in our families of origin and in relationships where we simply don't know what to do.

Most recent books on love suggest love should mean something different to men than it does to women — that the sexes should respect and adapt to our inability to communicate since we don't share the same language. This type of literature is popular because it doesn't demand a change in fixed ways of thinking about gender roles, culture, or love. Rather than sharing strategies that would help us become more loving it actually encourages everyone to adapt to circumstances where love is lacking.

—Bell Hooks

I hope one day I can go back to loving and enjoying sex the way I used to. I hope for the day when I can have sex and not have flashbacks of the times I was raped. I hope for the day when I can masturbate and have sex without feeling completely dirty and ashamed afterward. I hope for the day when I can do all of these things without having to drink to release my inhibitions. I hope for the day when I can experience joy in sex. I hope for the day when I can start adding more people and their astrological signs to my notes document again. I hope for the day when my friends go back to roasting me for how big of an ethical slut I am and that my partner will join in on that, as well, and no one will experience envy or jealousy. Or if we do, we will know how to navigate those tough emotions in a healthy way.

Just because the way I love is different than the way you might have been taught to love doesn't mean it's wrong. It's just different, and you might find, if you look inside yourself enough and you discover the way you want to love is different than the way you've been loving, it's okay to change your mind. It's okay to change what you believe.

What I find more often than not is, when my beliefs or ideas change, it's never that I was wrong before and right now. It's more about how, with each iteration, I become closer and closer to who I've always been. It has just taken me some time to get there.

Chapter 13

Happiness is the [Hard] Choice

"I figure life's a gift and I don't intend on wasting it."
—Jack Dawson in *Titanic*

I DON'T REALLY SEE the point in doing anything in life if you don't have passion. Now, you're not going to have passion every single day of your life, but if you don't have passion for what you're doing in your life currently, then it is time to reevaluate what you're doing.

It only makes sense this would be the hardest section to write and the one I would avoid until I absolutely had to write it.

A few months ago, I asked my friend Kelly to come by. I needed someone's opinion on a friendship of mine that had recently gone south. Kelly is the kind of person who will help you get down to the bare bones of a situation.

"Did you always feel this way about the friendship?" Kelly asked.

"Honestly, I felt bad for her from the beginning. There's nothing worse I can feel for someone than feeling bad for them. I hate that."

"Well, there's your answer. You say this is a pattern that keeps repeating in friendships and relationships in your past. It's repeating itself right now. From day one of this relationship, you chose the other person's feelings over your own. You chose to disrespect yourself by allowing someone into your life whom you knew you weren't really comfortable with in the first place, because you felt bad for them. Every time you choose to not hurt someone's feelings at the expense of your own, you are doing a disservice to yourself and setting yourself up for the pattern to continue."

I fucking love friendships like this. People who just tell me how it fucking is without worry of hurting my feelings.

There is a large disconnect between those areas I am and am not willing to advocate for myself. It is this disconnect that has kept me in a perpetual state of sadness and depression. It is my unwillingness to see and break the patterns that keep me in this cycle.

I believe it has been easy for me to love people my whole life. Maybe not in healthy ways, but I don't like to look back and say, "I thought I loved that person, but now I realize that wasn't love." Like people say in the movies or on *The Bachelor,* after they finally find "real love" in less than a month, in front of hundreds of cameras.

Instead, I like to say that I was in love for what I knew love to be at that time in my life. I do also believe I gave my heart fully to the men I loved, every time. From day one of preschool with Sawyer Hughes to my "high school sweetheart," Brian Bryers, my unsuspected, Benjamin Harisburg, and even Seth Stinger for a moment, to Langdon, Trevor Riley and Raymond Walter, who were summer loves. But Langdon always stayed in my heart and, to this day, is still there.

It's important to tell the story of Langdon and me from the beginning. I am warning you, however: it is painful and can be triggering. I also would like to say this is my side of the story. Also that, after everything we have been through, I still love this man.

I know most people might think me a fool or a hypocrite, but I can't explain love perfectly, because no love is perfect. I don't see loving someone as a waste of time, and I know love takes work. I also know, at any given moment in the past or even now, I could walk away from this man, never look back, and probably find the "ideal" in a relationship with someone else.

But I don't want someone else. I want him. And I don't know that any partner would ever be able to accept the love for Langdon that I hold in my heart.

On Jan. 2, 2022, I was sitting in a café in our now hometown of St. Pete Beach, Florida. He was at work at the Hollander Hotel, bartending, and I was sitting in "his" coffee shop, with his car and house keys... Yes, it is a little odd, spelling out things people naturally do in a relationship, but after I explain the past, how we got to this point, you will understand. Also, I will show how we were trying to navigate moving forward by unlearning the traumas taught to us in our pasts, including by each other.

In that moment, we felt like partners. In that moment, we felt like we were growing together. In that moment, he was mine and I was his. I didn't know how long that moment would last, but I wished I could take the past few days and bottle them for a lifetime.

At the time, being with Langdon was enough for me. I felt calm and relaxed, cooking dinner, playing boardgames, and just hanging out at home. I love the feeling of security in it. But I only feel that with him. He makes simple feel special. He makes simple feel like home. He makes me feel seen without having to do something or be someone. He was there at the beginning, and he's still here now. I don't matter to him because of what I've become. I just matter.

I don't remember the first time I met Langdon. He was my bartender at O'Connors in Delray Beach, Florida in 2011, where Seth and I had just moved. I was twenty-two and very quickly became the local barfly at the establishment. I say that like I was the only one, but the truth is anyone who went to the OC (as we liked to refer to it) was a barfly, because it was the locals' pub. It was the spot all the chefs and industry folk went to after work. I didn't know this ahead of time but was just lucky enough that Seth was a chef and introduced me to the place. I quickly claimed the spot in the "divorce" and started collecting chefs for friends. Genius for a poor girl who likes to eat bougie. Highly recommend.

Langdon was everybody's favorite bartender. Still is, and probably will always be. If you've ever been to O'Connors, or Hurricane in Delray Beach, Florida between the years of 2011 to 2017, you probably met him. He always knew your drink and charmed you right out of your flipflops. This is probably why I never liked him.

I didn't dislike him, but when I see a guy whom all the girls swoon over, I automatically find them less attractive. Being able to self-analyze pretty well, I think this has been a defense mechanism of mine for years. If I don't pay attention or allow myself to get caught up in the noise, then I can't get hurt. Put on the blinders and be yourself, and no one can get you.

The thing is, that is exactly the type of behavior that attracts people. So, while I was minding my business, planning a white-trash-bash birthday party for myself, Langdon planned his infiltration into my life.

As I've mentioned, the guys I have dated are pretty bottom of the barrel. It doesn't take a lot to impress me or make me feel seen. Someone doing the bare minimum for me used to feel like I was on top of the world. I am working on my standards, but at this time, they were *very* low. Still, I love how Langdon wooed me.

It started one night while I was very drunk (typical for this time in my life). Back then, I used to double-fist Guinness and Jägerbomb bombs all night long, sprinkled with an Irish car bomb here and there. Until I learned any more than two of those and I was guaranteed to pee the bed. The Jägerbombs at the OC came in stein glasses. It's a wonder how anyone survives their early twenties.

I was hungry, per usual, so Langdon threw a bag of peanuts at my face. Being the cool girl that I am, I caught them, obviously. I then told him, "If you throw nuts at my face every time I walk in this bar, I will never go to another bar again." This is how the dance began. I didn't have a car at this point in my life and walked to and from work. My job was on one side of the OC and my house was on the other. The next day walking home from work I passed by the OC and heard someone whistle from behind. I turned around to see Langdon and a bag of nuts flying toward my face.

I caught it.

This continued for weeks. I got to the OC for my birthday, decked out in leather pants, a leather vest, tits to the chin, black eye, and a fat lip, topped with a mullet. Langdon was waiting with a brown paper bag. It was filled with a gallon of milk, Flamin' Hot Cheetos, pork rinds, Junior mints, and some other liquid I can't remember. He had been paying attention and remembered all my favorite snacks, which I had talked about while drunk over the past few months. I know that probably sounds pathetic, to get so excited about this, but it was so unexpected and flattering. He made me feel seen in a way I hadn't felt before.

I had a wicked hangover the next day. I remember waking up at a friend's house and just lying on the couch until 9 p.m., eating junk food and sleeping on and off. I had no intentions of going anywhere or doing anything.

I went out for a cigarette and pulled out my sky app. Jupiter, Venus, and the Moon were all in alignment, and I decided to send a picture of it to Langdon. He convinced me to meet him out for a drink.

It had to have been midnight by the time I met him at OC. Ahhh, the days of getting ready to go out at 10 p.m. and not even getting to the bar until midnight. That'll never happen again in my life.

I was still heartbroken over Benjamin, but something about Langdon was so fresh and fun, it was easy to forget the pain.

He invited me to meet him at O'Connors, which surprised me, since I knew it would be filled with everyone we know, which meant we would be surrounded by every dude I had slept with in this town already. But fuck it, why not.

Sitting at the picnic tables in front of the bar like I had been doing for months on the daily, Langdon and I talked and acted as if we had already been together for years.

"What are you doing?" I asked as I leaned back when he leaned in toward me.

"I was going to kiss you..."

"Right here? Right now? In front of everybody?"

"Yes."

"Well, okay then." I had a grin that filled my entire face.

That was our first kiss. He chose me, and he chose me publicly.

We left the bar that night and broke into my favorite rooftop pool, went skinny dipping, and fucked like a porno over the railing of the hot tub. It was so hot. We went back to his place after that and continued to have sex for hours, on and off. The next day, we stayed in bed until 5 p.m., continuing to do the same.

Our chemistry was undeniable, and we were inseparable after that night. We immediately planned a weekday getaway in the Keys (weekends aren't weekends for the service industry) for the next week. I slept at his house every night.

Sitting on the beach one day, I explained to him how I can usually tell how a relationship with someone is going to work out, and whether it will be short or last a long time, plus how it will end. I used to do this with all my friendships, too. Even when I could tell something was off, I always wanted to give everyone the benefit of the doubt. I don't do this as often anymore. I have learned how important it is to protect myself. Sitting on the beach with Langdon that day, without knowing all the details, I could sense the pain from his past. He asked me what I thought of him.

"I hear you say you don't want to get married and have kids, but I think you say that because of the pain you have seen those things bring. I think you want marriage and a family more than anything else but are terrified to allow yourself to want those things. I think you're drawn to me because I don't let you stay on the surface level. And I think you're already in love with me," I added with a laugh.

Back then it was impossible for me to break eye contact with him. Nowadays, it can be hard for me to make eye contact with him. I miss those moments of eye contact. It created a feeling deep in my chest, making me never want to leave those moments.

"I want to tell you something," he said. "But I don't want you to get upset or weirded out." He took a deep breath. "I am changing my phone number. My last relationship did not end very well, and I think it is time she and I don't have contact anymore. I just don't want you to think there is anything going on there anymore. I want us to be together. I want you to be my girlfriend."

"Are you sure? I don't want you to feel you need to do this for me. I am okay with just continuing to have fun with each other. I don't want to make this a serious thing, unless you are ready," I replied.

"I want to be with you. I don't want to be with anyone else."

So, Langdon became my boyfriend.

People in Delray really did not like this. Langdon's ex-girlfriend especially did not like this. She started to show up at places where we were, including an event with a fashion show I was doing the hair for. She was relentless.

One day, when I was out of town, she and Langdon got together, and he cheated on me. In June 2012, I found an email from her to him.

> *Don't worry. I'm not going to tell your girlfriend you cheated on her that night at The Duck.*

She was bitter. He chose me. He cheated on me in the first month of our relationship, but he chose to stay with me as opposed to leaving me for her, after they were together for six years. I thought this meant something. I reasoned with it. I could understand how feelings for her wouldn't just go away, when I still grappled with my feelings for Benjamin.

When he got home from work that night, I confronted him. I just wanted to understand. We stayed together, but two weeks later, he decided to break up with me. He couldn't handle to pain of looking at me, knowing what he'd done to me. At least, that was his explanation. We then had break-up sex that led to my pregnancy.

After the abortion (the one that worked), I thought we would never talk again. But he kept coming around. From 2012 to 2016, Langdon and I were in a toxic, on-again, off-again relationship. He continued to cheat on me multiple times, both with the same ex-girlfriend and other women.

We were so good at enjoying each other's company and ignoring the shit, when we were together. He also protected and championed for me throughout those years. He helped me buy a car, and he paid my bills when I couldn't afford to. I fought him a lot when he did these things, because it always felt as though he was trying to buy my silence. That if he helped me with all he did, then he was allowed to do any extracurricular activities outside of our relationship.

Looking back on our relationship, my biggest problem was never the act of him sleeping with other women. It was the lying and always treating me like I was the one who had cheated, whenever I dated and slept with other people while we were separated. As though what he was doing was acceptable, but it was not okay for me to do it.

In the summer of 2014, we broke up for a second time. He couldn't give me more than date night on Tuesdays, refused to take a vacation with me, and wouldn't meet my family or parents. I found out later that night that he was going on a vacation with a group of guys he'd claimed to not like but was planning on not hanging out with them after the trip.

I texted him.

Glad to hear Kyle gets a trip to the Keys out of his break-up with you. What do I get?"
"What do you want?" he quickly replied.

I was sitting at the bar of my then favorite restaurant in Delray.

Norway, I typed.
Okay. Then we will go to Norway.

We were obsessed with *Chef's Table* on Netflix and more than anything wanted to go to Faviken, Magnus Nilson's restaurant. So, he booked it: ten days through Norway and Sweden at the end of October, 2014. And I stopped talking to him.

I am laughing as I write this, because this kind of game we used to play with each other was so typical of us. I stopped talking to him because I knew, either way, I had a flight and reservation at Faviken booked with my name on them, and neither was refundable. For once, I finally had the power in this relationship, and I was going to eat it up.

Two months after I stopped talking to him, I was sitting at 3rd & 3rd, my favorite bar. The bar is shaped as a large square. When you walk in, there are tables to your left, a small stage, and a door to the bathrooms. Directly in front of you is the bar. Opposite the front door on the other side of the bar is a back door that opens to a wooden patio, where people smoke and play large Jenga and Connect Four. It is very lounge-like, with couches in random places, and it's dark inside. I always sat at the same spot: the bar seat next to the service station, in front of the back door.

The back patio wasn't an open patio. It had an eight-foot wooden fence surrounding it, with no way to exit.

I was sitting in my usual spot with a friend of mine when Langdon and his roommates walked in. My heart sank. He smirked and waved awkwardly at me. I looked away.

The audacity he has, I thought, *to think he can just act like everything is normal!*

That's when the drinks started to appear. One after another, the bartenders brought me drinks Langdon had bought for me. I declined every single one of them.

I had still been sitting with that friend. But as I mentioned, everyone in that town loved Langdon, so my "friend" had already ditched me to go talk with him and his friends. They were sitting at the corner of the bar by the front door. I had no way to escape without walking directly past them. So, I decided to run for the bathroom and hide.

Just as I went to grab the bathroom door, I felt another hand. I looked up to see Langdon trying to open the door for me.

"What are you doing?" I exclaimed.

"I'm holding the door for you. What are you doing?"

"Clearly, I'm trying to go to the bathroom."

"Okay. Can I talk to you when you're done?"

"Fine."

I joined him and his friends when I finished pretending to go to the bathroom. He apologized to me for everything, and for the first time ever, he told me he loves me, and he swept me off my feet. It wouldn't be until the summer of 2020, when I lived in New York City, that I finally watched *Sex in the City*. Watching Carrie and Big do their little dance of love felt like I was reliving my entire relationship with Langdon

So, we went to Norway and had the most magical trip I have ever had in my life to this very day.

In May 2016, I found messages between him and another woman. Nothing had happened between them physically yet, but it might as well have. When I confronted him about it, he broke up with me and immediately started to sleep with her.

I still had keys to his house, so one night, before his roommates ever knew we had broken up, while Langdon was at work, I went into his house, took every gift he had ever given me and hundreds of pictures of us, and TPed his entire room and bathroom with all of it. Then, I took pictures of us, and in every book that he owned, I put one inside. (He is a big reader guy.) That way, anytime he ever tried to read a book of his again, he would be reminded of how shitty a boyfriend he was.

You might call this crazy, but to this day, I still think it is hilarious to imagine his reaction, coming home to this at 4 a.m., after a long shift of bartending. I even left a picture of myself giving a kissy face in his toilet to greet him at his next pee, and a bitmoji cartoon I made of him that said, "Langdon is the Batman." But I crossed out *the* and added *not,* instead. I'm a goddamn genius. This is the type of petty bullshit I do to people in retaliation. At least it makes me laugh forever, and I didn't hurt anyone in the process.

He had also just lent me $2,000 for school, and I decided to take that money, go buy my dream dog, and never pay him back. I know: I will rescue pets in the future. In this moment, though, I was the one who needed rescuing. I knew I wasn't going to be getting out of bed for anything, so I needed something to take care of, which in turn would help me take care of myself.

In September 2016, I got a handwritten letter in the mail.

> *Katie, I'm Sorry...*
>
> *Everything you said in the letter you left me was true. I've read it over and over, and it leaves me broken inside every time. I am realizing and reconciling the person I <u>think</u> I am with the one my <u>actions</u> clearly <u>prove</u> I am.*

You were right that I need help, and I am getting it. Maybe I don't know what it really is to love someone. I don't know if a person can love another person, if you don't know how to trust/believe/accept/be honest with that other person. I don't know why, but I am/was incapable of believing in myself or you. I'm so sorry for that. I allowed outside influences from the beginning to create negative beliefs in my already insidious mind, and I was never able to let them go. This was so unfair to you and us. I have allowed these insidious thoughts to guide my actions and decisions throughout our relationship, and for many years before that, for far too long.

I know I must break this selfish, misguided cycle if I am ever to be happy or make another person happy. I am so sorry I allowed this behavior to hurt such a wonderful person as you.

I've made many mistakes in my life because of what other people thought and how I viewed their importance and relevance. I've lost out on many things in life because of this.

I can live and accept many mistakes that I've made, for these reasons and others. The biggest mistake I've ever made is losing YOU. Never understanding and accepting the LOVE we had for each other is the worst mistake of my life. I never realized how much I loved you. I never admitted how much YOU gave me. I never accepted that I might love you more than anyone. I never allowed myself to believe that was possible. I've severed a piece of my body by losing you, and now I must live with that hole inside me because of my blind and selfish actions. I know I must learn from this ultimate mistake if I am ever to grow. I love you, Katie.

I hope you have endless happiness in your life. You are an extraordinary woman with the potential to change and heal the world. I know you were able to make me feel more than ever before. Stay amazing and beautiful.

I hope, one day, we can go on another adventure together.

My love, my Cleopatra, my Ophelia, my Dr. Beckett, my Katie...

Langdon Larkin Lytle

We didn't get back together. We decided to start seeing the same therapist. And decided that the part of our relationship that did not need any help was the sexual aspect. So, we agreed to be celibate for a year and work on ourselves.

I was celibate for a year, I even went back to church during this time. Langdon even came with me. We took a trip to Tampa right after the New Year, and he took me to Bern's Steakhouse and a hockey game. (I used to be a *huge* hockey guy.) He then took me by his favorite diner and pointed out the condos across the street.

"I imagine, when we move here, that is where we will live while you go to medical school and I open my own restaurant."

He was imagining our future together. After that trip, we continued to dream and plan the idea of moving to Tampa/St. Pete, together.

I spent the summer of 2017 working on Nantucket Island. When I got back, Langdon and I planned to have a conversation about our relationship.

"I have put a lot of thought into this while you've been gone," he began. "I realize I have an issue with commitment. So, I started to think of all the things I have always wanted to commit to but never have. I have always wanted to buy a brand-new car, I have always wanted to open my own restaurant/bar, and I have always wanted to be able to fully commit to you. So, as a way to learn how to commit to things, I bought a new Toyota 4-Runner."

He's got to be fucking kidding me, I thought.

I found out later he had been sleeping with other people during the entire time we'd said we would be celibate. I lost my damn mind.

Was this his way of controlling me? I wondered. *To make sure I wasn't sleeping with anyone else, while he got to do whatever he wanted? What the fuck is wrong with him?*

So, I started to date other people. It was that Halloween, 2017, when I ran into Langdon again at 3rd & 3rd. At that point, I brought up the idea of friends with benefits. We clearly did not know how to stay away from each other, I thought, so maybe, if we were just extremely honest with each other, this could work.

The only problem with being extremely honest with someone else was Langdon was not good at it. I had spent every Thanksgiving and Christmas with Langdon and his family since 2013. That year was not going to be any different. To my knowledge, Langdon was not seeing anyone other than me, which was why I was so surprised when his ex-girlfriend from all those years ago contacted me to inform me Langdon was spending Christmas with *her* that year. He was sleeping with her again. I also came to find out he was also sleeping with one of his coworkers whom we used to visit; she later become his next girlfriend.

So, at this point, I was done. I gathered up my Christmas gifts for his family, went to his parents' house, and told them everything he had done. I let them know I probably wouldn't be seeing them anymore. I left and immediately got online to send Langdon a glitter bomb. In the color of crimson, of course. His favorite football team's color, and the color of his brand-new Toyota 4-Runner, the car he chose to buy instead of committing to me. Remember?

The only thing I could not predict was where he would open this thing. Imagine the joy that overcame me when I found out, years later, he did in fact open that glitter bomb in that brand-new Toyota 4-Runner, which continued to have glitter inside until he sold it last summer, when I moved to St. Pete to be with him.

After that Christmas, we didn't speak for almost a year. I found out through the grapevine he'd moved to St. Pete during the summer of 2018. I was so proud of him. He'd finally escaped the toxicity of Delray. As happy and as proud of him as I was, I couldn't help but feel completely abandoned. I reached out to tell him how proud of him I was. The chat was friendly, but I quickly became adamant that he tell me if he was still in a relationship. He told me he was going to write me a letter to explain everything. This is what he sent:

> *Katie,*
> *I have so many thoughts on my mind when it comes to you and me and us. A complex subject, only because I made it so. Although there is great complexity within a simple and straight-forward idea or feeling or relationship. The simple and straight-forward idea of this letter is to apologize and express an understanding.*
> *I am so sorry for not allowing us the real chance at a long, loving honest relationship. I sabotaged our beautiful connection at every*

opportunity because of my scared and childish mindset and behavior. I was too concerned/obsessed with what others thought or said. I should have trusted my initial instincts, (something I'm just now being able to accomplish) and what I saw from and in you that brought us together. The times of clarity, where nothing interfered, when there was only you + me + us, were amazing. I was too scared to move forward or let go of the past to fully understand how amazing, at the time.

Sadly, I should have been concerned about what I was losing by not committing and understanding the amazing connection. I understand more and more that emotions and interactions from my childhood have created so much of this scared insecurity and mistrust of myself and others. But I think that also is a cop-out and excuse for poor behavior to some extent.

I am and will always be sorry and sad for how I mistreated and misunderstood you. You are a kind, loving, beautiful, intelligent, creative woman! I should have never doubted the purity of your emotions and intentions. I should have followed my instinctual heart that wanted to know you immediately.

That I allowed weakness to lead me instead is sad and awful and unforgiveable. I should have honored you instead of abusing you. And if I wasn't man enough to do that, I should have let you go and move forward. Ultimately, I was a weak child and could not do either. I am so sorry.

The mere fact you would still reach out to me or read this letter is a testament to your soul and persona and goodness. I must have been a blind idiot not to understand that for so many years. It is very difficult to reconcile the way I mistreated you with the man I believe and want to be. I am changing and understanding so much more because of the time spent with our therapist, and I have you to thank for that relationship, too.

I know I have apologized repeatedly, but again, I am sorry for mistreating you and your emotions, for not believing in the power of our connection, and for short-changing both of us for even more wonderful memories.

I am not seeking forgiveness, nor do I think I deserve it. I only want to express my understanding of what went wrong, what I took for granted, and the fault that belongs solely to me. And my understanding of what an amazing and beautiful person you were and are.

I am excited and happy for all the wonderful and inspiring things you are accomplishing. You will be an amazing doctor!

I am sorry and sad that it has taken me this long to understand and see the way everything was and is. I could go on but...
LOVE YOU ALWAYS,

Langdon (L-Cubed)

We continued to talk after I got that letter. He came to my apartment days before Christmas that year, to catch up. He was still with his girlfriend and former coworker. He didn't tell me any of that until I asked him, point blank in front of my face. So, I gave him until the end of the day to tell her, or I was going to. I wasn't going to let him do to another girl what he had done to me for so long.

He couldn't, so I sent her the letter and our texts from the previous couple of months. She moved to St. Pete to live with him a few months later, anyway.

The next year was my final undergrad year. This was the year I lost my Nana and Papa while living out of my car and when I graduated, all in the last three months of the year.

Langdon sent me a picture of my Nana and Papa playing Scrabble from a trip we took to San Diego in 2015 on his birthday, December 2, 2019. I got it the same day as my Nana's funeral. I was enraged. I had reached out to him before my Papa died, asking for him to send me that picture for them to see before they died. Because of the relationship he was in at the time, he did not respond, though. Instead, he sent it on his birthday, when he was alone, because everything was always about him.

This on-again, off-again situation with the girlfriend who moved to St. Pete to live with Langdon went on for a few years. Just like our relationship had. Anytime they broke up, he reached out to me. Then, they would get back together, and he would pretend to hate me again and block me on everything. Their relationship finally ended in the spring of 2021.

I know how hard he tried to be a better person for her. He tried to be and do all of the things he couldn't do for me, but he still didn't know how to be entirely honest even in that relationship. I know he was heartbroken when he ended it. But he could tell there was no going back: the trust was broken beyond repair, and they were both miserable. So, he left her because he loved her, not because he didn't.

We started to talk again in the summer of 2021, just as friends. Then, we came up with the idea that he would pay me $50 a week to be his "therapist" and he couldn't take anything I had to say personally. So, I tried to coach him through his relationship with this new girl he was into.

We were both seeing other people. Anytime he tried to make negative or judgmental comments, I would ignore him. His opinion on my relationships no longer impacted me. I knew what I wanted in my life and relationships, and I was confident in who I was and who I was becoming.

I invited him to one of my best friend's weddings in Florida in October, 2021. It was the first time we had seen each other in person since that day he visited my apartment, before Christmas 2018.

While we were drunk that night, he tried to fight with me over how little attention I was giving to him. I was a bridesmaid, and this was my best friend. In the past, with any of my former, emotionally abusive boyfriends, I would have given into a situation like this. But this time was different. I remembered who the fuck I was in that moment.

"This is my best friend's wedding," I said, standing up for myself. "You were invited as a guest. I am a bridesmaid for *her* wedding. This night is not about *you*. It is about her! So, if you don't like it, you can leave."

The game had changed, and for the first time we were on a level playing field. He stayed. I introduced him to ethical non-monogamy unsuccessfully, and he became a partner I could trust, ten years after the first time he threw nuts at my face. I moved to St. Pete in September 2022. Langdon, Charlie (the dog I bought with his money I never paid back), and I drove together from Cambridge, Massachusetts to St. Petersburg, Florida as a family.

Now, when I experience rage, I treat Langdon like he is the cause of all my problems. I domino everything he's ever done to me in the past onto what is happening in the moment and take everything out on him, even though I have chosen to be in this relationship and forgive him for the past.

It is unfair for me to do that. In every relationship, you will have to forgive the other person at some point. I don't think it is fair to stay in relationships where you are unable to forgive the other person and continuously bring up the past.

I have never wanted Langdon to feel indebted to me. I have always wanted to have a partnership that is equal. I have worked very hard to get to a place where I don't experience the rage and hurt that I experienced in my past. Unfortunately, when it comes to trauma, you don't always know when or why you will be triggered.

I do know being around my family triggers me. It's painful to be ignored, especially by those who are supposed to love you most. To me, my existence and who I am as a person has felt incredibly ignored by my family my entire life. What hurts even more is fighting for people who don't see you or understand you.

I spent most of my life believing I handled my pain appropriately. I always allowed myself to feel my sadness, but what I didn't realize is just how important anger is in the healing process. I never let myself feel angry until a few years ago. Once I entertained the idea of anger, the floodgates immediately burst open, and I was fucking pissed. I don't think I have stopped being pissed since. I have just learned better ways of managing my rage.

Rage hit me in the face the day I recognized how my family constantly tried to tell me how I felt and how I experience things, without ever once listening to what I was trying to tell them. I've been called a liar my entire life, as though I couldn't possibly know how I feel on my own without someone telling me how I feel and what I mean.

Sometimes, when I am around my family, I am reminded of how Langdon used to treat me as though I was a liar in the same way. As if the walls started to close in, and I'd lost my shit and I was right back in the days after leaving Havenwyck, twenty pounds lighter, floating through the world as though I'd just received a lobotomy.

My family, friends, and what felt like the world had tried to strip me of everything I am as a person, just to make themselves more comfortable. That is when the rage becomes uncontrollable, the second I feel like anyone is trying to put me back in a cage.

Giving in to my rage keeps me further from happiness more than anything else. I have chosen to be with Langdon despite the past. To hold on to the pain and anger of the past while staying in this relationship would be making the choice to torture myself. There are a lot of things in our lives we choose to hold onto that only bring us negative emotions. We hold onto the past so often, as though doing so will somehow impact the person who has done us wrong, instead of recognizing that the only person we are hurting is ourselves. We rob ourselves of joy and the ability to experience happiness when we do this.

So, when bad memories creep up or a triggering moment occurs that makes me want to lash out, or when I find the Lego dolls Langdon and his ex made of themselves, when they were together, which he still has, I try to take a moment. See it for what it is. Do I still have things from exes? Yes. Does it mean I still want to be with them? No. Do I care about them? Yes. Does my care for them impact the relationship I am in? No. And the same goes for him and his past.

Who are Langdon and I now? Who are we becoming? Are we continuing to grow together? These are the questions that actually matter to me in my relationship.

We all have a past, but I don't want to live in the past, and I sure as hell don't want to hold onto it. I will say I would not be with Langdon today if it weren't for his ability to have very hard conversations. Not only that, but his ability to be self-reflective and understand which parts of our past and his actions hurt and why. The awareness, growth, and his actions to make sure those things don't repeat themselves are why I am so proud of this man. It is so hard to make the choice to change.

It was very hard to have so many people know our entire story and know what judgement they must pass on us, but to decide to say "fuck it" anyway. But you know what was harder? Trying to stay away from each other for so long, based on what everyone else had to say about us, while ignoring what we intuitively knew to be true about each other.

I have no idea what people have to say about us now. I don't think he does, either. And honestly, both of us being writers, I bet we could come up with more entertaining stories about ourselves than our haters ever could.

We've chosen happiness. And choosing happiness is hard. Especially when everyone in the world likes to think they know better about your own happiness than you do. But you know. You always know what will make you happy. You have just gotta make sure you choose you.

Chapter 14

Fuck Personal Development

"There can be no keener revelation of a society's soul than the way in which it treats its children."

—Nelson Mandela

THE DOUBLE-EDGED SWORD and necessary evil.
It was 2017. I was twenty-eight years old and just recently enrolled in a Biological Sciences Pre-Med bachelor's program at Florida Atlantic University in Boca Raton. I was staring at the back of the rice-and-beans package at the Publix in downtown Lake Worth, Florida. I had been there for four hours. I was hungry when I'd gotten here and border-lining a migraine coupled with rage, as my stomach grumbled for the tenth time that hour.

This package has more than five ingredients in it and I don't understand more than half of what they are. Beans and rice are only a complete protein when eaten together, but I don't want to have to cook them separately. It's going to take too long if I don't buy canned beans, but I can't buy canned beans. I need protein, but I hate quinoa. I can't think straight.

All the food in my cart is fresh and going to go bad in a few days, and I live alone. Oh my God, I waste so much food. I'm so tired. I can't afford this much food just for it all to go bad. I can't buy these eggs, they need to be from a local farm. Even if the carton says free-range, that just means they're overcrowded in a building and not locked down. I can't find any raw milk in this area, and I can't continue using almond milk with how much water goes to waste. I can't be here anymore.

I walked around the grocery store, putting everything back where they belonged after spending the past four hours strategically picking everything out, based on my being vegan, gluten-free, with needed protein and close enough as I could to my budget, but I knew I still couldn't afford it.

So, I headed to my nannying job where I hovered over the kids as they ate dinner. Then, I ate their leftover scraps of chicken nuggets, French fries, and macaroni n' cheese, hating myself but at least I was not wasting food. I was exhausted by the time I got home and stressed to the max. Langdon had broken up with me months ago to sleep with another woman, and I'd thrown myself into personal development, to find the perfect way to eat for everyone else but me.

I woke up the next morning after crying myself to sleep, again, and walked into the bathroom. My hair was so thin, tangled, and dry. I was trying to brush through it when there it was... I should have known this was coming. I could have bet it was, if I was actually listening to my body like I should be. A perfectly circular bald spot the size of a half dollar on the side of my head. I'd been killing myself to be "healthy" and this is the proof.

I'd recently completed a course to become a certified holistic health coach and nutritionist, and I couldn't imagine ever wanting a client to treat themselves the way I had been treating myself. It was time to take a big step back before I hurt myself anymore.

But I'm not good at moderation. I am a zero-to-a-hundred girl. I didn't know how to merge a reclusive celibate homebody vegan, training for *American Ninja Warrior* and going back to school to be a doctor with the party-till-you-drop, chain-smoking sexual wild child. I had to choose one or the other, and to be honest, the only one I could actually afford financially and mentally at that moment was the wild child, because, let's be real, no full-time college student working four jobs can afford to eat healthy in this country, so fuck it. In the worst of times, I can always rely on my ability to turn on the full-blown survival mode, burning the candle at both ends plus in the middle. So, let's do it!

Which I did. For the next three years, I did exactly that, until my pseudo-seizure in February 2020, which brought me to a screeching halt. My body knew better. It knew I needed healing.

After Langdon and I broke up in the summer of 2016, I'd started to get a taste of alone time. I started to lean into what being alone looked like. But I had to be productive, and I didn't have time to love myself the way I should have been. So, it manifested in other ways.

Whether that meant taking out my sexual traumas on current partners by blowing up on them mid-intercourse or treating every man I came across as though he had wronged me the same way my ex did, it was going to come out one way or another. I didn't know how to love myself, yet I wanted everyone around me to love me the way I wanted to be loved. I couldn't imagine I was capable of hurting anyone because I couldn't imagine anyone caring enough about me to be bothered by anything I did. That's just how little I thought of myself.

I am so sick of the culture we have created around personal development. Somehow, in this insanely unhealthy culture of grind, we have managed to turn even our free time into to-do lists of self-discovery and joy! We must schedule time for joy in this day and age. Make sure you're meditating, doing yoga, working out, stretching, taking your vitamins, taking your supplements, drinking your warm water with lemon, definitely don't forget that tongue scraper, and oh, you're vegan? Well, you're going to be deficient in iron and B12 and so many other things, so you'd better switch to keto, but they say it'll take five years off your life, so actually we're doing Whole30 now. But you can't do any of that without first getting tested for all of your allergies, and I almost forgot, are you journaling every day? Wow, I can't believe you still eat dairy. Oh my God, and *sugar*? Sugar is the worst drug on *Earth*! Same with alcohol—we're all sober now! Don't forget to manifest, *Don't you dare forget to manifest*. You know you're manifesting every moment of the day, so you might as well be intentional about it. But before you do any of that, you must clear every single negative aspect of life that has happened to you through hundreds of lifetimes, then you can come back and make your vision board and start believing you actually deserve more in life, but don't start thinking too highly of yourself. You don't want your followers to think you're too cocky, definitely don't forget to humble yourself. And once you're done with that, make sure you're getting at least eight hours of sleep and drinking 120 ounces of water, but don't drink it too fast, because your body won't absorb it properly, and you'll just end up pissing it all out. Are you counting your macros? Are you spending time alone? Do you have good friends? What about therapy? Are you doing EMDR now? Because you can't simply be doing *just* talk therapy. Are you recycling? *Your town doesn't have recycling*?!

Are you tired yet? Because I am fucking exhausted. I am so exhausted, in fact, I honestly don't even feel like writing this right now. I am sitting at my desk and while typing this to you, all I can think about is how I haven't worked out in two months, haven't meditated in a week, my body feels weak, and I am not eating properly, but for the first time in my life, I am pretty okay with not hitting all the things I am striving to accomplish all the fucking time.

I can't lie and say self-help and personal development are bullshit, because they're not. It definitely has had a huge impact on getting me to where I am today. But man, the way we have tackled this industry is a nightmare. The fact that it's an industry is, like, what the fuck, man?

Here's the thing, though. I am extremely grateful for my journey and all the things I have learned to get me to where I am now. If it wasn't for all of the personal development I have done, I definitely would not be where I am today. However, if I was raised to believe certain things as a child, would I have needed to go through all this personal development?

We've spent our entire lives teaching ourselves what to hate about us, just to turn right around on this rollercoaster and decide, "Oh, shit, now I gotta go back and unlearn everything I've ever known." In the future, can we just raise our kids to love themselves, listen to themselves, and be whomever the fuck they wanna be in this world?

For the sake of humanity, I hope the generations living on Earth right now are the first and last generations to be inundated by personal development. If not, then we haven't actually learned shit, and personal development will become just another notch in our belts of comparison to say who is better than the person next to them. Seriously, this guru shit of comparing how to become more enlightened than the person next to them and who is right and who is wrong is just the modernized war between religions.

Let's just love all the kids all the time. Let's figure out how to love ourselves and how to be happy for others loving themselves, okay? Like, this could be a Barbie World and we could all be Barbie Girls, but everyone is so concerned with who is going to be the best Barbie! *We are all Barbie!*

Chapter 15

This World is Not Fair, but There is Peace in the Chaos

"There's no lemon so sour that you can't make something resembling lemonade."

—*This is Us*

I DON'T TALK MUCH about being a scientist. Just writing that sentence creates a pressure in my gut that ends at me biting both my upper and lower lips as I suck them in to stop myself from crying.

I loved science and math as a kid. Not in the same way I loved writing, creativity, and art, but in the way you love something that comes easy to you. It's easy to enjoy something you're good at, and science and math were my natural talents, although I tried to ignore that for my entire adolescent life.

The problem I had once going back to university at age twenty-eight was I was finally enrolled in courses that were challenging for me. They were going too fast to teach myself, and I was never a person who could learn science or math from my professors. I always saw my own patterns and understandings in how these puzzles worked, and trying to listen to anyone other than myself confused the hell out of me.

Getting into Cornell was something that was never on my radar. To be honest, it kind of just happened in the middle of a manic year filled with death, alcohol, graduation, and a pandemic. All of a sudden, I was going to Cornell, an Ivy League school with the university statement, "Break the rules." Fuck yeah!

But the more I tried to understand my peers over Zoom and learn from my teachers at a distance in the lab, the more I realized there was an unspoken set of rules everyone abides by in the scientific community. It's been predominantly selective, sexist, racist, and held to a code of ethics understood as part of the good ole boy's code of ethics. More or less, the idea is don't ask, don't tell, and we can publish. I don't want my words to be mistaken. I am a scientist. I believe in science. I also believe in good scientists. I also believe that 90% of the scientists I have worked with do follow an honorable code of ethics. If they didn't, I probably wouldn't be in the position I am today.

I spent my childhood looking at the stars with my dad every night before I would go to bed. He always would point out Orion's belt to me. The first time I ever saw the movie *Apollo 13,* I remember believing we were watching the news. I felt as though I was experiencing this moment of history in real time.

In fourth grade, we had to make our first diorama incorporating hydraulics based on a biography of our choosing. I chose Amelia Earhart, and I used the hydraulics to depict her airplane flying over the Bermuda Triangle. This was the first time I had used my scientific skills, along with my creativity, to build something I was ecstatic to show people. Why wasn't everyone else as excited as I was about creating this moment in time?

The next year, in fifth grade, we learned how electricity worked. Our task was to design a house on cardboard and figure out how to have all the lightbulbs connect, so that each individual room could be turned on and off separately from the others, while all maintaining the same power source. We finished ours so quickly and were the only group able to make ours work, so we started adding additional rooms and levels, just for the fun of it. No one was paying attention to me, because at the same time I had just transferred to a higher-level school, where our classes were a combination of fifth and sixth graders. I didn't know how to assimilate into my new environment.

The school was different, the classes were different, and people who I thought were my friends treated me as though I was a stranger. I have no recollection of who my actual friends were, but I do remember that house and the electricity I created.

In middle school, we had a science project about mold growing on bread. The experiment came and went, but I couldn't let it go. I needed to know what had happened to the bread, even after the experiment ended. I wanted to know the full cycle. I wanted to understand every detail.

In ninth grade, I got caught smoking weed during Labor Day weekend and was immediately sent to become friends with my brother and all his church friends. So, I dove head-first into Christianity in a way I never had in my life. I sought to understand the religious beliefs about evolution, as that was one of my major project topics for ninth grade biology.

I hope someone reading this got to see the PowerPoint presentation I gave about evolution and the Bible. It started with a photo of Jesus's face and the sound of a heartbeat, to really bring out the dramatics. I was fucking serious. I had been forced into a world where I wasn't allowed to believe in science, and I didn't know how to take it, other than to dive in head-first and hope for the best, I guess.

In tenth grade, I took an astronomy course. The sky never had any denomination or connection to faith, for me. The universe existed beyond the explanations of science or faith. I thrived on my connection to something that couldn't be defined as one or the other. Most people took the class as an easy elective. It was the class I took most seriously. Part of our homework was to watch the phases of the moon on a nightly bases and track it for the entire semester. I was the only person in the class to do this. I happily gave everyone my worksheets to copy, just so we wouldn't have to waste time with our professor being disappointed with the class, and we could get to discussion, talking about how fascinating the sky is. High schoolers falsifying tracking the moon phases is a battle I am willing to leave where it lies.

Then, I was heartbroken when the cube I created for the egg-drop contest failed. All I could think about for weeks was how badly I wanted to repeat the experiment over and over again until I got it right. But no one cared how it worked, not even the people who won, and no one cared about the moon or what happened to the bread after it got too ugly to look at. No one wanted to know why their light circuits didn't work or how to fix them. They just wanted someone else to do it for them which I obliged because to me it was fun. And no one wanted to know why hydraulics worked better than pneumatics for our dioramas, but I did. And no one ever noticed.

No one was paying attention, and much like my ability of understanding non-monogamy could be a thing or I was allowed to like girls, I was not aware or ever taught my creativity wasn't only allowed for painting, writing, drawing, charcoal, or clay; I could have been using my creativity for science and math the entire time, and the basis of both subjects lies in the ability of the scientist to have creativity, an open mind, and to believe that possibilities are endless.

As adults we are not paying attention. We are not paying attention to what our children need from us. As children, we don't have the capacity to know what is available in the world, other than what we were told we are allowed to strive for. Based on what parents want for their children, they are usually shown a narrow set of paths they are "allowed" to take in life. It's hard for me not to wonder what could have been possible, had we all been given the option of all possibilities from the beginning.

I wasn't seen. And I craved so deeply for so long to be seen by anyone.

The modern-day Church attributes who you are as a human to whom you associate yourself with. It denies morals you have exist, based on those associations. When I was friends with Janis, the heroin addict, I was automatically assumed to be one too. The Church rarely acknowledges Jesus's association with the "wildebeests" or "low-lifes" of the world. But ya know, whatever. I'm not here to debate that. If you've made it this far, I am pretty sure you don't need me to go into depth about the hypocrisy of the Church. By the way, I hope someone calls me a wildebeest. Fuck, yeah. I am a wild beast. I pray to be nothing less than a wild-ass fucking beast of a lady.

And for that, I was sent away. As you know. Conforming in the Christian religion is very important when being raised in a Catholic household. If you do anything other than conform, the assumption is there is something wrong with you and you must be saved (brainwashed) at all costs. Because the idea you could possibly think anything different means the devil must be at large.

Morals, ethics, science, and religion are probably the most commonly debated topics in all of history. Debating morals and ethics amongst scientists can become tricky.

And when you are the lowest on the totem pole, the last thing an energetic student or employee wants to do is cause disruption.

But I am a disruptor. I am the whistleblower, and I don't know why there was ever a point in my life when I thought I might be able to hide that in order to further my own self interests. Because, at the core of it all, whistleblowing *is* my self-interest. Disrupting is my MO. And the day I created a new Facebook page, pretending like there would ever be a way for me to separate my personal life from my professional life, was a fucking joke.

I was in the shower at the gym today and had a flashback to summer camp. I am not exactly sure which camp it was, and perhaps it was just a conglomerate memory of all the different bathrooms and outdoor showers I remember. I could smell the forest in summertime and look up to see the tops of trees and the blue sky, while rinsing off from whatever disgusting activity we had just done.

The bathrooms filled with old wooden stalls barely hanging on, with concrete floors littered with daddy longlegs. Those daddy longlegs came back to my mind especially. The absolute fear and terror I had while showering, keeping my eye on them the entire time, and never stopping to take in the actual serenity in the moment.

Although I will never have back those moments in my life, for a second today, I was able to go back there, to feel and to see it for what it really was. As if I had time-traveled just to go back and appreciate the serenity and peace that surrounded me even in the midst of fear and anxiety, though I did not know how to at the time.

I think we spend most of our lives not appreciating the time we have in the moment. I know I am guilty of this. I don't want to live life like that anymore.

I am thirty-four years old, and I don't want to wait any longer to accept the beauty of life, to only look back on good times or look forward to when I'm finally done dealing with this shit. There is always shit; there is always going to be shit. I want to be happy regardless of the shit. So, I am going to be. This is my pact.

Times will get tough, depression is sure to come, but I am going to do everything in my power to see the beauty and to remember how lucky I am to have this life. I will do everything I can to get the most out of it.

In my professional career as a scientist, it didn't take long before I came up against my first ethics-less lab mate. It took two weeks. Twelve ten-plus-hour days, a three-day blizzard in Manhattan, and almost twenty different protocols in January 2021, with only five people to accomplish it all. Which Covid testing protocol was going to be the best? Which were the top five, and which one should win the award, during the height of Covid, for being most accurate and fastest?

They all sucked. I think only one or two of them came out with accurate results, and I am happy to say most of the testing protocols we went through, I never saw as products most commonly used during the pandemic.

The day came for us to submit our data to be published into an article summarizing all of the techniques we had tested.

As I looked over the data that had just been turned in, I noticed the numbers on the protocols I tested did not match the data I had collected.

"We analyzed way more than forty-nine for that protocol, and I put all of them on the original spreadsheet." I texted TJ, the woman leading our project.

"Breathe. It's all good. It's done."

"But it's not right."

I contacted the person in charge the next day and informed them of the falsified data. The work we did for Covid testing protocols was never published and never will be. Meaning the majority of the work I did during my master's program will never be published.

No one would have known, had I never said anything. I was a nobody in that lab. Luckily for me, I had an incredible leader who was willing to take the losses with the wins and was willing to hear me out. That makes me proud to have been part of that lab.

It was later discovered that the same person who falsified data had also falsified her PhD during the height of Covid, to gain the position she had. While this person goes on being published and recognized in numerous articles, I have yet to be published in one.

Should my own personal research be published? Yes. Does that have anything to do with them? Not exactly. But I would be lying if I said this moment didn't impact my entire career as a scientist. That moment broke my heart in a way so hard, it's still impossible for me to follow anyone online in the industry of my dreams.

Trust in science is built the same way as trust in relationships is built. As far as my heart is concerned, the scientific community has cheated on me more times than I can count. At some point, your heart gets broken enough to not want to try anymore. I know I don't work the same way "classically trained" scientists work, but that doesn't make the way I work or understand things wrong.

I also have the common knowledge to know the difference between what is wrong and right and the willingness to speak out in its presence. So, as much as my heart is broken based on these circumstances, there is not a moment when I regret my decisions. I knew back then I never wanted to be associated with the person who caused these infidelities to the science gods. And if my only stance in the scientific realm comes from being the person who refused to be associated with this liar, just to make themselves look better, then I did the best I could with what I had without compromising my integrity.

If there is anything this moment in my life made me recognize, it was integrity rarely gets the screentime it deserves. Why aren't there awards for integrity? Why aren't people acknowledged for what they have done when faced with adversity?

My master's ended without any direction, and I was left to fend for myself, after being rejected by every PhD program I applied to, using the same method I had with the master's program: being poor and needing them to cover the financial portion of my application. No one wanted me except for the Air Force and the Navy. I spent the summer in New York City, hoping a position would open at the lab where I had done my master's, and while applying to positions all over the world. I was desperate. I applied to over 750 positions.

Through personal conversations at the small startup where I ended up, in Cambridge, Massachusetts, I recognized just how much of a wildcard I am. However, even with that recognition, all it made me think was just how weak the companies are that I have applied to. Especially the ones I really cared to make a difference at. Their unwillingness to imagine anything other than the norm and how hiring someone like me is a risk. I am a risk, but I am also the biggest reward, if you actually mean what you say. Do you keep your word? Because I keep mine. Even when it comes to my flightiness.

Honestly, how often is integrity a value that companies look for in their employees? Based on the system we are living in, it feels more like integrity is something to be feared, when companies have too much to hide, which, unfortunately, seems far too often these days. What is up with this pretending to be good people?

Evolving With Integrity

The combination of growing up, educating myself, unlearning, and healing throughout my life has led to this point of heightened self-awareness, which can be incredibly difficult to navigate. I want to write this book, but I also want this possibility to exist for everyone. I want others who have experienced pain similar to my own to heal, but I also recognize my privilege of being white. When friends come to me with their painful stories and traumas and immediately rescind or diminish them by saying how they realize that other people have it harder or that their story isn't as bad as someone else's, I immediately remind them that pain is relative to our own personal experiences. The hardest thing my friend has ever been through is still the hardest thing they've ever been through, regardless of what that looks like to another person's hardest time.

Not to negate or diminish other people, especially BIPOC experiences, because those are very different things. Looking at my own advice toward friends, it is time I take it the way I would want them to. I can't possibly help the world without helping myself first. I can't be the kind of person people can rely on, if I don't work out my own shit first. I can definitely multitask, but to ignore doing the tough inner work on ourselves in the name of (God, Christ, the Church, or whatever else you believe) is doing a very great disservice to the world and only contributing more to the pain of the collective conscious.

I am a multidimensional human being. I allow myself to flow in and out of my own dislikes and likes, because they are ever-evolving in the same way I am. I have so many labels. Scientist, product manager, analog astronaut, problem solver, drag king, sister, aunt, friend, lover, partner, neurospicy, autistic, ADHD, PMDD, pansexual, sexual, writer, entrepreneur, girlfriend, woman, feminist, womanist in training, ally, advocate, initiator, catalyst, difficult, etc.... The list goes on.

But I don't fit. Because not one of those labels encompasses the entirety of who I am. And not one of anyone's labels do. We are so much more multifaceted, and instead of looking at this as a superpower, we look at these things as burdens. That somehow, if we just fit somewhere perfectly, it would end all of our problems.

But that journey takes us far down the rabbit hole of philosophy and what it means to have free will. These boxes we have created for ourselves have become cages, not permitting us to change our minds at any given moment, out of fear of being labeled fake, disingenuous, or a liar. Somehow, changing our minds has become a character defect, instead of the recognition of the enlightenment it really is.

Giving yourself permission to change at any given moment is the freshest air one can ever breathe. As a collective, we are so afraid of change, yet the entire essence of life is exactly that. I am terrified of things staying the same. Nothing makes me feel more uncomfortable than stagnancy. I am bored to death, because the collective male consciousness decided to make dick contests and ego-puffing the basis of our society, instead of joy and peace.

I refuse to be put into any box, but I want to feel a sense of belonging more than anything else. The way belonging looks to me in the world isn't hitting the mark, though.

I am used to being the world's side piece. People really like me. They always have. I make life easier for people to be themselves, until that mirror I am becomes more than they can tolerate.

When I was younger, I allowed myself to be people's secret friend/lover/person. So, it was easier (for them) to put me away and take me out when it was convenient for them, in times of self-reflection and wanting to be seen. As I got older and started to recognize this superpower I had, I became less and less willing to be the world's side piece. It hurts to be seen fully yet never appreciated or respected.

I am capable of working just as hard as I feel. Yet my emotional intelligence has been used against me my entire life. Somehow, being able to articulate how you feel immediately labels a person as unstable or irrational.

You won't put me in a box.

I have already been sent to the loony bin unwillingly. I have been told to get married in order to afford the cost of living. My own parents grounded me when they found out I liked girls and then pretended my coming out on social media was a joke, twenty years later.

I am still here, and my position has not changed. I will not conform. And in the words of Rage Against the Machine, "Fuck you. I won't do what you told me."

We have created all these fucking rules in this world based on shit made up in our own heads. Made up by people who have been put up on a pedestal, because it is easier to follow than it is to create change (supposedly). We make shit so fucking complicated, it drives me crazy.

The Road Less Traveled

A&W Worker: "MOOOOOOOM! The new girl knocked over all the cups!"

Twenty-four hours later...

"Hi, this is Katie Dickieson, the girl who started training yesterday. I am not going to be able to make it in today."

A&W Owner: "Oh, okay. Why is that? When will you be coming in to finish training?"

"I just don't want to, and I am never coming back."

Five years later... Winter, 2010

To my boss at the first hair salon, where I worked with Seth: "I quit. I left the key in the tree."

Two years later... Winter, 2012

Five days post-abortion, after the first one failed and I had to hide it from everyone...

Janet: "You cannot go home for Christmas. The salon is too busy, and we need you."

"Then I quit."

I turned around to leave the salon. My friend and roommate, Jessie, was working reception, and by the look on her face, I could tell she'd heard everything. I passed her on the way to the door. Just as I made it outside, I felt a hand grab my arm and spin me around. It was Janet. She shoved a packet of papers into my chest.

"Here's your non-compete."

As I lifted my hands in the air, the papers fell to the ground, and I laughed as I walked past her.

Five years later... Spring, 2017

"I want to talk to you about how you speak to all of us who work here. It is demeaning and very hurtful. I can see you are frustrated, but speaking to us the way you do, especially in front of customers, is not conducive for a productive work environment. It actually has the opposite effect on our ability to do a good job in this hostile environment.

"I love this place, and I care about the people and want to see it thrive, which is why I am bringing this to your attention. I want to let you know I am putting in my two weeks' notice today, but I wanted to make sure I came to you with this information on behalf of everyone else who will still be working here."

Andrea said, "Why would you even come in and waste my time today? I don't need you. You should have just never showed up at all. You can leave now."

"I know we are understaffed right now, and I know you're in a difficult position. I am willing to stay until you have the coverage you need," I replied.

"We don't need this. You can leave."

Four years later... Winter, 2021

Qian: "If you want to be able to afford a place to live in the same city you work, I suggest you get married."

"My salary is over $30,000 less than every employee in this city with the same job title as I have and experience as I do. My salary does not even cover the cost of living. My 'raise' is half the amount of inflation, which is actually a pay downgrade. This is not acceptable, to treat employees this way, and I will not work for a company that does."

This world is not fair. I stand by every decision I have made as a disruptor in my professional career, because I stood by my morals and ethics. I am at peace now because I acted with integrity every step of the way.

I don't know exactly what is next in my journey as integrity seems to create side streets, and the road less traveled. Which can feel like a pretty long road, if you ask me. But I have faith there is a reason for it all. I was never supposed to be a scientist or an artist. I was always meant to be both.

Chapter 16

Change is a Drug Unlike Any Other

"The measure of intelligence is the ability to change."
—Albert Einstein

DARLENE PUSHED THE SCISSORS onto my desk and into my hand. I slowly brought them down to my cargo pocket. I was wearing my favorite Army-print cargo pants I'd stolen from my brother, which were four sizes too big for me and held up by the infamous, silver-studded, black-leather belt from Hot Topic. Mine had been broken for months and was being held together by staples and duct tape, which was fine, because it made me look even more hardcore.

It was 2002, and I tried to pretend Avril wasn't who had given me permission to start dressing like a boy, I had done it before it was cool. The original hipster, but ya know, punk-rock hipster.

I raised my hand to ask Mrs. Warren if I could use the restroom, and I headed out down the long hallway of lockers to change my life forever. I walked in and stared at myself in the mirror. It was go time.

I flipped my head upside down and pulled my hair tie from one wrist, to gather all my hair into a pony tail and flip it back up. I reached for the scissors in my pocket and, without thinking, grabbed the tail of my hair with my left hand while taking the scissors above the hair tie with my right and started cutting.

It was so much harder than I had imagined. The scissors were very dull, and I couldn't see what I was doing. My hand was cramping, and I was shaking.

The time it took, longer than expected, was enough to allow my doubt to sink in. I didn't want anyone to know the pain I was suffering. Doing this was the ultimate way to tell the world I didn't give a fuck, when in actuality I cared more than most. But I couldn't let them know that. I had to make the entire world believe this is what I wanted, because if they knew how sad I actually was, then they would know how weak I was, and I couldn't let them know the truth.

I was shaking.

Can't anything ever be easy?

"Do you want some help?"

A girl came walking out of one of the stalls. She had been watching me. She didn't even ask me why I was doing what I was doing. She just offered to help.

I went back to class, ponytail in my pocket. All eyes fell on me. Everyone laughed as I showed it to the class.

"I told you I would do it."

The bell rang and I headed to my locker. This was middle school in the early 2000s, so we didn't have cell phones, but gossip spread like wildfire before I could finish exchanging my books for next period. My boyfriend met me, the guy I'd been passing notes with for a few days.

I wouldn't allow him to reject me. I said, "I did this to see if people actually like me for who I am." But I didn't even allow the guy I was seeing to make up his mind about me cutting off all my hair. Instead, I ended things with him to avoid more pain and continued to internalize everything.

My group of girlfriends had been telling me what to wear and how to act for two years, and I was sick of it. Luckily, they were too embarrassed to be friends with the girl who dressed like a boy and cut off all her hair, so I became a loner. That was when I found my safety in Black women.

Camille had been my closest friend outside my group for all of middle school, and she continued to be my friend even after I cut my hair. She invited me to sit with the only group of girls who made me feel accepted and didn't seem to be afraid of my being a lesbian: the Black girls' table.

We were in the suburbs of Detroit, where our friend groups and cafeteria seating assignments were categorized by your group's interests or sports, unless you were a Black girl. In that case, that was all you were. And somehow, people say segregation no longer exists.

My internal story was very different from what I portrayed outwardly. The thing was, though, I was both at the same time. Outwardly, I was this chick screaming "fuck the world" boldly and declaring I don't care what anyone thinks of me. I dropped my entire life from before. I didn't want friends or boyfriends who didn't like me for who I was, and I wore my tough exterior like armor, hoping someone would love me enough to penetrate it without ever really knowing who the real me was. Having to grow up faster than others makes it difficult to find space to develop joy.

I have always been a catalyst for change, because I know first-hand how big change is easier if you just jump without looking or calculating first. We will never be ready for what taking the leap will throw at us. We just have to trust in ourselves to know we've handled what we have in the past and then believe in our abilities to do the same in the future.

Begging to be loved but terrified of being hurt: this is a dangerous and lonely place to be. I forced myself to grow up too quick, because I had to protect myself. Chopping off all my hair threw me to the wolves of reality in this world. I already had known just how unkind the world can be, so I made a statement that acknowledged it, accepted it, and made me a magnet for those who felt the same, so I collected fellow misfits along the way.

I wasn't going to survive in the world I was born in. That is what people who don't understand me don't realize. I was thirteen years old and had already tried to kill myself multiple times. *As a child.* I couldn't control any aspect of my life, and no one was listening to me. Everything I did was looked at as wanting attention, as though there was something wrong for wanting my parents to see me for who I truly was.

But wanting attention as a child is one of the worst sins you can commit, and once you are guilty of it, you will forever be treated like every move you make is for that same attention. "Attention-seeker" will overshadow every aspect of your human existence until the day comes (if it does) you finally gain your parents' respect and they are willing to start listening to you.

It took a master's degree from Cornell University before my mom finally looked at me one day and said, in awe, "What have you done with my daughter?" As though that little girl who wrote seven-page-long letters begging for communication in a family, that angsty tween who chopped off her hair, or that teenager who was sent away couldn't possibly be the same person who earned a master's degree from an Ivy League school.

"I am the same person I have always been. You just didn't listen."

This is my way of saying enough is enough, it's time for me to rid myself of this self-inflicted cage once and for all. If I strip myself naked in front of the world, then maybe other people might gain the courage to do the same.

I can't think of a more beautiful world to live in than one where everyone is safe enough to be their truest selves entirely. The only way we get to that point in the world we're living in today, though, is by radical acts of self-love that, unfortunately, put us in very vulnerable positions to be punished, labeled, and ridiculed for being exactly as we are.

I am ever-changing, ever-evolving, always learning, and always growing into the next phases and chapters of my life. I give myself the permission to change. To change my mind, change my hair, change my relationship preferences, change my passions—to change anything I want to at any given moment, because this is my life. I want to empower you to give yourself the same permission.

By giving ourselves the permission to change, we are then also giving ourselves the permission to have been in the wrong without ridicule. To be able to admit mistakes without fear. So often in this world, when people admit to their shortcomings or the mistakes they have made, their opponents want to point fingers, as though somehow berating a person after they've already acknowledged their limitations or errors will somehow set in stone just how right *"we"* were and just how wrong *"they"* were. We pride ourselves more in being right than in celebrating the joining and community of people coming together. And we wonder why it's so difficult for people to admit when they've been wrong.

If we want this world to change, if we want our communities to change, we need to be willing to allow people to admit to their wrongdoings without execution. It's exhausting, trying to teach people how to love you. It's not a Black person's job to teach a White person how to not be racist, and it's not a woman's job to teach men how not to be misogynistic. No one wants to have to beg to be loved properly, nor should they have to. But we live in a society that has been built on thousands of years of these painful ways of living being the norm. They cannot just be erased. We need education, empathy, and compassion more than anything right now. And it starts in the adults. It starts with us, because if we don't heal as a whole, these cycles will be passed on for generations, just as they were passed on to us.

Right now, I am giving myself permission to change. For the first time in my life, I am sitting in a life where I am not just surviving any longer. I am not where I want to be, but I am safe. I could spend the rest of my days working up the corporate ladder, buying a house, getting married, having kids, retiring, maybe traveling the world some, and then die. I know that. I also know those things alone will not fulfill me.

I am fucking terrified to take a chance, now that I feel safety is something I have to lose. That safety isn't real, though. That life I just described is the prescribed life we've been fed our entire lives, as the "right way" of living, like there's some fucking rule book on life. There's no fucking rulebook, and you can change your mind whenever the fuck you feel like it!

Chapter 17

The Synergistic Flame

"Sometimes life has a way of pointing us in the right direction."
—Mr. Feeny in *Boy Meets World*

"**D**O YOU OWN A microscope?"
This was a question I had been dying to hear for almost ten years.

In 2014, I earned a certificate as a health coach for holistic nutrition. A year later, I took a course in live blood analysis. The intention was to do live blood analysis as part of my process in assigning protocols for cleanses to people, under my new LLC, The Origin of You.

The problem was, I didn't believe in myself. Not only did I not believe in myself, but I didn't want to charge people for my services, because I wanted everyone to have access to the information I had to help them.

I never had a single paying client. I did analysis for all of my friends and family and anyone else I would talk to who seemed interested. Then, just as quickly as it started, it ended. I didn't feel confident defending the science, when I hadn't been to school for that type of science. I wanted to be able to defend what I believed in and to help people with both Eastern and Western medicine.

I was sitting on the side of a fjord in Geiranger, Norway when the inspiration clicked. Mountains have that effect on people. If you're ever indecisive and at a crossroads in life, go stand on top of a mountain. I am sure you'll find your next steps there.

"I am going back to school for nursing. I will figure out the steps and enroll the second we get back," I proclaimed to Langdon, the Seven Sisters, and the rest of Norway.

I got back from Norway and did exactly what I said I was going to. I found the best nursing program I could find in the area and went to the registrar's office. Here's the thing, though. I didn't know how any of this process worked. I didn't even know you could only join college at certain times in the year. I didn't know who to talk to, how loans work, what the fuck a grant is, or how to find what classes I needed to take. These were the hardest and most tedious parts about going to school, and they don't teach you any of this information in high school. I certainly didn't get this information the summer going into my senior year, which I had spent under the Baker Act.

I had failed so miserably the only year I attended college (besides the few classes I took for business, right after cosmetology school), straight out of high school, that I had to complete an associate's degree from scratch. I had to retake all the classes I had already failed twice before, classes I had already taken in high school, when I was bored. I took eighteen credits a semester and had my associate's within a year.

I went back to school to become a nurse. I thought, at the age of twenty-eighty there wasn't much I was allowed to do with my life, at that point. So, I settled for second-best. I don't know about you, I don't know where you are at in your journey. If you're already following and conquering your dreams and have forged your way ahead, you probably will remember what I am about to describe. As for those who are still in the beginning of your journey, there are going to be moments that come along, once you start to align yourself with the universe. In those moments, doors are going to start opening like you've never seen or experienced before, as if the universe is on your side and telling you, "Keep going!" It's going to feel that way because *it is*.

I knew I wanted more than to become a nurse, but that didn't stop me from becoming the best I could, in order to become the best nurse I could possibly be. When I went back to university, I was taking eighteen credits a semester, working three jobs, and getting no less than a 4.0 GPA. I was on a mission. I was inspired, and I was on track.

In pursuit of your dreams, there are multiple stages that become transformative and pivotal moments, which you never expect. Moments that will put everything you've been working toward directly in front of your face, asking, "Is this what you really want? Or have you just grown so comfortable on this path, you're afraid to pivot/change/redirect your efforts?"

Just as fluidly as the weather patterns change, we, as humans, change every second of every day. Our dreams, beliefs, ideals, wants, and needs are constantly changing. They should and they need to, in order for us to grow. If we fight that need to adapt and evolve into our higher self, we become stuck in a place we're not meant to be. We forget how to move. The universe stops giving us those *keep going* signs, and life becomes a loop of stagnant energy. The universe is not always going to say, "Keep going" all the time. This is something to remember. I will touch more on it later. But right now, it is really important to home in on the moments when the universe is pushing forward for you and recognize how to embrace these moments and signs.

I was in my third and final semester at Palm Beach State College, finishing my associate's degree before moving on to nursing school. It was April 2017, and I had all my boxes checked, signed, and ready to be reviewed by my advisor, in order to apply for the nursing program. I was *pumped*. Not only had I finished my associate's degree in three semesters, but I had a 4.0 GPA, I was killing it, and most definitely was going to be accepted for the program.

I walked into the advising office, signed in for my advisor, Carol. She was the woman in charge of the nursing program, the only person I'd ever spoken to, whenever I went into the office. I sat down and waited.

A few moments later, a different advisor walked out of her office and called my name. I told her I appreciated her wanting to help me, but that I was waiting for my advisor, who needed to be the one to help me. My advisor was in with someone else, and I didn't mind waiting, but this new advisor was pushy. She insisted she would be able to help me, and my advisor would not have time to see me that day, due to her schedule.

I was so annoyed. I hate when things disrupt the way I expect them to go. This was supposed to be a smooth transition. I was supposed to walk in there, impress the hell out of my advisor to make sure she remembered me when it came time for admittance into the program, and walk out knowing I had it in the bag that day. *Who the hell did this advisor think she was?*

I tried to leave, saying I would come back at a different time. Eventually, I gave in to this new advisor and decided, what the hell, I will meet with her and can reschedule a meeting with my advisor for a different time.

This new advisor's name was Cynara Stubbs. I walked into her office, shut the door, and sat down.

Cynara asked, "Student ID?"

I replied, "K15108995."

"What program are you trying to apply for?"

"Nursing," I said. "That is why I needed to meet with Carol, since she is the head of the program."

Cynara said, "Okay, okay, let me just take a look at your records quickly..."

I was growing impatient. I was so annoyed, feeling like my time was being wasted.

"Kathryn, your record and your grades are very impressive."

I replied, "I know. I worked really hard to make this happen."

"Why do you want to be a nurse?"

What was up with these questions?! I thought. *Why do I need to validate what I want to do with my life to this woman? Who does she think she is? She doesn't even know me.*

I continued, "Well, I am twenty-eight years old, I finally came back to university last year, and I figure this is my best option, given the place I am at in my life."

"Do you want to be a nurse?"

"I mean, it's better than what I have been doing. It's a good career and will put me in a position of stability for the rest of my life.'

Cynara pressed me again. "But do you want to be a nurse? Your grades are good enough to get you into medical school, if you want to. Do you have any kids?"

"No."

"Do you have a husband?"

"No."

Cynara asked, "Have you ever thought about medical school?"

"I mean, of course I have," I said. "But given the point I am at in my life, I never thought of that as a possibility or even something that was acceptable for me to do. I am over the amount I am allowed for student loans, and I have no way of paying for this."

Cynara said to me, "You are graduating with your associate's degree and a 4.0 in your last three semesters. Your new grades will replace the old from your first year in college. It will only take you two more years, maybe even less if you keep on the same track, to get your bachelor's from FAU, which you can transfer directly from here to there. I can do it for you today. So, let me ask you again, because I don't want you making a decision you don't want to make, but I also don't want you thinking your only option is this. Because right now, you can do whatever you want to do. You worked for this opportunity. Don't think about anyone else right now. What do you want?"

I took a deep breath and then said firmly, "I want to be a doctor. Tell me everything I need to do."

Cynara Stubbs changed my entire life in less than twenty minutes. A woman I met one time, a woman I tried to ignore, a woman I was annoyed by saved me from making a decision I would have unknowingly regretted for the rest of my life.

A woman I met one time for twenty minutes saw who I was and what I was capable of. She didn't need to know my past, she didn't need to know my story, my age, or my background. She saw my determination and passion and didn't question who I showed her I was. She questioned why I was trying to hold that part of me back. In that moment, she gave me the approval I had been seeking my entire life.

I am forever grateful for her pushiness. I am forever changed by that single moment in my life. I never made another appointment with my nursing advisor. In fact, I never stepped into that office ever again. I didn't even go to my graduation. I started my bachelor's of biological sciences pre-med program at FAU that fall, and that was still only the beginning.

Six years later, and on the other side of the state, in St. Petersburg, Florida, Langdon and I are fully living with each other for the first time in our eleven-year, on-again, off-again relationship.

"I don't think you understand my sexuality. I don't think you realize that I don't just want to fuck another dude. Like it could be a woman with a penis. And when I talk about being interested in two men at once, I'm not talking about just fantasizing about being with two men. I am also talking about fantasizing as a voyeur, watching two gay men.

"I can't respond to your comment about exploring in the future together, when I have kinks and fantasies that I know you wouldn't enjoy. So, am I allowed to disclose the fantasies that wouldn't include you? Or am I only allowed to talk to you about the things that do?"

Langdon replied, "It's hard for me to hear what you are saying and not take personal offense to it, when we barely have sex, and you're telling me you want the freedom to be able to have sex with anyone."

"This is a microcosm of a macrocosm I have to explain to you in levels, for you to fully grasp what I am trying to explain to you. The past year, I have been really working to uncover and deal with all the trauma I have suffered. More specific to this, the sexual trauma I have endured. I have done EMDR on the times when I was raped. I have done therapy and Vipassana (a two-week-long silent meditation retreat). All of these things have bubbled years of suppressed energy to the surface.

"Along with all of this resurfacing comes the lifetime's worth of shame I know I don't need to feel, but it is not something I can control. It is difficult for me to have sex without thinking about every negative remark I have ever heard in regards to slut-shaming, religion-shaming, sexual orientation-shaming—the list goes on. I don't know how to have the hot and steamy sex I used to love without being drunk enough to not be worried about all that comes up for me.

Not to mention, but this is the first time I have ever felt really insecure in my own body. That has also decided to pop up this year, as well. So, when I have sex, I am also thinking about every position, every roll, and how every detail of my own body turns me off, because it's impossible for me to enjoy sex if I do not feel sexy. Sex I used to enjoy is now triggering for me. I don't know if that kind of sex will ever be something that is comfortable for me again. I sure as fuck hope it does, but in case it doesn't I wouldn't want you to miss out on your fantasies or the things you enjoy, just because I am incapable of it anymore."

A few months later, Langdon and I are now in couple's therapy. We don't fight or debate like we used to on these topics. We are understanding and open to listening to each other's experiences and feelings. It's a wonderful feeling to be on a journey with someone you love, where you both take the time to fully understand each other, without always taking everything they do personally.

It's taken us some time to get to this point, but it didn't really take us that much time once we both fully chose each other, chose this relationship, and chose to put in the work.

Chapter 18

Disruptors Get a Bad Rap

"Sometimes being brave means letting everyone down but yourself."
—Glennon Doyle, *Untamed*

DISRUPTION IS HOW I create change for myself and other spaces.

People see me as being free when I see myself as being caged.

When people compliment how outgoing and authentic I am, it makes me cringe. It physically hurts me to hear people think such lies about me. Because the truth is, for the most part, what people actually see is the caged version of me. I try so hard to see every single angle of every single problem that comes across my brain. I can feel and see and understand it from every fucking side. And I so badly want everyone to be happy, so I have fucking killed myself, trying to make the world an easier place for anyone and everyone however I can, in any way, shape, or form, for my entire life.

How can I make everyone as comfortable as possible?

How can I bring some common ground to this conversation?

How can I make this easier for everyone else?

How can I make this quicker and more efficient?

And yet, with my mind running a million miles a second, at a pace to protect everyone I can think of in every possible way I can think of, I still manage to piss every single one of you off. Because me at my "best" and trying to please everyone around me on the scale of being a "good girl," I still rank as a disruptor. I still rank as difficult, challenging, demanding, exhausting, complicated, stubborn, troublesome, annoying, mentally ill, and anything else a woman might be labeled for speaking her mind.

I get labeled these names when I am in the middle of bending as hard as I possibly can, because I wouldn't survive if I had to bend any harder, and I still like myself enough to be here. I still care enough for other people who have felt the same way I have felt about staying here. But I cannot bend anymore. Writing this book is the biggest step I have taken toward never bending again. I had no idea how exhausted I was from bending for so long, until I stopped.

The most important people in my life, my parents, haven't been able to recognize how far I have bent since childhood to make them more comfortable. Why would I bend more for anyone else than I have bent for them? When even my own parents don't entirely accept me for who I am. It's laughable, honestly. To think anyone would think I could be tamed, if my own parents couldn't do it. What makes anyone else more important to me than them? I've lived with my family labeling me the problem child my entire life. If there is anywhere I feel most comfortable, it is as the problem.

We are capable of being so much more than we are being, and I am not talking about production value. I am talking about being human beings and experiencing this life we have been given.

The chance to recognize and connect to all the other humans around us at all times. We don't have to worry about robots; we have become the robots we've feared would take over the jobs we don't even want to do. What the fuck are we doing? This can't possibly be it. This can't possibly be the life you dreamed of. This can't possibly be the world you imagined as a kid.

Even as a kid locked in their bedroom, I created a world in my imagination to escape to, so I didn't have to feel the pain of what being locked in that room did to me. I imagined, because I knew there were beautiful people, ideas, and places outside of the walls I was confined within.

And they did exist. I've met them, and I know there are so many more I have left to meet. I know, if you are reading this book, then you are one of those people, too. I know it because I am one of those people, and I'm just a nobody who is somebody, just like all of you. It's not supposed to be like this. It doesn't need to be like this.

Chapter 19
Remember Who the Fuck You Are

"Remember who you are."
—Mufasa, *The Lion King*
"Beeeee Yourself."
—Genie, *Aladdin*

I AM NOT THE SAME PERSON I was when I started writing this book.

Currently, I am going through the process of being diagnosed as autistic or on the spectrum. It was as if a key was dropped directly in front of me that unlocks the door to understanding all the missing links of my life.

While it feels that way, it is not the truth. Whether or not I am diagnosed as on the spectrum, it will not change anything about who I am as a person. I am still the exact same person I have been this entire time. It changes nothing other than my awareness and the possibility of understanding how to mitigate and manage certain symptoms.

It is the same as when I was finally diagnosed with PMDD. I had PMDD all along, but knowing made me better equipped. Because knowledge and understanding are everything in this world.

I hate labels, as I have said, because if we were all more understanding and accepting of our differences, I don't think we would need labels. Labels pack us into groups that eventually become "us versus them." That isn't helpful toward making this experience more beautiful for all. But much like death and taxes, labels exist. We can use them to our advantage, as opposed to using them as targets.

I am a pansexual, privileged cis White woman, and I have ADHD, PMDD, and Major Depressive Disorder, and I am potentially on the spectrum of autism. ADHD, PMDD, MDD, and autism are all tricky to diagnose correctly, when they are all present, because so many symptoms overlap. I am also a survivor of rape and both emotional and physical abuse. I am 6/2 Manifestor, Aries sun, Libra moon, Capricorn rising. I am a scientist, author, and entrepreneur. I am a product manager in corporate until I break free. I am a disruptor. I am a feminist working to be a better womanist. I am a liberal for what that means in 2023. I am a daughter, sister, cousin, and aunt. I hope one day to be a mother.

These are just a few of the labels I know I can be categorized under. These are the labels people pinpoint to plan their attack or attachment. My understanding of these labels helps me to navigate my daily relationship with self and the rest of the world. These labels help me to understand that, at one point, I didn't have certain labels, but they existed anyway, which makes it easier for me to be more understanding to others who may not have labels to understand themselves yet.

Playing in the dark in a world that wants to put you in as many boxes as possible is terrifying, because we all want the ability to explain ourselves and have understanding. If I am capable of working to better understand who I am as a person and can label myself quicker than the world, then the world is going to have a hard time telling me who I am when I already know.

Knowing who we are before the world tells us who we should be is the key to being free from the metaphorical chains that society tries to put us in. This starts with our children. This starts with the way we raise our children, but our society is broken. Our society wants to control.

The Upper Limit Problem tells us that we each have a threshold of how much happiness we are willing to allow ourselves. We have a tendency to limit our own happiness, because we don't think we deserve things to go well all the time. The unfortunate aspect of this is that a lot of this comes from preconditioning as a product of our childhoods and the ways in which others have made us feel unworthy.

"Your need for acceptance can make you invisible in this world. Don't let anything stand in the way of the light that shines through this form. Risk being seen in all of your glory."

—Jim Carrey

Being seen in all of your bigness can feel like a very scary place sometimes. This is why it is so important to block out the noise. In the past couple of years, I have become very adamant about fighting this theory. I do everything I can to ignore anything that wants to see me unhappy, which even includes my own subconscious, sometimes.

Sometimes cutting off the things that hurt us are necessary so we can develop on the path we are seeking. At some point, I found it necessary to unfollow everyone on Instagram. This is something I battle with doing every single day. I recently started refollowing people again, and I am flirting with what is supportive of others and healthy for me. I don't see unfollowing people as being unsupportive of others, but more as being supportive of myself in moments when I need to clear out the noise.

It's unfortunate that social media has become something we use as a catalyst to start fights and arguments that might not even exist. I know many people whom I have unfollowed who noticed, were upset by, and even stopped talking to me after insisting they unfollow me, too, just to prove who is boss or something. Like a pissing contest. But I don't care. The whole thing is dumb.

"Whatever your dream is, whatever your goal is, you're not going to be able to make it happen if you don't have a dream party every day. Like you gotta have a dream session. You gotta go in a room, close the door, and you've gotta actually see yourself doing it. You've gotta feel yourself doing it. You've gotta actually walk in the future, live it out, come back in the present, and start working toward it. Before you can do the impossible, you gotta do the possible. Will the real Eric Thomas please stand up?"

Will the real Katie Dickieson please stand up?
"Stop being afraid to take a test.
Stop just waking up like an accident.
You not average. Why are you being average when you are not average? Why are you being good when you are not good... You're great.
When are you going to step up to the plate?
To be able at any moment to sacrifice who you are for what you will become.
Don't cry to quit, cry to keep going, you already in pain you already hurt, get a reward for it.
Focus on your solutions."

Eric Thomas's words play on repeat in my head most days.

Because fighting White supremacy means fighting capitalism, and fighting capitalism means fighting systemic racism, and fighting systemic racism means fighting for freedom and equality, which means fighting for freedom and equality is the fight to protect the three unalienable rights: life, liberty, and the pursuit of happiness. Which means the fight against White supremacy is not just a fight for POC or people in the LGBTQIA+ communities. It is a fight for anyone and everyone who has been a victim of capitalism and the way it has divided and conquered our ability, as a collective, to live, be liberated, and happy, due to the economic injustices of this world.

"Fuck you. I won't do what you tell me!" Can you imagine what might happen if we all just said *no*? I think it's time to fuck shit up. And when I say fuck shit up, I mean in a good way. Let's throw figurative bombs and piece it back together as we go. Let's throw a wrench in the cog and be entertained at how quickly the faces of our superiors humor us, when they realize we've grasped onto our own power.

You don't have to be an asshole to create a boundary or advocate for yourself. But sometimes, doing these things can feel like you're the asshole. I dunno what to tell you here, though. Ya kinda gotta get comfortable with being the asshole. You're not really an asshole, though. You're just "difficult," supposedly.

Chapter 20

The Great Dance of Nostalgia

"We just don't recognize life's most significant moments while they're happening. Back then I thought, *Well, there'll be other days*. I didn't realize that that was the only day."

—Dr. Archibald "Moonlight" Graham,
Field of Dreams

D O YOU KNOW THE TASTE of your first cigarette? The one you didn't know how to smoke? And yet, even if you haven't smoked in years, if you go back to that place, all of a sudden, when you take one hit of a cigarette, you are transported to that time.

For me, it's the first cigarette I ever smoked on Bradley's front porch with my friend Donovan, pretending I knew what I was doing. The cigarettes I smoked before water polo practice, driving around the high-class neighborhoods where I grew up. Every cigarette I smoked to be part of the social group at Guitar Center. The countless cigarettes I smoked while playing chess and Blokus on my phone, when I had to live with my parents again, obsessively playing Call of Duty in Benjamin's basement. And the countless cigarettes I smoked on the back patio of 3rd & 3rd.

Also, the cigarette I smoke now at Flatbread and Butter in downtown St. Petersburg, to remember every person I have been up to who I am now and how each and every one of them made me who I am today. You can hate that I was a smoker; even I can hate that. But not to acknowledge the impact smoking had on my life would be a lie as to who I have become.

Back in the summer of 2014, I started a major health kick. I was in holistic nutrition school and I abruptly quit smoking cigarettes. Now, I will smoke the random cig just for the nostalgia.

On August 11, 2014, I walked out of the gym and got into my white 2007 Toyota Camry, threw my yoga mat into the backseat, and grabbed my phone from the cup holder. I always kept my phone in the car when I took classes at the gym. Zero distractions, especially on the nights when I took body pump followed by yoga.

I turned on my phone, and before the screen could even load, an incessant vibration began. I couldn't even open my messages, because they wouldn't stop loading. The screen flashed with each new message notification. But then there was my phone log: sixty-some calls from family members, friends, and my boyfriend.

In my gut, I knew something was wrong before looking at a single message.

I called Langdon first, and before he could say anything, I asked, "Was it Robin Williams or Jim Carrey?"

"It was Robin."

I went home, collected all the Robin memorabilia I could find, put it on my coffee table, and poured myself a glass of wine. I couldn't bring myself to watch a movie or anything else, for that matter. All I could think in that moment was, if he couldn't make it out of this life without killing himself, then there was no hope for me.

I never let anyone know this. I sat in my pain yet with the solace of knowing someone actually did understand how I felt. There was comfort in knowing it was Robin, and I was not alone.

I sat on my couch, staring at the man who'd raised me through screens. Etheric cords are energetic cords, attached from our chakras to people as well as animals, inanimate objects, and places where we have relationships. This can include people we have never met but feel connected to. For me, Robin Williams was one of those people I feel this with strongly.

I went to bed and dreamed I was in the most beautiful, light-filled, octagonal, wooden chapel I had ever seen. It was glowing through stained glass, and the ceiling rose to a point in the center. Robin stood in the middle of the chapel behind an easel, painting.

I noticed noise coming from outside and could see thousands of people through the windows, waiting for their chance to come in. I looked at Robin. He looked up and smiled. I know this was his way of saying, "I see you," while having so many other people to see, as well.

Robin's Wish came out in September 2020, smack dab in the middle of the pandemic, during my deepest moments of solitude. I was living in Ithaca, New York, working on my master's degree at Cornell. When I finished the documentary, I felt like I had lost the man who raised me through screens all over again. The grief was different this time, however. Robin had Lewy body dementia. He didn't kill himself.

Keep going.

It's been three years since I watched that documentary, and I have been advocating intensely for my health and wellbeing ever since. I have come to recognize the moments of nostalgia as they are happening now, and not just after they're gone. My life has reminded me that every moment we are in will soon become a moment that is remembered, which has made the present so much more meaningful to me now.

Today is August 4, 2023. I just turned in my manuscript for editing, and I am in my final appointment with the doctor who's been taking me through the testing for autism.

"I have diagnosed you with autism, PTSD, and conversion disorder, and reconfirmed your original diagnoses of ADHD and PMDD."

Ten minutes later, the phone rings. It's my sister.

"Did Mom and Dad tell you they're selling the house?"

"No."

"Aren't you upset?"

"No."

I couldn't make up a more perfect ending to this book.

Keep going.

Move Dates

    2007: Aug—Southfield, Michigan to Traverse City
    2008: Aug—Traverse City to Birmingham
           Oct—Birmingham to Ferndale
    2010: Dec—Ferndale to Southfield
    2011: May—Southfield to Delray Beach, FL
           Aug—Delray Beach, NE 4th Ave.
    2012: Aug—Delray Beach NE 8th Ave
           Sep—Delray Beach, NE 8th Ave
    2013: Aug—Delray Beach, NE 7th Ave
    2014: Apr—Delray Beach, Federal Hwy
           Dec—Delray Beach, NE 14th St
    2015: May—Delray Beach, Andrew's Ave
           Nov—Delray Beach (homeless)
    2016: Jan—Delray Beach, NE 4th Ave
           Feb—Lake Worth, K St
    2017: May—Lake Worth, N St
           July—Nantucket
           Sep—Boca Raton, Mizner Blvd
    2018: Apr—Delray Beach, Andrew's Ave
           Sep—Delray Beach, Franklin Club Dr
    2019: Aug—Delray Beach, Avenue L
           Sep—Delray Beach (homeless)
           Nov—Delray Beach, Santa Clara Dr
           Dec—Lake Worth, Hillcrest Ave
    2020: Mar—Santa Barbara, California
           Apr—Asheville, North Carolina
           May—Southfield, Michigan
           Aug—Ithaca, New York
    2021: Jul—New York City
           Aug—Cambridge, Massachusetts
    2022: Sep—St. Petersburg, Florida
           Apr—St. Petersburg, Old Southeast
           May—St. Petersburg, 5th Avenue NE

References

988 – National Suicide Prevention Hotline
800-799-7233 or Text START to 88788 – National Domestic Violence Hotline
1-800-273-TALK (8255) – 24/7 Crisis Hotline: National Suicide Prevention Lifeline
Text TALK to 741-741 – 24/7 Crisis Text Line
Send a text to 838255 – Veterans Crisis Line
1-800-662-HELP (4357) – SAMHSA Treatment Referral Hotline (Substance Abuse)
1-800-656-HOPE (4673) – RAINN National Sexual Assault Hotline
1-866-331-9474 – National Teen Dating Abuse Helpline
1-866-488-7386 – The Trevor Project

Finding mental health care
American Psychiatric Association
American Psychological Association
National Association of Social Workers
SAMHSA Mental Health Provider Locator
Veterans Affairs

Additional Resources by Mental Health Condition

Alcohol & drugs
Substance Abuse and Mental Health Services Administration
National Institute on Drug Abuse

Narcotics Anonymous
Alcoholics Anonymous
Physicians for Responsible Opioid Prescribing (PROP)
National Institute on Alcohol Abuse and Alcoholism
Start Your Recovery
Detox Local's Drug Withdrawal and Detox Guide
Addictionresource.net
Narcotics Anonymous

Anxiety disorders
National Education Alliance for Borderline Personality
Teen's Health
Anxiety Disorders Association of America

Bipolar disorder
Depression and Bipolar Support Alliance
National Education Alliance for Borderline Personality
Teen's Health

Borderline personality
BPDVideo
National Education Alliance for Borderline Personality

Self-Injury
Teen's Health
Self-Abuse Finally Ends

Depression
Depression and Bipolar Support Alliance
National Education Alliance for Borderline Personality
Families for Depression Awareness
Teen's Health
American Psychiatric Foundation
National Alliance on Mental Illness
HeadsUpGuys

Eating disorders
Teen's Health
Overeaters Anonymous
National Association of Anorexia Nervosa and Associated Disorders
National Eating Disorders Association
Eating Disorders Anonymous
Proud2Bme
Understanding Eating Disorders
National Alliance for Eating Disorders

Emotional health
Let's Erase The Stigma
Love is Louder
Half of Us
Veterans United
American Psychiatric Foundation
Active Minds
OK2TALK
Make The Connection
Inspire USA Foundation
National Dialogue on Mental Health
Each Mind Matters
Befrienders Worldwide
Veterans Affairs Training
Veterans Affairs Mental Health Toolkit
Veterans Affairs Mental Health

Schizophrenia
Schizophrenics Anonymous
Schizophrenia.com
National Alliance on Mental Illness

Stress
Veterans United
Stress Management-HelpGuide.org
Teen's Health

Suicide prevention
American Association of Suicidology
The Dougy Center – The National Center for Grieving Children and Families
How to Talk to a Child about a Suicide Attempt in Your Family (Rocky Mountain MIRECC)
The Jason Foundation
The Jed Foundation
Lifeline Chat
Man Therapy
Mental Health America
My3 App
National Action Alliance for Suicide Prevention
National Organization for People of Color Against Suicide
National Suicide Prevention Lifeline
Now Matters Now
Parents, Families, Friends, and Allies United with LGBTQ People (PFLAG)
Safety Planning Tools
SAVE
The Society for the Prevention of Teen Suicide
StopBullying.gov
Suicide Prevention Resource Center
Teen's Health
The Tyler Clementi Foundation
Veterans Crisis Line
Wounded Warrior Project

LGBTQ Resource List

Political
Equality Federation
Human Rights Campaign (HRC)
National LGBTQ Task Force
Victory Fund
Bisexual
BIENESTAR
BiNetUSA
Bisexual.org
Bisexual Resource Center

Youth
Gay, Lesbian & Straight Education Network (GLSEN)
GSA Network
LGBTQ Student Resources & Support
Point Foundation
Safe Schools Coalition
The Trevor Project

Military
The American Military Partner Association (AMDA)
American Veterans for Equal Rights
OutServe-Service Members Legal Defense Network
Palm Center
Transgender American Veterans Association
Veterans for Human Rights

Transgender
National Center for Transgender Equality (NCTE)
Sylvia Rivera Law Project
Transgender Law Center
Transgender Legal Defense & Education Fund

Aging
National Resource Center for LGBT Aging
Services and Advocacy for Gay, Lesbian, Bisexual & Transgender Elders (SAGE)

Legal
American Civil Liberties Union (ACLU)
Lambda Legal
The LGBT Bar
National Center for Lesbian Rights (NCLR)

General
Anti-Violence Project
CenterLink
COLAGE
GMHC
Matthew Shepard Foundation
Movement Advancement Project
Out & Equal
Parents, Families and Friends of Lesbians and Gays (PFLAG)
Straight for Equality
The Williams Institute

Anti-Racism Books to Read

Caste
So You Want to Talk About Race
How to be an Anti-Racist
Between the World and Me
Me and White Supremacy
White Rage
Why Are All the Black Kids Sitting Together in the Cafeteria
Why I'm No Longer Talking to White People About Race

Thanks

THANK YOU TO:
The late Ann Smyth, and the entire Smyth family, I would not be who I am today without all of you.

Cynara Stubbs for seeing me when I couldn't see myself and changing my life in an instant.

Samantha Joy, my publisher, and Landon Hail Press, for knowing I had a bigger story to tell and taking the time to pull it out of me.

My late Nana and Papa (Joyce and Tom Dickieson), who taught me how to work hard and love hard.

My Grandma (Pat Bean) for encouraging me to be as wild and free as possible. And for questioning, "Why are you going ninety miles an hour? You'll get there, if you go fifty and stop to smell the roses."

Cammie Williams, for being my friend when no one else would, picking me up when I didn't think I could make it, holding space for me, and for checking me when I need to be checked. You are my greatest teacher.

My partner, Langdon Larkin Lytle. You are my very best friend. Thank you for finding me again in this lifetime. Thank you for loving me even when you hate me. Thank you for being my person. Thank you for celebrating my bigness. And lastly, thank you for going on the rollercoaster with me that was writing this book and experiencing/working through all of the emotions for a second time. I am so grateful we continue to choose each other every day. I love you forever.

And finally, my dog Charlie, thank you for saving my life.

About the Author

MEET KATIE DICKIESON, an individual with a zest for life, a confluence of science, creativity, and unyielding spirit. As a licensed hair stylist in two states and a certified holistic health coach, Katie's mantra has been, when artistry and science merge, remarkable transformations unfold. Grounded in biological sciences pre-med and later propelled into the stratosphere with a master's in biomedical engineering from Cornell University, she's explored topics as vast as the cosmos itself, from Martian regolith's dance with plant life to the deepest aspects of human sustainability.

But to pigeonhole Katie merely as a scientist or a creative would be a disservice to her vast journey. Having relocated thirty-three times in just sixteen years, and facing the raw realities of being unhoused twice, her narrative is a testament to resilience and the unyielding strength of the human spirit. This story finds voice in *Remember Who the Fuck You Are: Who Were You Before the World Told You What to Be*, an unfiltered reflection of her trek, celebrating authenticity and the power of undaunted perseverance.

In the world of entrepreneurship, Katie collaboratively crafts Wing, a disruption to the online dating world. Distinct from the superficial swipe culture, Wing reimagines the dating paradigm, promoting connections founded on shared passions and authentic engagements rather than mere appearances.

Katie's commitment to living authentically isn't confined to pages or platforms. Embracing her neurodiversity, as someone diagnosed with autism, ADHD, PMDD, PTSD, and conversion disorder, she's delved deeply into understanding herself and the vibrant tapestry of neurodivergent minds. These insights have fostered a profound passion for mental health advocacy and the celebration of unique minds.

Today, with gratitude as her compass, Katie stands poised to explore uncharted territories, driven by an unwavering desire to indelibly impact our world. She's more than just an entrepreneur, scientist, or artist; she's a beacon of boundless potential. Join her on this enthralling journey—where every connection, every insight, every venture is a step closer to weaving together the vast, intricate tapestry of life.

Find more about Katie and her work at: www.katiedickieson.com.

www.ingramcontent.com/pod-product-compliance
Lightning Source LLC
Chambersburg PA
CBHW031615160426
43196CB00006B/138